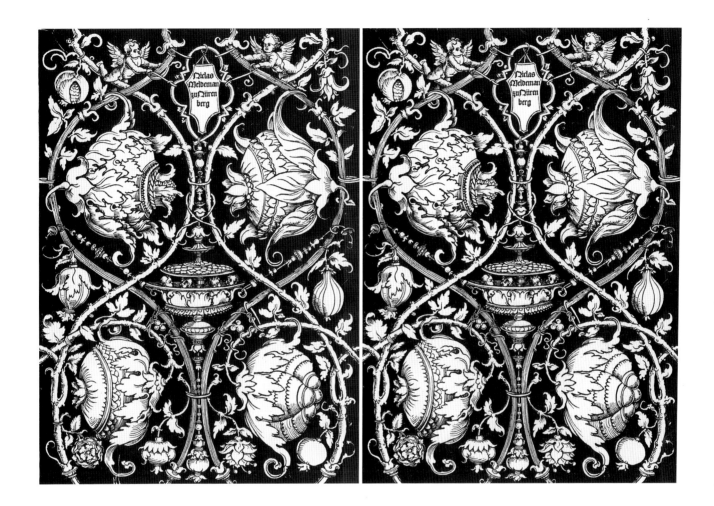

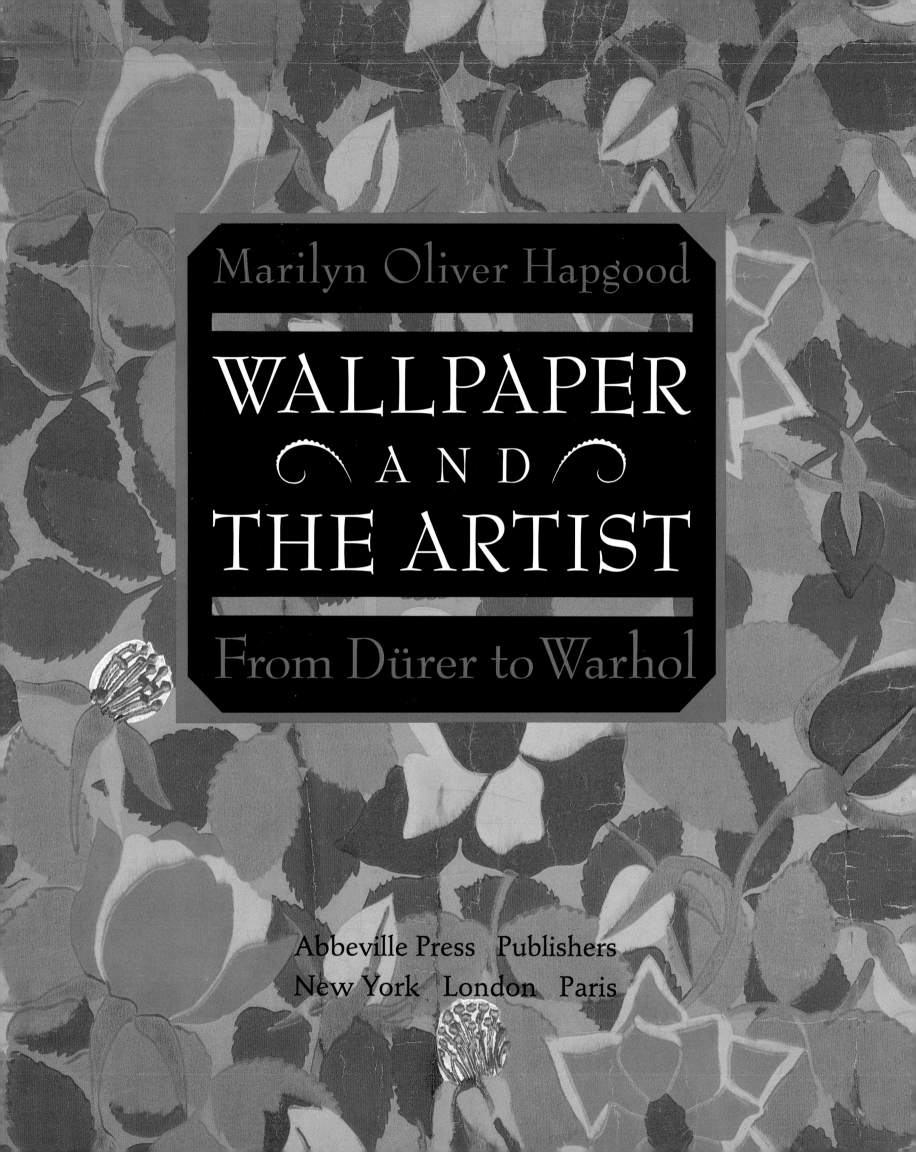

Marilyn Oliver Hapgood

WALLPAPER AND THE ARTIST

From Dürer to Warhol

Abbeville Press Publishers
New York London Paris

FOR ROBERT

COVER: E. A. Seguy (active c. 1900–1933). Wallpaper design. From *Samarkande,* 1920. See plate 153.

ENDPAPERS: William Morris (1834–1896). "Fruit" ("Pomegranate"), 1862–64. See plate 48.

PAGE 1: Hans Sebald Beham (1500–1550?). "Pomegranate," c. 1520–25. See plate 7.

PAGES 2–3: Martine. "Les Roses roses," 1912. Wallpaper, cylinder printed, Paul Dumas. Bibliothèque Forney, Paris.

PAGE 5: Jean-Baptiste Réveillon (1725–1811) and Jean-Baptiste Fay (active 1775–1789). Wallpaper panel, wood-block printed; from a series entitled "Coq et Perroquet," 1785–88. See plate 12.

EDITORS: Jacqueline Decter, Constance Herndon, Amy Handy
ART DIRECTOR: Renée Khatami
DESIGNER: Barbara Balch
PRODUCTION EDITOR: Cristine Mesch
PICTURE EDITORS: Maya Kaimal, Deborah Abramson
PRODUCTION MANAGER: Dana Cole

First edition

Library of Congress Cataloging-in-Publication Data
Hapgood, Marilyn Oliver.
    Wallpaper and the artist : from Dürer to Warhol / by Marilyn Oliver Hapgood.
        p. cm.
    Includes bibliographical references and index.
    ISBN 0-89659-933-7
    1. Wallpaper—History. I. Title.
NK3400.H37 1992
747'.3—dc20   92-14717

CONTENTS

ACKNOWLEDGMENTS   6

PREFACE   8

ONE   From Dürer to Rowlandson (1500–1800)   13

TWO   Before William Morris: The Grammar of Ornament, Instruction, and Illusion (1800–1860)   31

THREE   William Morris and His Followers: The Moral Power of Art (1860–1895)   51

FOUR   The Art Nouveau Style: The Force of Nature in Line and Form (1890–1905)   87

FIVE   Movements toward Restraint (1900–1960)   115

SIX   The Art Deco Years: From Elegance to Exuberance (1910–1940)   143

SEVEN   The Wallpapers of Charles Burchfield (1921–1929)   175

EIGHT   From Surrealism to Spoof: Later Twentieth-Century Artists (1950–1980)   185

NINE   Art and Wallpaper   209

APPENDIX A   Artists' Wallpapers for Children (1860–1980)   235

APPENDIX B   Artists' Wallpapers: A Guide to Manufacturers and Shops   257

NOTES   259

BIBLIOGRAPHY   265

INDEX   269

ACKNOWLEDGMENTS

I have numerous people to thank for the journey this book has taken me on. The subject of the book has almost invariably provoked a spark of surprise and even personal involvement. Many have apparently not forgotten the impact of a wallpaper in their lives, and for them considering wallpaper in the category of art is a challenging and appealing idea. Thus I have been the lucky recipient of a warmth and good will that have made researching and writing this book a genuine adventure. Although I cannot thank everyone here by name, I send my gratitude to the many people who helped me along the way.

Some I must single out for special thanks. The scholarly world of art historians, curators, and librarians is made up of extremely generous people. I began with a summer of research in Washington, D.C., working in both the Art Library of the National Gallery and at the Library of Congress. Both institutions were treasure troves, their staffs most helpful. In the White House I was able to study the wallpapers through the courtesy of William Allmann, archivist. The Freer Gallery of Art made important contributions through its unique Whistler holdings.

Fortuitously, two of my five years of work on the book were spent in London when my husband was assigned there. Jean Hamilton and Lionel Lambourne welcomed me to the National Art Library at the Victoria and Albert Museum and its dazzling collection of historic wallpapers in the Print Room. At the Drawings Collection of the British Architectural Library of the Royal Institute of British Architects, Neil Bingham was helpful with Voysey and Burges. The library itself was an unsurpassed resource for Pugin, Olbrich, Wright, Le Corbusier, and other architects. The Witt Library at the Courtauld Institute allowed me to see exciting holdings of the Bloomsbury group. At the British Museum Department of Prints and Drawings, Frances Dunkels and her staff showed me their great collection of Rowlandson and Dürer. It was there I met by chance

Christian von Heusinger of the Herzog Anton Ulrich-Museum, Braunschweig, who with Horst Appuhn has done pioneering work on early wallpapers of Dürer's time. Dr. von Heusinger's special work on Dürer has enriched art history, and his generosity to me is most deeply appreciated.

At Walthamstow on the edge of London, Norah Gillow of the William Morris Gallery shared her expertise on Morris, the gallery's splendid collection of Mackmurdo and Morris wallpapers, and its excellent library. Outside London, at Charleston, the curator Vicki Walton gave me a host of good suggestions; Antony Wells-Cole, curator of Temple Newsam, contributed information on Audubon; Heather Woods and Jessica Rutherford helped me on Robert Jones and the Royal Pavilion at Brighton; at an early stage, Christine Woods, curator of wallpapers at the Whitworth Art Gallery, Manchester, and Joanna Banham, curator of the Leighton House, London, gave me general information that I relied on throughout my work.

In Paris, Veronique de Bruignac of the Musée des Arts Décoratifs allowed me to see a superb collection of Art Deco artists' wallpapers. Daniel Marchesseau at that institution gave me invaluable help on Laurencin; Marie-Noël de Gary did the same for Bénédictus. At the Bibliothèque Forney, Marie-Catherine Grichois showed me the distinguished collection and volunteered excellent suggestions. At the Musée d'Art Moderne de la Ville de Paris, Danielle Molinari guided me on Delaunay. The staff of the Cabinet des Estampes at the Bibliothèque Nationale was helpful with numerous artists, especially with Denis. In Saint Germain-en-Laye, the curator of the Musée Departemental du Prieuré, Marie-Amélie Anquetil, was instructive on Denis as well. And my thanks to Jacqueline Jacqué at Musée des Impressions sur Etoffes, Mulhouse, and Bernard Jacqué, Musée du Papier Peint, Rixheim, for their insightful correspondence.

In Brussels, Anne Adriaens-Pannier of the Musées Royaux des Beaux-Arts de Belgique assisted me with Magritte. Also in this city I was guided through the Tassel House by Madame Delhaye of the *Musée Horta*. Jean Delhaye, whose courageous vision rescued the Horta legacy in Brussels, was most helpful in correspondence.

In Germany, Ernst Wolfgang Mick of the Deutsches Tapetenmuseum in Kassel has been indefatigable in responding to my numerous requests and, from the excellent collection at Kassel, munificent in his support. I am most grateful to him.

In Vienna I was privileged to see an expansive collection of the Wiener Werkstätte at the Osterreichisches Museum für Angewandte Kunst, and I thank Angela Völker and Ruperta Pichler for this courtesy. In Bassano del Grappa, Italy, the staff of the Museo Civico allowed me to pore over the Reimondini Collection of domino papers of the eighteenth century.

In the United States, Nancy Weekly, curator of the Charles Burchfield Center, Buffalo, has been continuously helpful, and Janet Byrne at the Metropolitan Museum of Art, New York, kindly helped me a number of times with problems. I also want to thank Ann Dorfsman, former curator of wallpapers at the Cooper-Hewitt Museum in New York, for her guidance, and the present curator, Joanne Warner, for her enthusiasm and wide range of information. Christopher Monkhouse, curator at the Art Museum of the Rhode Island School of Design, gave me fascinating material on Calder and Warhol. Charles Stuckey, of the Chicago Art Institute, was always full of stimulating ideas, in correspondence and in person. I also thank Sally Pierce, curator of the Print Room at the Boston Athenaeum; in Hartford, Marianne Curling of the Mark Twain House and Margherita Desy and Beverly Zell of the Stowe-Day Foundation. My grateful appreciation to the library staffs of the Fine Arts and the Houghton at Harvard, the Museum of Fine Arts, Boston, and the Sterling and Francine Clark Art Institute in Williamstown, Massachusetts. Above all, my heartfelt thanks go to my home University of New Hampshire Library in Durham and its unfailingly courteous and forgiving staff, whence came the hundreds of books that were the backbone of my study.

I extend my sincere thanks to living artists and to galleries who have contributed work to this book. Wallpaper companies have been immensely helpful: please see them listed in appendix B. Individuals were important contributors: Jill Ford, Ray Watkinson, and John Riely responded with correspondence far more generous than anyone could deserve. I also owe a debt of gratitude to Julius Hummel and Reinhard Backhausen and to Colin White. And I shall not soon forget the privilege of interviewing Leo Castelli on Warhol, Judy Taylor on Beatrix Potter, Dominique-Maurice Denis on his father, Maurice Denis, Robin Tanner on Edward Bawden, Rosalie Mander on Morris, and Elizabeth de Haas on Emory Walker and Morris. My friend Susan Edwards has from the beginning given me her expertise on writing and editing, and has consoled and counseled me with innumerable walks, talks, and cups of tea. I am deeply grateful to her and to my friends Kathleen O'Neil and Vera Trafton, who willingly supplied me with German translations, and to my friend Akemi Maeda for her unending support.

I salute Abbeville Press and its imaginative, meticulous, hardworking staff: Mark Magowan, who first saw possibilities in this book; Constance Herndon, Jacqueline Decter, and Cristine Mesch, who sensitively shepherded it; Amy Handy, who helped edit; Maya Kaimal and Deborah Abramson, who did the picture editing; Philip Reynolds, who copyedited; and Renée Khatami and Barbara Balch, who designed it.

Finally, the book is dedicated to my husband, Robert, who more than once took it under advisement in his professional way and rescued it from oblivion.

Look to your walls!" said William Morris, the greatest of wallpaper artists, and so we do, whether we mean to or not, especially if the walls are covered with wallpaper. Humble and perishable as it may be, wallpaper can have an extraordinary presence in our lives. It can cast a Proustian spell: "Those giraffes!" exclaimed George Plimpton in a television discussion of childhood memory.[1] Proust himself recalled the power of a wallpaper that "succeeded . . . in imprisoning me in the heart of a sort of poppy, out of which to look at a world quite different from in Paris."[2] Queen Victoria in 1885 was described as "content with nothing but the same patterns in the same colours and materials—because of the sad and fond memories associated with them."[3]

At times we may be strangely and totally absorbed in a wallpaper pattern. We have all experienced despite ourselves the kind of laborious intensity of observation with which Raskolnikov is transfixed in *Crime and Punishment:* "How many petals [had the white flower on dirty yellow wallpaper], how many ridges on each petal, how many of the small brown marks?"[4] Everyone, too, has no doubt seen imaginary images on an old papered wall with "its old, suspicious-looking stains," as described by de Maupassant.[5]

Ordinarily wallpaper is the last thing we would care to look at with such intensity. Jokes about the worthlessness of wallpaper seem to be everywhere. "An expensive variety of wallpaper," was John Updike's comment about a Diebenkorn painting.[6] A music critic accused Andrew Lloyd Webber's *Aspects of Love* of a "uniform welter of orchestrated dialogue" resembling a "dramatic-musical wallpaper."[7] When a Picasso painting was auctioned for record millions, a BBC announcer declared in mock disparagement, "Well, it wouldn't have gone with my wallpaper anyway." We jest about papering walls with devalued money or bonds, indicating that wallpaper is virtually worthless—thus Henry Miller complained: "The wallpaper with which the men of science have covered the world of reality is falling to tat-

ters."[8] One nineteenth-century critic offended by the abstraction of Monet's *Impression: Sunrise* declared that *unfinished* wallpaper was better painted![9]

Particular wallpapers come in for their own disparagement. In *The Yellow Wallpaper,* Charlotte Perkins Gilman's heroine expresses her loathing in precise and eloquent detail: "I never saw a worse paper in my life. One of those sprawling, flamboyant patterns committing every artistic sin. . . . It is dull enough to confuse the eye in following, pronounced enough constantly to irritate and provoke study, and when you follow the lame uncertain curves for a little distance they suddenly commit suicide—plunge off at outrageous angles, destroy themselves in unheard-of contradictions."[10] Oscar Wilde was more succinct, joking: "My wallpaper is killing me. One of us will have to go!" and true to Wildean wit, he then died.

It is clear that wallpaper patterns can make remarkably powerful statements. Since time immemorial artists have made patterns, in the beginning no doubt meaningful shorthand messages. Gradually the messages became motifs, meaningful universal symbols. In the last few hundred years wallpaper patterns have interested a surprisingly large number of important artists and architects who have tried their hands at designing them. Wallpapers by more than seventy-five such artists are surveyed and illustrated here, extending over almost five centuries from the time of the earliest surviving wallpapers to the present. Prominent throughout are the many artists best known for their paintings who also created wallpaper patterns. A few painters have been interested in scenic or mural wallpapers. Another group consists of celebrated architects, mostly of the nineteenth century, when wallpaper was widely accepted. As the importance of wallpaper declined in the early decades of the twentieth century, architects ceased to think of it as a wall covering of sophisticated choice, although surprisingly both Le Corbusier and Frank Lloyd Wright designed wallpaper at midcentury. But distinguished artist-designers created wallpapers during these years and earlier, as did gifted illustrators, who most often contributed wallpapers for children.

For certain artists, such as William Morris and Charles Burchfield, work on wallpaper was important to their livelihoods. For many others it was a brief challenge, sometimes involving only a few designs that tend to be neglected by art historians. Yet artists' designs for wallpapers are as varied and distinctive as their other works. As analysis will show, artists' wallpapers typically demonstrate the same creative impulses that radiate throughout their work. This finding and the new perspectives that it affords are a major focus of this study. Along the way, the artists' involvement with wallpaper provides some new glimpses into their lives and times. The wallpaper patterns themselves relate interestingly to trends in design and issues in art history. These relationships are another main focus. Beyond such points of interest, many artists' wallpapers are works of intrinsic value and beauty in their own right. They are—however small—works of art. Above all this book celebrates these triumphs.

The great majority of the wallpaper artists to be discussed are major figures, or involved importantly in major art events. In general, at least one respected book has been written about each. For the most part their wall patterns were intended for paper, but a wall textile will on occasion be considered: Morris particularly admired textiles as wall coverings; Raoul Dufy used one of his own textiles as a wall covering and then depicted it in many of his paintings. Walter Crane, Le Corbusier, and Louis Comfort Tiffany, among others, designed paper coverings for ceilings as well as walls; Albrecht Dürer contributed to actual paper monuments for walls and created wallpapers as well. And Henri Matisse's paper cutout murals could not have been overlooked.

The subject of artists' wallpapers has not been treated before, and I have not undertaken to be all-inclusive. Except as it has impinged on the West, Eastern wallpaper art has regretfully been omitted, as has the work of a host of minor Western artists and a few more important ones. Nor have I sought to sift out works of artistic merit from the multitude of attractive wallpapers created by designers who are not otherwise well known as artists; that would require another

book in itself. The fact that the wallpapers considered here were designed by notable artists is of the essence: by juxtaposing wallpaper and the artist, this study seeks to map a hitherto unexplored part of the important area where the fine and decorative arts meet.

A bird's-eye view of the five centuries under consideration suggests how very differently this area has been conceived. At the beginning of the sixteenth century, what we now call the decorative arts and the fine arts were considered equally important. Dürer made a wallpaper pattern as seriously as he attempted any woodcut; to him everything he created was "fine" art, generally intended for many people. His woodcuts were sold in great numbers, very cheaply. Similarly, Thomas Rowlandson at the end of the eighteenth century used much the same style and figures in his wallpaper borders that he used in his watercolor caricatures. Both kinds of work were sold cheaply and were available to everyone. Rowlandson did not concern himself with a difference between fine and decorative art, although by that time (1800) other people regretted for him that he did not. For the equality between the fine and decorative arts was beginning to change with the advent of the Industrial Revolution, and its impersonal and even debased industrial decoration.

In the middle of the nineteenth century William Morris reacted to this problem by demanding a finer, handcrafted, more meaningful ornament. Morris referred to the decorative arts as "the lesser arts," yet he himself produced only one canvas that has survived, while designing several dozen celebrated wallpapers, even more textiles, some tapestries and stained glass, furniture, and many ornamental designs for books. He focused on these areas because he was deeply convinced that, for a better society, art must enter the everyday lives of all human beings. In "The Beauty of Life" he stated: "You will want pictures or engravings, such as you can afford, only not stopgaps, but real works of art on the walls: or else the wall itself must be ornamented with some beautiful and restful pattern."[11]

At the end of the nineteenth century, Maurice Denis and others in the group known as the Nabis turned the relationship between art and ornament around. As interested in decorative as in fine art, and wanting to bring the two together, they held that a work of fine art should aspire to be decorative—an ornament—but in a spiritually meaningful way. ("Art is an abstraction," Gauguin declared.)[12] Gradually, however, abstract line, color, and form in art became more important than "meaning," which might have to be brought to the work from outside it, thus not allowing the work to stand on its own. In the twentieth century, fine art has been freely allowed purely abstract meanings, or even no meaning. We have been moved by many of these works: to call abstract art "decoration" has been in the late twentieth century a scathing criticism. Eventually at midcentury and after, the meaninglessness of abstract art has become an ironic art message. So too has Andy Warhol's "Cow" wallpaper become art. Its parody of both wallpaper and art traditions—remote traditions that in the late twentieth century are almost like tribal customs—is meaningfully banal. The "Cow" wallpaper has meaning beyond its own banality, yet its banality is a key part of its meaning.

The relation of wallpaper to the other decorative arts has also been variously conceived. The idea that wallpaper in a room should be part of a selective, unified plan for its ornamentation is a comparatively recent one. In Morris's own rooms, for example, he seems to have welcomed many patterns in the furnishings. (So do some avant-garde artists today.)[13] Not until the end of the nineteenth century on the Continent did the idea of a *gesamtkunstwerk,* or totally designed art environment, gain currency. We will examine Hector Guimard's suite of wallpapers for the Castel Béranger and Josef Hoffmann's work at the Palais Stoclet in this light.

Amid these changing conceptions, all wallpaper artists have had to come to terms with certain constants of a demanding art form. For one thing, they have had to operate under severe technical and commercial constraints, more confining than they have faced in creating their fine art. They have needed to take into account the limited number and quality of colors available, the width and quality of the paper, its vulnerability to dampness, heat, light, and dust, plus some regard for the market—artists' wallpapers have often sold badly. More fundamentally, artists designing wallpaper have had to consider two special features: in most cases the wallpaper is meant to cover all the wall space of a room, and the same pattern is usually repeated throughout (the chief exception being scenic wallpapers, which are quite like murals). The artistry of the patterned designs depends in large part on the handling of these two features. How can any pattern, known in wallpaper parlance as a "repeat," survive such insistent repetition? In the latter part of the nineteenth century, artists approached this problem with extra patterns—for dado and frieze as well as filling. In the early twentieth century the Bauhaus approach to the problem was to design with minute patterns that were basically textures with subtle color blendings almost like solid colors.

Generally the wallpaper viewer is in an enclosed space. If the wallpaper repeat is too insistent, the viewer may feel trapped; if it is too muted, the walls may seem barren and uninteresting. Le Corbusier, the architect who once held that walls should be "pure" white, later designed some large-scale, dramatic, geometric wallpapers himself. The task of the wallpaper artist is to strike the precise balance that will help create a desired environment, whether of repose or excitement, cozy domesticity or magisterial formality.

That a wall covering is made of paper is an important factor in itself. A wallpapered room has a different feel from one in which we are surrounded by plaster or wood or leather or stone or even silk. Most wallpaper seems (and is) ephemeral. To create an atmosphere of permanence a design on paper requires some authority and vitality and some slight depth. The repeats must link together well. The design must give the onlooker a sense of well-being.

Wallpapers do not look at all the same on the wall as in a pattern book. How a pattern looks when extensively *repeated* is integral to its artistic success. As Ernst Gombrich has pointed out, the motifs of a pattern, when repeated so many times, will appear to the eye to provide their own order that will overwhelm any individual motif.[14] One of the secrets of Morris's successful designs was their combination of a luxuriant dominant motif with a richly conceived but subdued background pattern. He urged the artist to provide some mystery so that the eye did not see everything in a design at once.[15] He was also skillful at giving just enough depth to his designs to allow the observer a satisfying sense of space and at the same time a comfortable awareness of the wall's flatness.

When Morris observed that wallpaper must have meaning he meant that it must remind the viewer of something beyond the wall. He urged meaningful "repose."[16] He believed that plant motifs provided both beauty and rest, but on rare occasions he integrated an animal form into the design. The Art Nouveau artist Alphonse Mucha, like his mentor Eugène Grasset, was insistent that both animals and plants could provide decorative subjects; his animal designs, however, often seem misguidedly naturalistic while his flowering wallpapers are imaginative, vigorous, and welcoming.

Yet it is difficult to think of an important post-1950 artist who has used plant motifs in wallpapers, although some have tried animals. The self-consciousness of contemporary life allows only a spoof of wallpaper traditions: wallpaper design has been interesting to artists of our time precisely because it gives them opportunities for being deliberately provocative. On the other hand, there are contemporary "pattern" artists who have made an artistic statement by choosing to make their paintings look like wallpaper.

Most of the artists under consideration, particularly those working in the last two hundred years, have considered their wallpaper designs less important than their major works. Nevertheless, they have endowed their designs with something of themselves. Few artists have expected to create "high art" in a wallpaper pattern; work in the decorative arts has been regarded by almost everyone as minor art. For the most part I accept these judgments both in general and where wallpaper is concerned, but with two important provisos: When created by a major artist, a wallpaper has a special interest in the realm of decorative art. In addition, certain artists' wallpapers can transcend the ordinary limits of decorative art to enter the realm of great art.

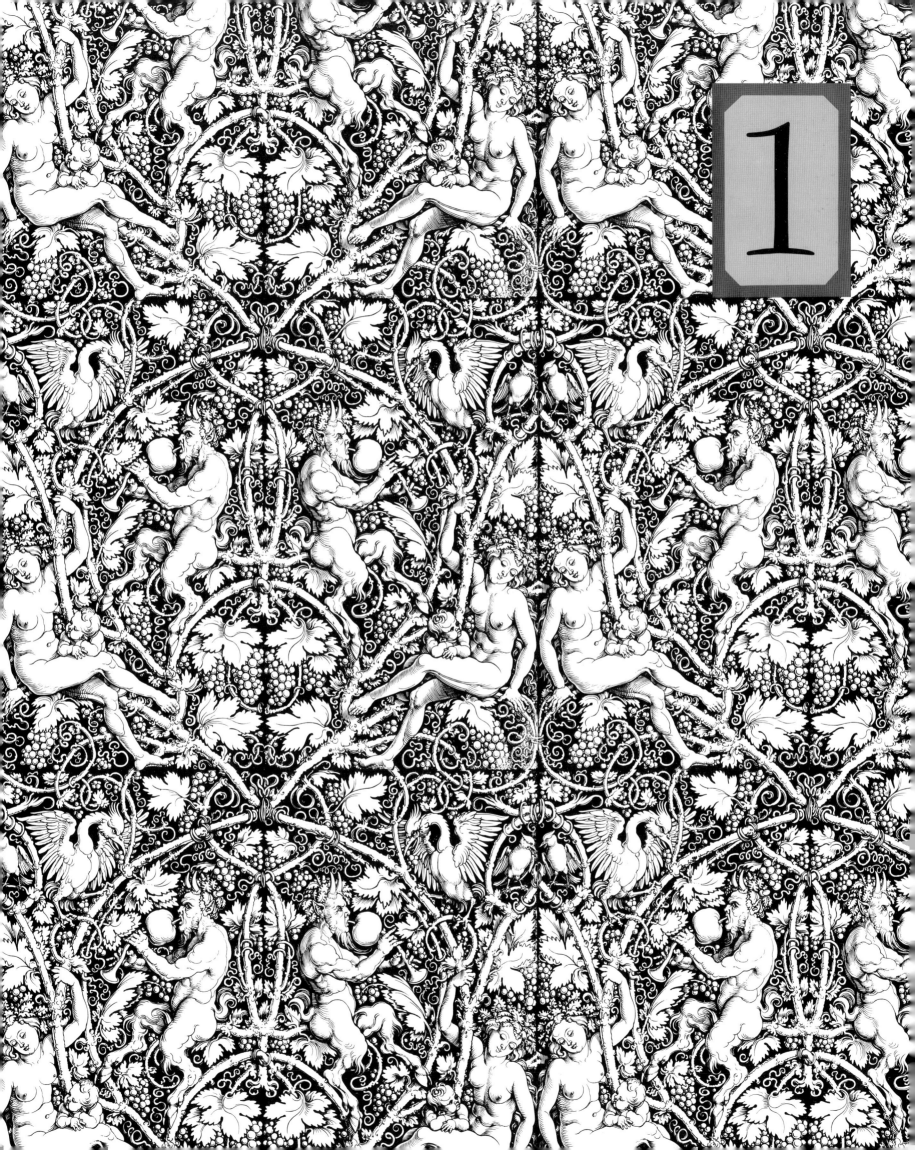

FROM DÜRER TO ROWLANDSON

(1500–1800)

Plate 1 *Preceding pages*
ALBRECHT DÜRER (1471–1528)
"The Satyr Family," c. 1515.
Wallpaper woodcut in montage as repeating
wallpaper, each side: 20⅞ x 12¾ in. (53.2 x
32.4 cm). Montage devised by Christian von
Heusinger. The Metropolitan Museum of Art,
New York; Rogers Fund, 1922.

Plate 2 *Opposite*
ALBRECHT DÜRER (1471–1528)
The Satyr Family, 1505.
Metal engraving, 4½ x 2¾ in. (11.4 x 6.9 cm).
The Metropolitan Museum of Art, New York;
Fletcher Fund, 1919.

he earliest great wallpaper artist known is Albrecht Dürer. His wallpapers may have survived precisely because he was a renowned artist in his own time. Painstaking research by a German scholar, Christian von Heusinger, has recently identified two of Dürer's woodcuts as wallpapers.[1] Of these the more remarkable is the "Satyr Family." Dated around 1515, the wallpaper may have been created for a wedding, possibly by imperial commission from Emperor Maximilian I: there are lovebirds in the pattern, and history records a double wedding of Maximilian's grandchildren in Vienna on July 22, 1515. The wallpaper's subject is bold and bacchanalian, portraying a satyr, his wife, and their child—an ensemble Dürer had earlier depicted in their exact positions in his small metal engraving *Satyr Family* of 1505 (plate 2). He brought the satyr motifs back to Nuremberg from Italy and used them several times in his art; their meanings for him remain mysterious to us.[2]

For the larger wallpaper design, Dürer embellished this ensemble with a phoenix and other birds, grapes, leaves, and an intricate forest of twisting vine arabesques, additions that make up about two-thirds of the design. The intertwining branches, which outline male and female sexual forms, emphasize the Dionysian implications of the satyrs and grapes. Dürer formed a most ingenious complete pattern by turning over the design, the whole having been conceived in such a way that the two sides, when combined, create the decorative and symbolic patterns with grapevines. Miraculously, both sides of the design still exist, the right half more crudely cut than the left. Recently the full version with a black background has been discovered as well (plate 1).[3]

Clearly we are in the hands of a great master with this wallpaper. It is all the more remarkable because it is among the earliest surviving wallpapers. Dürer's work is a stunning contrast to the work of the anonymous northern European artists who fashioned wallpapers in the sixteenth and seventeenth centuries. Before they created paper hangings, they commonly designed canvas or leather wall hangings for warmth and sturdiness. They were most influenced by tapestry art, for which all their materials were an attempted cheap substitute. Their figurative motifs were often crudely drawn, whereas Dürer's are consistently fine.

It is the extremely sensual sexuality of the "Satyr Family" that chiefly sets it apart from much of Dürer's work. The same may be said of the other woodcut that von Heusinger persuasively conjectures to be a wallpaper, the "Grosse Säule" ("Great Column"; plate 3). Done in the same year as the "Satyr Family," it too may have been an imperial commission. The column, with its phallic suggestions, is surmounted by a naked satyr and embraced by harpies, who in turn are held up by putti encircling a turnip root, another sexual symbol. Von Heusinger suggests that the column could have been repeated at intervals as wallpaper around the upper part of a room and could have been colored.[4] The column, on four paper woodblock-prints, is six feet high by three feet wide.[5]

There is no question that Dürer himself did the colored cartoon for the "Grosse Säule," a work now in the British Museum. By its side in the same frame is a much cruder woodcut print based on the drawing, dated 1517 and probably executed by a member of Dürer's workshop. Similar images are found in Dürer's drawings for the remarkable prayer book he made for Maximilian and on a decorative frame he presented to his good friend Pirckheimer in 1513.

Dürer's pupil Hans Sebald Beham, who had long been considered the creator of the "Satyr Family" wallpaper, is credited with a pomegranate-pattern repeating wallpaper, two candelabra patterns that could be used vertically as columned wallpaper, and a group of remarkable wallpaper borders. A simple and charming wallpaper border of cherubs' faces (c. 1520–25) has a version for vertical use and another for use horizontally (plate 4). Another border of the same date depicts tritons locked fiercely in combat with their two tails and one hand of each bound together—their free hands flail at each other with tied fish (plate 5). The motif is from Andrea Mantegna's *Battle of the Sea Gods,* 1485–88.[6] Beham is also credited with the "Grosse Girlande"

Plate 3
ALBRECHT DÜRER (1471–1528)
"Grosse Säule," c. 1515.
Woodcut, 63 x 9⅛ in. (160 x 23 cm).
Herzog Anton Ulrich-Museums,
Braunschweig, Germany.

Plate 4 *Top*
HANS SEBALD BEHAM (1500–1550?)
"Cherubs," c. 1520–25.
Horizontal wallpaper frieze,
woodcut, height: 7⅝ in. (19.3 cm).
Herzog Anton Ulrich-Museums,
Braunschweig, Germany.

Plate 5 *Bottom*
HANS SEBALD BEHAM (1500–1550?)
"Tritons," 1520–25.
Wallpaper frieze, woodcut, height: 8⁹⁄₁₆ in. (22 cm).
The Metropolitan Museum of Art, New York;
Rogers Fund, 1922.

("Great Garland") of 1520–25 (plate 6), which is an exquisite long paper border of many Dürer images: grapes, a harpy, an animal skull, a satyr. Beham's pomegranate-patterned repeating wallpaper (plate 7) has entwining vines much like the "Satyr Family" design but is less successful, in part because there is a gap between repeats, which the artist has partly solved by thongs. The resulting grapevine image, von Heusinger points out, is not of a heart, but of the turnip sexual symbol.[7] The pomegranate, which is shown as both flower and fruit in this design, was an important symbol of

Plate 6   *Above and below*
HANS SEBALD BEHAM (1500–1550?)
"Grosse Girlande," 1520–25.
Wallpaper frieze, woodcut. Herzog Anton Ulrich-Museums, Braunschweig, Germany.

Plate 7   *Left*
HANS SEBALD BEHAM (1500–1550?)
"Pomegranate," c. 1520–25.
Repeating wallpaper on black background, woodcut, height: 15⅜ in. (39.2 cm). Herzog Anton Ulrich-Museums, Braunschweig, Germany.

fertility and immortality to Emperor Maximilian, who is in fact shown holding a pomegranate like an orb in two of his portraits by Dürer.[8]

Another contemporary of Dürer's, Albrecht Altdorfer, is credited with a columned wallpaper of about 1515.[9] Between the columns is a repeating S-shaped acanthus design ending in a mask (plate 8). Altdorfer was a famed artist of Regensburg, but little is known about him today. His masterpiece is the epic painting *The Battle of Alexander* (1529), now in Munich.

Dürer, with Altdorfer and other artists, was connected with two major projects commissioned by Maximilian that cannot properly be called wallpapers yet involve extremely large designs created by combining many woodcuts and intended to be displayed, possibly pasted, on walls, like wallpaper panels.

Plate 8   *Right*
ALBRECHT ALTDORFER (1480?–1538)
Column with acanthus for repeating wallpaper,
woodcut, 14 x 10¼ in. (35.6 x 25.9 cm), c. 1515.
Herzog Anton Ulrich-Museums,
Braunschweig, Germany.

The famous *Triumphal Arch* (1512–15) was made of 192 woodcuts, the sheets pasted together to form a gigantic paper monument 3½ by 3 meters (11.5 by 9.75 feet), long considered the largest woodcut in the world (plate 9). Dürer designed much of the ornament and a few of the figures, and was in charge of the overall design. This awkward yet imposing work—Erwin Panofsky quotes Vasari in calling it "not beautiful but miraculous"[10]—depicts the emperor's life, family, and great deeds, and exalts him by placing his likeness over the central arch of majesty. The *Triumphal Arch* was to be placed in public buildings, carrying to his subjects the emperor's wish to be glorified through woodcut. The commission was an honor for Dürer, but the labor was heavy and the promised payment hard to come by. In response to the artist's pleading letter, the emperor consented to make yearly payments through taxes from Dürer's hometown of Nuremberg; by 1520, however, after the emperor's death, the town fathers had refused to pay Dürer his annuity, and he was writing of his poverty.[11]

The *Great Triumphal Car* is a large woodcut panel by Dürer showing the emperor in an elaborate chariot drawn by twelve horses, the horses themselves led by such allegorical figures as Moderation, Alacrity, and Magnanimity, and the chariot crowded with virtues such as Constancy, Prudence, and Truth. This work was originally conceived as part of a monumental, fifty-four-meter-long paper frieze. A collaboration of many artists, the frieze is known as the *Triumphal Procession*. The emperor ordained that one section portray a great procession of the people and stipulated that "all of them shall have laurel crowns on."[12] At the emperor's death in 1519 the frieze was still incomplete. Dürer published his own *Great Triumphal Car* from it in 1522. The finished frieze was not published until 1526 and included a *Small Triumphal Car* by Dürer, a celebration of the wedding of Maximilian to Mary of Burgundy in 1477.

The high artistry of Dürer's woodcut wallpapers and paper monuments derives in part from their association with the august and revered imperial court. But the skill he expended upon them also derives from his whole view of art. He chose deliberately to produce works that could be reproduced; that is why he left relatively few paintings but many engravings and woodcuts. Also, as Lewis W. Spitz suggests, Dürer "preferred etching to painting on the grounds of profit alone," and these works brought him fame.[13] Moreover, he was able to bring even to his celebration of worldly matters a religious sense of dedication: "For work well done is honoring to God, useful, good, and pleas-

Plate 9 *Opposite*
ALBRECHT DÜRER (1471–1528) and others
Triumphal Arch for Maximilian I, c. 1512–17.
Woodcut, 138⅞ x 119¾ in. (351 x 304.3 cm).
Graphische Sammlung Albertina, Vienna.

Plate 10
Domino wallpaper, stencil and wood block, 18th century. Courtesy of the Reimondini Collection, Museo Civico, Biblioteca e Archivio, Bassano del Grappa, Italy.

Plate 11
Queen's Drawing Room flock wallpaper, Hampton Court, 1735. By courtesy of the Board of Trustees of the Victoria and Albert Museum, London.

ing to men. But to labor contemptibly in art is wrong and properly condemned, it is hateful in small works as in great."[14]

Dürer was creating wallpapers very soon after paper first became widely manufactured in Europe, at the end of the fifteenth century. After such an auspicious beginning for wallpaper art, there is no major artist to consider until the end of the eighteenth century, although there are important wallpaper traditions and lesser artists. Unfortunately, few wallpapers have survived the sixteenth and seventeenth centuries.[15] Indeed, paper may not have been commonly used on walls until the end of the seventeenth century, a century ravaged by war, fire, and pestilence. Early in the eighteenth century, however, Savary des Bruslons reported, "There is not a house in Paris, however grand, that does not contain some example of this charming decoration, even if only in a wardrobe or other private room"[16] (plate 10). Some of the credit for this popularity of wallpaper must go to Jean Papillon, who worked from 1688 on in his Parisian shop at the sign of the Butterfly and was known as a *dominotier*. (The wallpaper patterns *dominotiers* created were called *dominos*.) His son left a treatise praising his father as the creator of *papiers de tapisserie,* which made extended use of repeating wallpaper woodblock and stencil techniques by joining a pattern on multiple sheets—even at times using more than one sheet for a complete design, as Dürer had done much earlier.[17]

The *papiers de tapisserie* included some flock wallpapers. Early in the eighteenth century, according to one report, these admired wallpapers were "as dear as damask." Those made in England were considered the finest in Europe. They were made especially sturdy by gluing wool fibers to a printed design; thus they resembled cloth or tapestry rather than fragile paper. Madame de Pompadour exchanged the damask and tapestries lining her wardrobe and the passage to the chapel at Versailles for English flock wallpaper in 1754. A most beautiful example of these anonymous wallpapers is the giant pattern of vertical floral motifs used in 1735 for the Queen's Drawing Room at Hampton Court, near London. This famous pattern once hung in many of the stately houses of Britain, and in 1985 was reproduced for the *Treasure Houses of Britain* exhibition (plate 11).

By the middle of the eighteenth century in France, a

genius wallpaper manufacturer, Jean-Baptiste Réveillon, produced some of the world's most beautiful wallpapers (plate 12). Pompeii and Herculaneum had only recently been uncovered and with them Pompeian-style wall painting. In many of his wallpapers, Réveillon, with the help of artists Jean-Baptiste Huet and Jean-Baptiste Fay and others, used Pompeian arabesques to set off the small pictured scenes, thus forming graceful patterns in elegant colors. Réveillon's factory was destroyed by a mob early in the French Revolution, but his successor continued to produce wallpapers. One of Réveillon's own wallpapers is titled "L'Eau et le feu" (c. 1780; plate 13). A similar theme was presented by Thomas Sheraton in his 1793 *Cabinet-Maker and Upholsterer's Drawing-Book*. He pictured a Réveillonesque wallpaper panel, which he described charmingly as "a temple set on fire by Cupids, whose intentions are defeated by the interposition of certain genie, who pour down water to quench the flames."[18]

Since heavy taxes discouraged the importation of French wallpapers in England, a new fashion in English wallpaper had emerged. Known as the print room, it entailed pasting paper scenes or portraits with paper frames on a wallpaper background. These decorations grew partly from the work of John Baptist Jackson, who had worked in France for a time for Papillon's son, then traveled to Italy where he began making small wallpaper copies of master paintings by Titian, Tintoretto, and Veronese (plate 14). Jackson used what he considered a new technique: color with oil paints and chiaroscuro achieved through use of multiple woodblocks. After his return to England in 1746 he wrote a self-important, bombastic broadside, *An Essay on the Invention of Engraving and Printing in Chiaroscuro* (1754), praising his own work extravagantly. The tastemaker Horace Walpole, while disparaging these wallpaper creations ("barbarous bas-reliefs"), used them all the same in his neo-Gothic villa, Strawberry Hill, thereby popularizing the print room. In fact, Walpole apparently thus wallpapered many rooms in this "plaything" house and wrote proudly of them in 1753, describing "the little parlour hung with a stone-colored Gothic paper and Jackson's Venetian prints . . . a bedchamber hung with yellow papers and prints framed in a manner invented by Lord Cadogan, with black-and-white borders printed; [a second] bed-chamber, hung with red in the same

Plate 12
JEAN-BAPTISTE RÉVEILLON (1725–1811) and
JEAN-BAPTISTE FAY (active 1775–1789)
Wallpaper panels, wood-block printed; from a series entitled "Coq et Perroquet," 1785–88. A complete set of these wallpapers is at the General Lafayette House, Chavagnac, France. By courtesy of the Board of Trustees of the Victoria and Albert Museum, London.

manner . . . the room where we always live, hung with a blue and white paper, adorned with festoons."[19] This fashion of pasting ever more elaborate ornamental paper decorations around prints continued throughout much of the century (plate 15). James Boswell's *Life of Samuel Johnson* refers to Mrs. Thrale's print room hung with William Hogarth's *Midnight Modern Conversation.* Thomas Chippendale decorated print rooms of his clients with rococo paper borders, which can be seen in the 1762 edition of his *Gentleman and Cabinet-Maker's Director.* There is a record of his decorating Lady Knatchbull's dressing room with verditure (greenish-blue) wallpaper adorned not only with the paper borders for prints but also with swags of fruit, satyr and lion masks, knots, and chains, all in paper.[20] Eventually, there were even wallpapers printed to imitate the look of a print room.

No survey of notable eighteenth-century artists' wallpapers would be complete without mention of wallpapers from China and attempts to copy or evoke them. Exquisite hand-painted panels on paper were imported into Europe from China even before 1700 and throughout the eighteenth century. In England owners of great houses were known to remove their Jacobean paneling and replace it with "painted paper of Pekin," as Lady Montagu called it. John Evelyn's diary entry for July 1699 mentions "hangings of Chinese papers" for Queen Mary at Hampton Court. Chinese wallpaper art was greatly admired, despite John Baptist Jackson's fulminations against its lack of perspective: "Lions leaping from Bough to Bough like Cats, Houses in the Air, Clouds and Sky upon the Ground, a thorough Confusion of all the Elements."[21] These exotic papers, with brilliant colors and exquisite stylized details of birds and flowers or Chinese scenes, set off a room to perfection (see plate 26) and were prized as well for their costliness. Cheaper chinoiserie wallpapers in the form of European copies soon became widely available. In 1737 Thomas Hancock wrote back to England from Boston to request a paper in the Chinese style. "Get mine well Done and as cheap as Possible and if they can make it more beautiful by adding more Birds flying here and there, with some landskips at the bottom, should like it well."[22] The style endured. In the late eighteenth century Jean-Baptiste Pillement created chinoiserie wallpapers for Réveillon.

At Harrington House, Gloucestershire, there was hand-painted chinoiserie wallpaper with grotesque, winged car-

Plate 14
John Baptist Jackson (1700?–1777)
Wallpaper, chiaroscuro wood engraving, c. 1740. After *The Crucifixion* by Jacopo Tintoretto (1518–1594). Whitworth Art Gallery, University of Manchester, England.

Plate 13 *Opposite*
Jean-Baptiste Réveillon (1725–1811)
Wallpaper, chiaroscuro color print from wood blocks, c. 1780. Based on Réveillon's "L'Eau et le feu" with slight variations. By courtesy of the Board of Trustees of the Victoria and Albert Museum, London.

touches that were originally created by Antoine Watteau in a drawing (engraved by Gabriel Huquier in 1730) known as "L'Innocent badinage" ("Boys at Play").[23] Watteau, a consummate painter of the early eighteenth century, is also known for his decorative designs, particularly those in the tradition of the Roman grotesque, which Raphael had found useful in

Renaissance decorative art. The style uses bizarre, fantastic human and animal figures with decorative scrolls, masks, and foliage. Watteau's *singeries* (monkeys embodying human characteristics) at Château de la Muette in France were notable examples of the grotesque; unfortunately, only engravings of them remain. At Harrington House, his winged motifs for the cartouches on the wallpaper were among the most daring of chinoiserie grotesques.

Interest in the grotesque in the first half of the eighteenth century led to interest in caricature in the latter half. At the very end of the century the artist and caricaturist Thomas Rowlandson engraved some grotesque wallpaper borders. Rowlandson was one of a group of English artists whose caricatures were so renowned that he failed to paint the conventional paintings expected of an artist so gifted. Instead he created thousands of watercolors, mostly carica-

tures, in a characteristic style his biographer Joseph Grego admired and carefully described: "[Using] his famous reed pen in a tint composed of vermilion and Indian-ink, the general effect was rapidly washed in, so as to produce an effective chiaroscuro; and the whole was colored in tender tints with a most harmonious arrangement of color."[24] Rowlandson, born in midcentury, was very much at home in the colorful surroundings he recorded. He was the son of moderately well-to-do parents, was precocious in drawing, and studied at the Royal Academy, where his talent was immediately recognized. He was described as both genial and honorable, but addicted to gambling and continually in debt. Grego related that "for too many years he was too indolent to seek employment."[25] However that may be, the sheer volume of his work is staggering, and in the great mass of the Rowlandson oeuvre, the wallpapers have been almost overlooked.

Rowlandson's wallpapers, issued by his benefactor and publisher, Rudolph Ackermann, in 1800, are border strips titled "Grotesque Borders for Screens, Billiard Rooms, Dressing Rooms, etc, etc. Forming a caricature Assemblage of Oddities, Whimsicalities and Extravaganzas with appropriate labels to the Principle Figures." They were considered grotesque because in many of them human heads are overlarge; they were caricatures because they lampooned the society of the times. Rowlandson's satiric style is almost as tolerantly detached as the "tender" colors of pale blue and rose that so often comprise his palette. The borders, however, were garishly hand-colored by others in a workshop. They were printed in strips, three to a page, twenty-four pages in a set, some to be arranged horizontally, others vertically. Meant to be cut apart, pasted together, and placed around panels of plain wallpapers, around doorways or windows, or used on screens, they were sold for pennies. They were drawn first by another caricaturist, G. M. "Mustard George" Woodward, but etched by Rowlandson. Grego assured his readers that anything Rowlandson touched was endowed with his own style, and the borders appear to be so. Ronald Paulson explains a "Rowlandson" as a style, "a way of treating subject matter—as we see in the many cases where he simply etched someone else's anecdote or design."[26]

Rowlandson's art is often zestfully bawdy and on occasion licentious, characteristics deplored by later biographers. The wallpapers, however, are relatively discreet. They are a

Plate 15
Print Room, Rokeby Manor, c. 1760.
Thomas Chippendale is thought to have decorated
this room with wood engravings for both prints and frames.
Rokeby Manor House, Yorkshire, England.

great deal like comic strips except that each small scene has little to do with any other and is complete in itself. The comedy is coarse; the scenes on the wallpaper are lively in the Rowlandson manner. Although the borders appeared in several advertisements, there is no record of any room in which they were used. Since the strips are about four inches wide, no one more than a foot away from the wall would be able to read them! Yet, closely observed as they are, they themselves reward close observation. They certainly obey no wallpaper traditions for borders, traditions that prescribe a definite repeated pattern. Nevertheless, on a wall these small figures in brash colors would have a rollicking rhythm very close to pattern. The borders have the same eloquent line of the reed pen that Rowlandson's watercolors are noted for, and they reflect the tendency in all his work to portray the pretty as well as the comic, grossly exaggerating the grotesque in some figures while allowing others, most often young women, to be attractive but often silly.[27] In their class-consciousness, misogyny, and folk philosophy, they (like Rowlandson's watercolors) comprise a microcosm of fashionable London society of the late eighteenth century, rendered with delightful verve and trenchant yet benign wit (plate 16).[28]

The words of Rowlandson's diminutive figures are etched above their heads. A couple, made to look as ludicrous as the artist can manage, is crowned with the motto "Ah sure a pair was never seen, so justly formed to meet by Nature." An admiral with his spyglass on a pretty young girl says to himself: "If I may judge by the stern, That seems to be a tight little frigate ahead, I'll throw out a signal and . . . " A young woman in a shepherd's smock dress minces: "Shepherds I have lost my waist. Have you seen my body? Sacrifice to modern taste. I am quite a Hoddy Doddy." A middle-aged couple has an argument: "Woman: I'll divide the house with you. Man: With all my heart my dear. I will take the inside and you shall take the out!"

It is remarkable that in this early period there should be wallpapers by such masters as Rowlandson and Dürer. Few could view their wallpapers as other than fine art. Dürer's wallpapers exemplify all the rules of design in use of space, variety of tone, superb line and form; they also masterfully respond to wallpaper's special concerns with unifying design and the intricacies of repetition. In contrast, Rowlandson's wallpapers conform to no rules at all. That is their charm. They are decorative with an eloquent line that exhibits wit and joie de vivre. As different as these two artists are, however, they are not without points in common. In fact, Rowlandson was enough interested in Dürer's "Satyr Family" wallpaper design to make a sketch of it; the sketch survives at the Huntington Library (plate 17).[29] The two artists shared a view of art that made no distinction between fine and decorative arts, and each sought wide and inexpensive dissemination of his work. It was thus as natural for them to practice their artistry in wallpaper as in any other form.

Plate 17

THOMAS ROWLANDSON (1756–1827)

Sketch, sepia pen over pencil, 8½ x 6¾ in. (21.6 x 17.1 cm), c. 1800. After Dürer's "The Satyr Family" wallpaper motif. The Huntington Library and Art Gallery, San Marino, California.

BEFORE WILLIAM MORRIS

The Grammar of Ornament, Instruction, and Illusion (1800–1860)

Plate 18   *Preceding pages*
JEAN-GABRIEL CHARVET (1750–1829)
"Rediscovery of the Sandwich Islands," 1804.
Wallpaper panels (based on Captain Cook's voyages),
from the panoramic "Sauvages de la mer Pacifique,"
twenty lengths printed in color from wood blocks,
Dufour. Courtesy of the Philadelphia Museum of Art;
Gift of Anne Mitchell McAllister in memory of her father
William Young McAllister.

Plate 19   *Opposite*
LOUIS LAFITTE (1770–1828) and MÉRY-JOSEPH BLONDEL
(1781–1853)
"Psyche Intending to Stab the Sleeping Cupid," 1816.
Wallpaper panels, from the panoramic "Cupid and Psyche,"
twenty-six lengths printed in grisaille from wood blocks,
Dufour. Deutsches Tapetenmuseum, Kassel, Germany.

To some the phrase "wallpaper and the artist" may bring to mind the remarkable scenic wallpapers produced in France during the nineteenth century, the first ones in 1804, the last around 1860. These wallpapers were deliberately designed to look like hand-painted murals rather than conventional wallpaper with its repeated patterns. Their panoramas typically have a theatrical look, displaying exotic lands, "savages," architectural phenomena, mythological subjects, great battles. "Sauvages de la mer Pacifique," or the "Captain Cook" wallpaper, is one of the earliest (plate 18). Designed by Jean-Gabriel Charvet and published by Dufour in 1804, it is one of the most brilliant in color and imaginative in execution; the oranges and greens are intense, the "savages" wear Roman costume, and the variegated flora are detailed and tropical. This wallpaper was in fact accompanied by a booklet describing it proudly and pedagogically as "living lessons in history and geography."[1] (Théophile Gautier once referred to scenic wallpapers as "useful encyclopedia[s] to study while waiting for the soup.")[2]

The artists who were involved in creating scenic wallpapers are not well known today: Jean Broc, Jean-Gabriel Charvet, Jean-Julien Deltil, Xavier Mader, Pierre-Antoine Mongin, Carle Vernet. The historian G. L. Hunter cites Jacques-Louis David as the artist responsible for the dazzling grisaille scenic series "Cupid and Psyche" (plate 19), but that attribution has proven to be mistaken.[3] The true creators, however, had styles in many ways similar to David's elegant neoclassicism: Louis Lafitte, winner of the Prix de Rome in 1791, and Méry-Joseph Blondel, a Prix de Rome winner of 1793. Lafitte's and Blondel's designs for this favorite myth were printed on twenty-six wallpaper panels in 1816 and were so continuously admired that Desfossé and Karth produced this series until 1931.

Jean Broc, a pupil of David's, is credited with Dufour's famous "Monuments of Paris," which lines up the great buildings of Paris along the Seine (plate 23). The foreground figures are thought to be by the artist Carle Vernet. The famous bronze horses shown here on the Arc du Carrousel were returned to St. Mark's, Venice, in 1815. The wallpaper was made in 1814.

The scenic wallpapers required great enterprise as well as artistry. Several years were needed to cut the hundreds, sometimes thousands, of blocks necessary, in addition to the painstaking printing process. Once cut these blocks could last for decades, however, and some early-nineteenth-century designs are still being reprinted from the original blocks. The first scenics were printed on rolls of paper composed of sheets glued together; the rolls or panels were then joined to form a scene. Their layout was not unlike the Chinese wallpapers except that an area of sky on the French wallpapers was left undecorated and made in extra length so that the panels could be trimmed to fit a given room.

Not surprisingly, considering the great labor of cutting the blocks, scenic wallpaper makers sometimes used their backgrounds more than once. Two Zuber scenic wallpapers sharing a background are now in the White House: "The American Revolution" (plate 20) of 1852 in the presidential family dining room is a recycle of the 1834 "Vues d'Amérique du Nord" ("Scenic America"; plate 21), in the Diplomatic Reception Room. The panel showing a stage-coach with genteel passengers in front of the Natural Bridge in Virginia becomes in the military version a troop of red-coated soldiers massed against the same background. The artist for both series was Deltil.

Plate 20   *Opposite*
JEAN-JULIEN DELTIL (1791–1863)
"The American Revolution," 1852.
Panoramic wallpaper, thirty-two lengths printed
in color from wood blocks, Zuber; *in situ*,
Family Dining Room, The White House, Washington,
D.C., President Richard Nixon and his family in the
foreground, the Natural Bridge of Virginia in the
wallpaper background, 1969. National Archives and
Records Administration, Washington, D.C.

Plate 21
JEAN-JULIEN DELTIL (1791–1863)
"Stagecoach and the Natural Bridge," 1834.
Wallpaper panel, from the panoramic "Vues d'Amérique
du Nord," thirty-two lengths printed in color from wood
blocks, Zuber. This original panel was changed in 1852 to
show soldiers in the foreground for the panoramic
wallpaper "The American Revolution." In the Diplomatic
Reception Room, The White House, Washington, D.C.
Courtesy of Deutsches Tapetenmuseum, Kassel, Germany.

Two American presidents are associated with French scenic wallpapers: President Monroe used the exotic garden scenes of the 1848 Zuber "Eldorado" in his Virginia home, Oak Hill, and President Jackson, retiring from the White House to his new home, the Hermitage in Tennessee, chose the 1823 Dufour "Telemachus" wallpapers for the entrance hall, where they may be seen today (plate 22). Scenic wallpapers were also popular in more modest American homes; they were often given as wedding presents. Not everyone, however, has had a high regard for them. Honoré de Balzac reviled them as "a grotesque and shabby invention" and in his novel *Le Père Goriot* (1835) described dilapidated boardinghouse wallpapers containing the "Telemachus" scenic series in a dining room as "the saddest sight of all," and "the subject of ribald jokes."[4] Nevertheless, the fine workmanship and verve of the French scenics has for the most part

Plate 22
"Telemachus on Calypso's Isle," 1823.
Panoramic wallpaper, twenty-five lengths printed in color from wood blocks, Dufour et Leroy; *in situ,* the hallway of President Andrew Jackson's home, The Hermitage, near Nashville, Tennessee, c. 1892. The Hermitage; Home of Andrew Jackson, Hermitage, Tennessee.

Plate 23   *Opposite*
JEAN BROC (1771–1850)
"Monuments of Paris," 1814–15.
Panoramic wallpaper, thirty lengths printed in color from wood blocks, Dufour et Leroy. Foreground figures after Carle Vernet (1758–1836). By courtesy of the Board of Trustees of the Victoria and Albert Museum, London.

been held in high esteem; they are in fact among the most cherished wallpapers in history and today are sold for princely sums.

Art wallpapers figured prominently in the Royal Pavilion at Brighton, the grand folly of the Prince Regent, who was to become King George IV. Begun in 1795 in a neoclassic style, the pavilion became instead a splendid Oriental fantasy that absorbed the talents of the finest architects and decorators for its adornment: the architect John Nash, Augustus-Charles Pugin (father of the architect Augustus Welby Northmore Pugin), the Crace firm, the painter Robert

Jones. The gifted but elusive Jones designed many of the wallpapers for the pavilion, including original and magnificent chinoiserie for the Prince Regent's private apartments. Very little is known about Jones. He is believed to have worked for himself as well as for the important London wallpaper firm of Eckhardt. Much of the most imaginative work in the pavilion is his, including, it is thought, the trompe l'oeil bamboo wallpaper frames around the Chinese paintings that were pasted directly over the chinoiserie dragon wallpaper in the Red Drawing Room, the many bamboo dadoes, and all the dragon wallpapers.

The dragon wallpapers are like no others. Inspired no doubt by Chinese art, they are nevertheless a totally original creation, understated in color but alive with fantastic dolphins, flowers, dragons, and phoenixes, held together by the rhythmic pulse of the artist's wavering, repeated arabesque line. Also grandly effective are the ingenious matching paper bamboo dadoes, designed by Jones to have a background of the dragon wallpaper. This wallpaper, echoing throughout the pavilion, unifies it. In the dazzling Banqueting Room flamboyant hand-painted Chinese scenes on Jones's subdued, small-patterned wallpaper in cobalt surmount the brilliant bamboo dadoes in red (plate 24). The large-patterned damask dragon papers (12 by 10 feet) for the private apartments were designed by Robert Jones in green and gray. For reproduction, the pattern was silkscreened and handpainted. Unused examples of identical wallpapers in chrome yellow and gray are among the Crace papers in the Cooper-Hewitt Museum in New York (plate 25). The ballroom of the pavilion is now believed to have once been hung with the yellow wallpapers and will be restored.

The Prince Regent greatly admired imported Chinese wallpaper and used it lavishly in his original decor for the pavilion. We know that he gave a set of Chinese wallpapers to Lady Irwin of Temple Newsam, Leeds, in 1806, after falling in love with her daughter. The daughter, the Marchioness of Hertford, hung the wallpapers at Temple Newsam in the 1820s, embellished with birds she had cut out from John James Audubon's first series of *Birds of America* (plate 26). She cut apart ten of the one hundred sheets and pasted on her walls twenty-five Audubon birds, also taking a few birds from a dark corner of the Chinese wallpaper itself! Audubon wrote his family about this with amazement but hope for more sales: "A Mr. Blydes continues the set of the Marchioness of Hereford [*sic*] who you Know has had the whole of the first Volume cut out and pasted on the walls of one of her Suberp [*sic*] Rooms!—Therefore he may yet want the first Volume himself."[5] In the end the marchioness ordered no further volumes. In 1802 the Prince Regent himself had decorated the blue and silver Chinese wallpaper of the Royal Pavilion's saloon with extra birds. The Crace Ledgers entertainingly record that in December 1802, Frederick Crace "attended the Prince in . . . fixing up and cutting out the Birds, etc. on the paper in Saloon."[6]

Plate 25
ROBERT JONES (active c. 1800–1825)
"Dragon and Bamboo," 1820.
Wallpaper, printed in color from wood blocks;
from the Royal Pavilion, Brighton, England.
Courtesy of Cooper-Hewitt, National Museum
of Design, Smithsonian Institution; Gift of Brighton
Art Gallery and Museum/Art Resource, New York.

Plate 24   *Opposite*
ROBERT JONES (active c. 1800–1825)
Wallpaper and Chinese painting, 1820; *in situ,* the Banqueting
Room (west wall), Royal Pavilion, Brighton. Royal Pavilion Art
Gallery and Museums, Brighton, England.

Plate 26
<small>UNKNOWN CHINESE ARTISTS</small>
"Chinese Garden," c. 1800.
Hand-painted wallpaper, hung c. 1827 with pasted-on birds
from John James Audubon's *Birds of America* (1827–38); *in situ,*
Chinese Drawing Room, Temple Newsam, Leeds, England.
Leeds City Art Galleries, Temple Newsam House, England.

Another important monument of English architecture was decorated with outstanding wallpaper art in the second quarter of the nineteenth century. The Houses of Parliament in the Palace of Westminster were destroyed by fire in 1834, and the rallying cry at the Royal Academy was "Hurrah boys, now's your chance; the Houses of Parliament are in flames."[7] Artists were needed for the many interior designs, which eventually included hundreds of wallpapers. The firm of Crace and the artist-architect Augustus Welby Northmore

Pugin (1812–1852) were chosen. For this massive task Pugin toiled ceaselessly, prodigiously, for many of the last years of his short life, creating every design himself. "Clerk?" he once said, "My dear sir, Clerk? I never employ one. I should kill him in a week."[8] Pugin had contributed to Charles Barry's winning commission for this building, but the two colleagues separated unhappily in 1837, and Pugin returned to the overwhelming task only at Barry's urging seven years later.

Plate 27
A.W.N. Pugin (1812–1852)
"Tudor," c. 1850.
Wallpaper; for the Houses of Parliament, London.
By courtesy of the Board of Trustees of the
Victoria and Albert Museum, London.

Plate 28
A.W.N. Pugin (1812–1852)
"Lion," c. 1850.
Wallpaper; for the Houses of Parliament, London.
Boston Athenaeum.

Pugin's Houses of Parliament wallpapers are even more Gothic than the architecture (plates 27; 28; 29). Their strong colors give them depth (some are flock), and their flat patterns are filled with heraldic animals and symbolic medieval motifs. All are formal; many are based on a geometric trellis. On the vast walls of the Palace of Westminster they have a presence and authority remarkable for paper designs. The stately pomegranate design for the Queen's Robing Room and the Royal Gallery is very similar to a fifteenth-century velvet at the Victoria and Albert Museum (plates 30; 31). "I am always on the look out," Pugin once wrote to Crace, "and I saw on the walls of a house built in the 15 cent that was falling down at Salisbury the ground work of the 2 patterns I send you stencilled on the walls. I thought they would make excellent patterns for papers and I have accordingly set them out in a variety of ways." Thinking lions "too peculiar for a general paper," he used birds in the alternative spaces instead, and thought the "movement of the pattern" admirable.[9]

Throughout his short, frenzied, overproductive life Pugin filled many sketchbooks with careful drawings of artifacts seen on his travels, and he used these for the thousands of designs he made. When at the age of fifteen he was spotted in the British Museum Print Room making a copy of a Dürer print, Pugin was offered a job designing plate. Shortly afterward his father suggested him for a commission to design Gothic furniture for George IV at Windsor Castle. In his twenties Pugin converted to Roman Catholicism and fervently believed throughout his life in its social and redemptive power; he once said there was "nothing worth living for except Christian architecture and a boat!"[10] He built two Gothic houses for himself, expressed the wish for a little "Gothic boy or girl" for his first child, and spoke of his third wife as "a first-rate Gothic woman."[11]

In 1837 when Pugin was twenty-five, he was commissioned to refurbish Scarisbrick Hall, Lancashire, a task he worked on until 1845, turning it into one of the first examples of domestic Gothic Revival. For the Red Drawing Room, he designed a splendid wallpaper of red flock on gold with a very large repeat of over two and a half feet, inspired by a fifteenth-century Venetian velvet brocade. He decorated other great houses with wallpaper, somehow finding time for more designs amid incessant architectural activity

Plate 29
A.W.N. Pugin (1812–1852)
"Lion," 1850.
Wallpaper, printed from wood blocks; *in situ,* Prime Minister's
Room, Houses of Parliament, London, 1903. Farmer
Collection, courtesy of House of Lords Record Office, by
permission of the Clerk of the Records, London.

that was to have influence for a good part of the nineteenth century. His wallpapers for Chirk, Lee, Lismore, Lough Cutra, and Windsor castles are bold, vigorous, and powerful, and—like the Houses of Parliament wallpapers—formal, geometric, and stylized. Many of Pugin's wallpapers are

available today; some are printed with the original blocks (see appendix B).

"All ornament," Pugin believed, "should consist of enrichment of the essential construction of a building."[12] The form and meaning of the ornament he saw as inseparable from

the architecture. His flat, perspectiveless wallpapers are very different from the popular pseudo-Gothic patterned papers he detested: "wretched caricature[s] of a pointed building . . . repeated from the skirting to the cornice."[13] His was a very advanced design theory, which he felt only the Middle Ages had fulfilled. But Pugin was rarely satisfied: "I have passed my life in thinking of fine things, studying fine things, designing fine things and realising very poor ones," he said.[14]

William Burges, a later self-styled "Goth," saw Pugin as his hero, "that wonderful man" who was, as the historian Mordaunt Crook expressed it, "the lode star of a generation of Goths."[15] Burges, the most Gothic of the followers, was a major architect in the third quarter of the century, a superb craftsman, a virtual scholar of the Middle Ages, and a magpie collector. Burges was so notoriously Gothic that when Jeffrey, the famous wallpaper company, invited him to design wallpapers, the public thought the firm had gone mad.[16] However, one can see a superb Burges wallpaper at the Château-sur-Mer, in Newport, Rhode Island (plate 33).

Burges's own Tower House on Melbury Road in London, "a model residence of the thirteenth century," still looms up just off the road, a small medieval castle-fortress. It is difficult to imagine wallpapers in that house but they may well have been used, since there are extant samples of wallpapers in heavy paper with Gothic designs by Burges marked

Plate 30   *Opposite*
A.W.N. PUGIN (1812–1852)
The Queen's Robing Room wallpaper;
in situ, Houses of Parliament, London.
Woodmansterne, Ltd., Watford, England.

Plate 31
A.W.N. PUGIN (1812–1852)
Wallpaper, block printed in flock c. 1850; for
the Royal Gallery and the Queen's Robing Room,
Houses of Parliament, London. Reprinted from
the original blocks by Arthur Sanderson and Sons,
Ltd. Courtesy of Arthur Sanderson and Sons, Ltd.,
Middlesex, England.

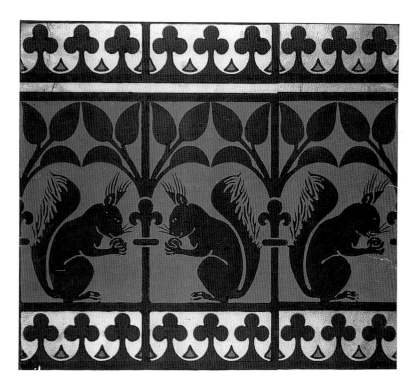

Plate 32
WILLIAM BURGES (1827–1881)
"Squirrels," 1872.
Wallpaper frieze, height: 14⅜ in. (36.3 cm), Jeffrey and Co. By courtesy of the Board of Trustees of the Victoria and Albert Museum, London.

"Melbury Road" (plate 32). Burges himself much preferred painted mural decoration and as architect for both the ruins of Castel Coch and the partly restored Cardiff Castle in Wales for the wealthy Lord Bute he used costlier, more medieval materials. Indeed, he abhorred "wretched" wallpaper "abominations."[17]

Nevertheless, Burges designed some lively and unique wallpapers, which luckily have survived. Some of these, including "The Daisy and the Snail," were published in the *Building News* in 1872 but accorded less than glowing praise:

> We are not quite sure that a repetition of masks is in any place a desirable decoration, and we certainly do not relish the idea of a face peering at us from every part of the room. The snails among the daisies are suggestive of our climate, it is true, but it is questionable whether any one wants this sort of reminder. Indeed, the introduction of any members of the animal kingdom in wall-

papers, involving, as it necessarily does, such an amount of repetition is always dangerous. . . . We would suggest to Mr. Burges the possibility of his designs being improved by a little more refinement.[18]

One doubts that Burges was at all impressed or offended by these remarks, when what he was after was an evocation of the passion, humor, and vitality of an idealized age. He used medieval animals in his friezes and even in his fillings quite blithely. There is dignity and authority in his use of masks. He was concerned with metaphor and symbolism, not just pleasant natural forms. One of his wallpapers includes motifs for earth, air, fire, and water, the four elements of the medieval universe. He loved little jokes in his decoration, as in the library of his house where he created an alphabet frieze in stone for the fireplace, dropping the *H* as in the Cockney dialect. He added a frog in a frieze with a bottle of cough medicine for his throat, and depicted the early bird and a worm on his guestroom door. His use of "unrefined" snails among daisies in his wallpaper designs shows the same droll amusement.

Although anti-Gothic, the architect Owen Jones was at midcentury, like Pugin, a student of design history. Jones believed that the styles of the past should serve the present rather than the reverse. His *Grammar of Ornament* (1856), "an attempt to gather prominent types of ornamental art," was wide-ranging and vastly influential, respected even by Morris. A design theorist, Jones revered truth in structure: steel columns should not be made to look like stone, architecture and design should grow out of the age, and the decorative arts "should arise from and be attendant upon architecture."[19] On the other hand, he concluded, "To form a style independently of the past would be an act of supreme folly."[20]

Although he designed very few buildings, Jones was commissioned to build the Viceroy's Palace in Cairo in 1863. For the interior, which he regarded as his masterpiece, he created fifteen sets of designs for wallpaper fillings and friezes and dadoes, described by the *Builder* in 1874 as "a style as perfect and exact as is exemplified in the tombs of the Caliph in Old Cairo."[21] Jeffrey produced a special catalog of these designs. Jones's travels in the Near East and Egypt as a young man powerfully influenced his design theories. He regarded the Egyptian style as the soundest and oldest, and at the Crystal Palace in London, built for the Great Exhibition of 1851, he designed an Egyptian court. In his published description he contrasted the stylized Egyptian lions in the court with the more naturalistic lions of the sculptor Antonio Canova, boldly concluding: "The superior-ity of the Egyptian idealized form over the attempted imitation of a natural lion carved in stone, will be very apparent."[22] Furthermore, he wrote forthrightly in the *Grammar of Ornament:* "The Egyptians dealt in flat tints, and used neither shade nor shadow, yet found no difficulty in poetically conveying to the mind the identity of the object they desired to represent."[23]

Plate 33
WILLIAM BURGES (1827–1881)
Reproduction of Burges's wallpaper with border of medieval hounds; *in situ,* second-floor bedroom, Château-sur-Mer, Newport, Rhode Island. The masks in the original pattern have been replaced with winged dragons. Courtesy of the Preservation Society of Newport County, Rhode Island.

Besides the Egyptian, Jones also greatly admired Middle Eastern geometric ornamental forms, many of which can be seen in his most surprising wallpapers (plate 35). Asserting that "all ornament should be based on a geometrical construction," Jones was able to make any wallpaper motif very flat and formal on the wall.[24] He suggested that "paper hangings" should not call attention to themselves, but remain as a background for the paintings, engravings, and other artworks.[25] Yet, as a student of ancient patterns, he was to give his own designs a striking primal shorthand. His "Queen Jones" pattern (plate 34), for instance, contains ancient motifs both Gothic and Moorish amid unexpected colors. Jones's carefully devised color theories produced some wallpapers with adventurous color schemes, in this case burgundy, mauve, red, and beige. He urged artists in the decorative arts to blend colors so that the whole presented a "neutralised bloom."[26]

Jones enjoyed the admiration of many. His use of color on the iron framework of the Crystal Palace in 1851 was particularly acclaimed.[27] His wallpapers, with their "bloom" and flat, abstract forms, have appeal today, and some are still being produced.

Wallpaper art flourished during the nineteenth century as never before or since. Even without the work of its dominant figure, William Morris, it would still have artistic importance. It covered the walls of the mighty and the humble with a wide variety of styles, many of them inspired by distant times and places. This historicism even reached the otherwise quite original scenic wallpaper artists, who often turned to the past for their subjects. Among the architects who designed wallpaper during this period, there was a developing interest in interior ornament as an integral element in architectural design. This work and the other developments surveyed in this chapter provide a rich context for understanding the accomplishments of Morris, preeminent in the last half of the century and beyond.

Plate 34 *Opposite*
OWEN JONES (1809–1874)
"Queen Jones," c. 1870.
Wallpaper, wood block, and flock, possibly printed by Woollams and Co. Whitworth Art Gallery, University of Manchester, England.

Plate 35
OWEN JONES (1809–1874)
"Diamonds and Hexagonals," c. 1860.
Wallpaper, printed in color from wood blocks.
By courtesy of the Board of Trustees of the Victoria and Albert Museum, London.

WILLIAM MORRIS AND HIS FOLLOWERS

The Moral Power of Art (1860–1895)

Plate 36 *Preceding pages*
WILLIAM MORRIS (1834–1896)
"Daisy," 1864.
Wallpaper, block printed, Jeffrey
and Co. William Morris Gallery,
Walthamstow, London.

Plate 37 *Opposite*
WILLIAM MORRIS (1834–1896)
"Willow," 1874.
Wallpaper, wood-block printed,
Jeffrey and Co. William Morris Gallery,
Walthamstow, London.

illiam Morris's prodigious work in wallpaper design, spanning roughly thirty years, is unequaled by any other artist. His remarkable story has been told again and again. A rich man's son, Morris was apprenticed to an architect but then—under the influence of his friend Dante Gabriel Rossetti, and with his lifelong friend Edward Burne-Jones—he decided to become an artist. He built a house—Red House—and having found so little that was beautiful to buy for it, furnished it with the help of his artist friends, then decided with these friends to start a firm specializing in the decorative arts. A royal commission to decorate the Armoury and Tapestry Rooms at St. James's Palace, carried out in 1866–67, helped his fledgling firm, later to be called Morris and Co., to make a start. Much of the wallpaper and textile design in the company was done by Morris himself; he also succeeded in mastering embroidery, textile printing and dyeing, weaving, stained glass, tapestry, manuscript illumination, and finally, fine book printing. His massive work as a writer, poet, and lecturer would have been career enough for most men. Yet in addition, he is known equally for his work as a socialist, writing tirelessly for this cause and giving hundreds of speeches. He died at the relatively young age of sixty-two from, as his doctor stated, "overwork, and being William Morris."

Morris's comments on designing wallpaper give a sense of the man as well as his ideas. In "The Lesser Arts of Life" (1878) he stated,

> I am bound to say something on the quite modern and very humble, but as things go, useful art of printing patterns on paper for wall-hangings. . . . I think the real way to deal successfully with designing for paper hangings is to accept their mechanical nature frankly, to avoid falling into the trap of trying to make your paper look as if it were painted by hand. Here is the place, if anywhere, for dots and lines and hatchings; mechanical enrichment is the first necessity in it. After that you may be as intricate and elaborate in your patterns as you please: nay, the more mysteriously you interweave your sprays and stems the better for your purpose, as the whole thing is to be pasted flat on the wall, and the cost of all this intricacy will but come out of your own brain and hand.[1]

Morris forthrightly followed his own advice. In this same lecture he concluded: "I do not want art for a few, any more than education for a few, or freedom for a few." He might have added that he did not want rewarding work for a few. He revered the Middle Ages as an era when a great part of society created art that was rewarding both to the community and to the individual. In his own career Morris emu-

THE SIX-MARK TEA-POT.

Æsthetic Bridegroom. "It is quite consummate, is it not?"
Intense Bride. "It is, indeed! Oh, Algernon, let us live up to it!"

lated the medieval artist; in his lectures he encouraged others to do so.

How much did Morris's decorative art influence people's lives? As for his own times, his work did without doubt make a difference in the decor of the homes of the well-off: toward the end of his life, Morris made a bitter remark about having spent his life "ministering to the swinish luxury of the rich."[2] The poor could not afford his kind of beauty, and probably would not have chosen it if they could, since in the 1870s and 1880s Morris wallpapers were popularly associated with the Aesthetes, who considered themselves the avant-garde in taste (plate 38). This avant-garde had indeed been considerably inspired by Morris's ideas on the importance of art in daily life. Gilbert and Sullivan's operetta *Patience* (1881) good-naturedly parodied them:

> Though the Philistines may jostle, you will rank as an
>   apostle in the high aesthetic band,
> If you walk down Piccadilly with a poppy or a lily in your
>   medieval hand.

Yet during the last decades of the century many people of moderate income who could afford to buy a Morris wallpaper or textile did so. Robin Spencer has analyzed the contemporary success of Morris's designs as "the legacy of one of the few art movements supported by the middle classes."[3] Surely this was part of Morris's hopes and intentions.

A tour of existing Morris houses and collections reasonably near London can illuminate his work in wallpaper as well as in the other decorative arts. Red House is an important architectural landmark, Morris's first house and the only one he built. Designed by Philip Webb in 1859, the towered, red-brick house in Upton, Bexleyheath, Kent, is an easy journey from London. This house was the site of Morris's greatest happiness in the early years of his marriage, from 1860 to 1865, and his two daughters were born in the house. It was the center of much affectionate revelry with artist-friends. Accounts abound of "Topsy" (Morris) laden with wine bottles coming up from the cellar beaming, and of the many practical jokes played on him (his waistcoat was once taken in to convince him of his sudden increased girth). Morris decorated the house with painted ceilings and wood paneling and massive, medievally

Plate 39   *Above*
WILLIAM MORRIS (1834–1896)
"Willow," 1874.
Wallpaper; *in situ,* Morris's bedroom, Kelmscott Manor,
Oxfordshire. Courtesy of the Society of Antiquaries, London.

Plate 40   *Right*
JEAN FROISSART (c. 1337–1404)
Manuscript of the fourth book of the *Chronicles,* fifteenth
century. This miniature presents "The Dance of the
Wodehouses," showing dancers celebrating a wedding feast.
Their costumes of flax and pitch were ignited by accident; the
background tapestry was the inspiration for Morris's embroi-
dered hangings in Red House, and for the "Daisy" wallpaper.
By permission of the British Library, London.

Plate 41
WILLIAM MORRIS (1834–1896)
"Sunflower," 1879.
Wallpaper, wood-block printed, Jeffrey and Co.
By courtesy of the Board of Trustees of the
Victoria and Albert Museum, London.

inspired painted furniture. Although Red House was not decorated with wallpapers during his years there, some Morris papers are hung in the house now. One of his first wallpaper designs, "Trellis" (1864; see appendix A), a pattern of wild roses on a very solid and square-shaped wooden trellis, was inspired by the rose trellises bordering the garden quadrangle. This garden with its medieval well and the congenial life at Red House inspired Walter Crane's painting *Tea at Red House.*

Kelmscott Manor, Morris's country house, is a sixteenth-century stone manor house in a tiny village on the upper Thames, in the southwest corner of Oxfordshire. The house is unforgettable, surprisingly modest and at the same time an evocation of the late Middle Ages and of Morris's years there. Architecturally, the house, gardens, and barns have layers of history; inside, the old house has been arranged much as Morris left it—filled with his own wallpapers, drawings, weavings, embroideries, and textiles. It shelters Morris's great bed with hangings embroidered for him by his wife and daughter (plate 39). Nearby is the famous Tapestry Room, lined with faded seventeenth-century tapestries of the life of Samson, which Morris found in the house in 1871 when he took joint tenancy with Rossetti, who lived there until 1874. A painting of Jane Morris by Rossetti, *The Blue Silk Dress* (1866–68), now hangs in the house, an eloquent reminder of the romance between Morris's wife and his friend, and of Morris's ensuing grief and despair. The classic Morris wallpaper "Willow" (1874; plate 37), in shades of blue, is hung in his own bedroom. This wallpaper of muted willow branches against a background of small, underplayed hawthorn blossoms is both reticent and rich. A similar Morris wallpaper in the house is "Willow Boughs" (1887; see appendix A) in Jane Morris's bedroom, more naturalistic than "Willow," in green and brown on a pale green and unusually plain background. Its effect is of summer light and air. "Sunflower" (1879; plate 41), one of Morris's rigidly symmetrical "turnover" patterns, is in a small room off the White Panelled Room, part of a circa 1670 addition to the house.[4] This pattern, popular for decades, creates a sense of order when repeated on the wall that has its own meaning beyond the individual pattern. It is a kind of hymn to nature, with flowers and fruit intertwined in a formal monochrome, adorning the flat wall with elegance and grace.

Morris's favorite way to decorate a wall was to hang fabrics in slight folds; he used this method many times in his own houses as well as for clients. Two rooms at Kelmscott Manor are decorated this way: "Kennet" of 1833 hangs in the Green Room and "Strawberry Thief" of the same year adorns the Old Hall. These are indigo-discharged dyed fabrics of simple cotton, yet their rich and warm designs make them sumptuous. The two formal pairs of birds in "Strawberry Thief" are a Gothic echo; "Kennet" is a bold, meandering vertical in which one of the imaginative principal flowers is suggestive of the textile work of Raoul Dufy. The original blue serge hangings from Morris's Red House (embroidered by his wife and friends) are preserved in the Garden Hall. The design of these hangings was inspired by a Jean Froissart manuscript (plate 40) in the British Library; one of Morris's first wallpapers, "Daisy" (1864; plate 36), was based on this pattern. It is the least complex yet one of the most cherished of all the Morris wallpapers: simple clumps of multicolored hedgerow flowers on a lightly hatched background. Altogether the old house is an extraordinary experience, the embodiment of Morris's love of beauty and reverence for the Middle Ages.

A number of Morris wallpapers may be seen *in situ* at Standen, a late Philip Webb house in East Grinstead, West Sussex. The house was meant to be simple and "anti-Victorian," and is ornamented in almost every room with

Plate 42
WILLIAM MORRIS (1834–1896)
"Sunflower," 1894.
Wallpaper; *in situ,* the drawing room, Standen House, East Grinstead, West Sussex, England.
Courtesy of Standen House.

Plate 43

WILLIAM MORRIS (1834–1896)

"Larkspur," 1874.

Polychrome wallpaper, wood-block printed, Jeffrey and Co.

William Morris Gallery, Walthamstow, London.

Plate 44
WILLIAM MORRIS (1834–1896)
"Bird," c. 1878.
Wall covering, double-woven wool; *in situ,* Morris's
Hammersmith drawing room. Hammersmith and Fulham
Archives, London.

Morris and Co. textiles, carpets, embroideries, tapestries, and wallpapers. This distinguished house, finished in 1894, was the country home of the Beale family, who bequeathed it to the National Trust in 1972, with almost all of its late-nineteenth-century decoration intact. In the gentlemen's Billiard Room is the original 1864 "Fruit" or "Pomegranate" wallpaper, one of Morris's earliest and most naturalistic (and most popular) patterns; in the drawing room, his classic monochrome "Sunflower" in green (1879; plate 42) serves as a perfect background for paintings; in the stairwell, a varnished "Bachelor's Button" (1892) wallpaper, a late design of art nouveau sinuosity, circled with swirling acanthus leaves

enclosing rounded petaled flowers. Once, before the varnish yellowed the paper, this stairwell must have been a bower of swirling blue blossoms. Each of the twelve bedrooms of the house has Morris wallpaper, including a polychrome "Larkspur" (1874; plate 43), with its gently rhythmic waving fronds. Since "Larkspur" has most often been a monochrome wallpaper, this beautiful version is not often seen. The ladies' Morning Room is hung in the approved Morris way, with "Daffodil" chintz (1891) loosely draped from frieze line to skirting. The stunning "Daffodil," now thought to be by Morris's brilliant assistant, John Henry Dearle, is characteristic of Morris's late decorated meander-

ing band patterns, naturalistic in its daffodil background, very stylized and bold in the plants of the foreground pattern.

Wightwick Manor, in Wolverhampton near Birmingham, dating from 1887, is an example of a Victorian house for which the owners chose Morris's decorative fabrics and wallpapers themselves, relying on their own taste for the furnishings that could be ordered from Morris and Co. catalogs or from the showroom in London. The Mander family, for whom the house was built, was wealthy and artistic and the house is admirable. Now owned by the National Trust, the original furnishings were augmented by both the Trust and Sir Geoffrey and Lady Rosalie Mander. Burne-Jones's glowing painting *Love Among the Ruins* looks at home here, as do the many photographs of Jane Morris by Rossetti. One of Morris's woven silk-and-wool double cloths, "Dove and Rose" (1879), an intricate iridescent bird and palmette design with great presence, is used in the drawing room as a wall covering in the Morris-approved style of loosely draped folds. In the library is the "Larkspur" wallpaper in monochrome; in the bay window of the Great Parlour is an especially fine color pattern in browns of the stately and elaborate "Acanthus" wallpaper (1875). "Acanthus" was one of Morris's most expensive wallpaper patterns, requiring thirty blocks. At one time it was used in shades of blue in the Speaker's House in the Palace of Westminster.[5]

Upstairs can be seen the expertly hung Honeysuckle Room (plate 45), named for the Morris wall chintz (1876) that was placed there in 1893. This design is one of Morris's most ambitious printed textiles, about which he wrote: "This Honeysuckle pattern has cost us a lot in blocks and is one of the most important we have or are likely to have."[6] The background in this pattern is particularly intricate with plant growth that complements the large, overblown tulips of the foreground, but Morris felt that his use of natural dyes at this stage had not yet been perfected. Nevertheless, the design is masterful, an example of Morris's turnover, or mirror-image, patterns and of his wish for a natural sense of growth in design.[7]

Next door, one arrives at the important but small Acanthus Room (plate 46), with the elaborate and almost overwhelming Morris wallpaper of that name. "All noble patterns should at least look large," said Morris.[8] The great

Plate 46
WILLIAM MORRIS (1834–1896)
"Acanthus," 1875.
Wallpaper, printed from thirty blocks, Jeffrey and Co.; *in situ,* Acanthus Room, Wightwick Manor, Wolverhampton England. Courtesy of Wightwick Manor.

Plate 45   *Opposite*
WILLIAM MORRIS (1834–1896)
"Honeysuckle," 1876.
Wall chintz, block printed, Thomas Wardle; *in situ,* Wightwick Manor, Wolverhampton, England. The portrait is by Frederick Sandys (1829–1904). Courtesy of Wightwick Manor.

acanthus scrolls on the walls illustrate his belief that small rooms can "look best ornamented with large patterns." Further, he said, "If properly designed they are more restful to the eye than small ones."[9] In this room are treasured bed hangings from Kelmscott Manor embroidered by Morris's daughter May, sold to the Manders in the 1939 Kelmscott sale after her death.

In London the place to begin a Morris tour is Kelmscott House, Morris's townhouse in Hammersmith, where the William Morris Society is located. Its setting on the Thames (from which Morris and his family once set out on a week's journey by boat for Kelmscott Manor) is majestic, and the path to the house along the river atmospheric. This house, once hung with Morris wallpapers and textiles, was the family home from 1878 (plate 44). Today the house cannot be visited, but the staff of the society, housed in the coach house nearby, is extremely helpful about providing the locations and schedules of places associated with Morris, and regularly holds small exhibitions related to Morris and his followers. The coach house was once the site of Morris's looms and of Hammersmith socialist meetings; now it shelters a considerable Morris collection.

A Morris tour in London should include the Green Dining Room at the Victoria and Albert Museum, as well as other Morris exhibits elsewhere in the museum. The Morris wallpaper collection in the Print Room is excellent. Another important site is the Linley Sambourne house in Kensington, built in the early 1870s and lived in for four generations by the family of Linley Sambourne, a cartoonist for *Punch*. This artist sometimes caricatured his aesthetic age as being preciously self-conscious about dress and furnishings, yet his

Plate 47

WILLIAM MORRIS (1834–1896)

"Fruit," c. 1874.

Wallpaper; *in situ,* the dining room, Linley Sambourne House, London. Linley Sambourne, London.

Plate 48
WILLIAM MORRIS (1834–1896)
"Fruit" ("Pomegranate"), 1862–64.
Wallpaper, block printed, Jeffrey and Co. William Morris
Gallery, Walthamstow, London.

own house contains the required Morris wallpapers and the usual "aesthetic" display of blue-and-white porcelain (plate 47).[10] The most notable wallpaper here is the early "Fruit" or "Pomegranate" (1862–64; plate 48), which can be seen in several variations in the hall, the dining room, and the morning room. This magnificent wallpaper was designed in four distinct large squares almost like tiles; on the wall they blend with an easy movement that links all four areas together. In production, the peach spray area replaced an olive spray, which was less colorful and less well balanced. The shading in the fruit was accomplished with nailheads in the wooden blocks used to print the pattern, a favorite Morris device.

At St. James's Palace, Morris carried out an early commission to redecorate rooms (1866–67) with a scheme that did

not include wallpaper. However, when a second commission from the Crown was granted for redecoration of the State Apartments of the palace in 1880, he created the regal "St. James" wallpaper (plates 49; 50) for the Grand Staircase, the Banqueting Room, and the Queen's Staircase. This wallpaper required twice the ordinary width for the full pattern and sixty-eight blocks for printing. Lesser rooms were decorated with "Jasmine" in light tones, and "Mallow" and "Sunflower" predominantly in blue; "our chrysanthemum paper," as the firm described it, was used for the boudoir in strawberry.[11] "Chrysanthemum" was the closest Morris ever came to a Japanese-inspired design; as of 1949 it was still in the palace. Each of these wallpapers, with its intricate tracery of pattern on pattern, has a stately simplicity and stature. No

Morris wallpaper, however, was ever again as dominant and splendid as the "St. James," with its large golden plant forms symbolic of the royal family and interestingly entwined with vines reminiscent of Dürer's. A few years later, in 1887, when Morris designed a flock wallpaper for Balmoral Castle (plate 51) the pattern was simpler and more reminiscent of Pugin, with crowns and thistles and the initials of Queen Victoria enclosed in large diamond outlines. The penciled note on Morris's design states: "Their majesties prefer this design with the diamonds as big again."[12]

The William Morris Gallery is housed in Morris's boyhood home in Walthamstow in outermost London. The gallery's collections of Morris, including most of the original Morris wallpapers, are unsurpassed; the permanent exhibitions are of major importance, and there are frequent special exhibitions.

What can be said of Morris's wallpapers in general? They are first and most significantly based on natural forms, but they are not slavish imitations of nature—they incorporate imagination, even fantasy. Morris felt that the ordinary man, whom he wished to see as artist, must give to nature and other human beings something of himself, "to give . . . [the seeker of beauty] some part of the infinite variety which abides in the mind of man."[13] This is one of the most original and moving of Morris's thoughts; he insists that ordinary human beings have something to give to life through art and that a literal copy of nature in art cannot satisfy the seeker of beauty if it lacks something of the unique complexity of the one who made it.

Second, Morris ensured that his designs were texturally somewhat complex, so that the eye does not see everything in the pattern at once. He advised: "In all patterns which are meant to fill the eye and satisfy the mind, there should be a certain mystery."[14] At first he disliked intensely the idea that the eye would grow restless looking for a pattern repeat. In many early patterns he carefully masked the repeats; in the later ones, he felt that "much ingenuity was spent, and not a little wasted, in doing it."[15] He came to believe that the repeat added to the vitality of the pattern. Yet virtually all Morris's patterns are ingeniously designed. They have a very slight depth: from the pattern on pattern, from the outlines, and from some judicious color contrast. These devices keep the designs from being totally flat, but they do not allow the

eye to penetrate as into a picture based on perspective. The colors in his drawings are pleasing and mellow, not overbright, but far from pastel. The colors in the Morris wallpapers, all produced by Jeffrey and Co., appear soft and natural, although even the originals were printed with chemical dyes. There are major themes and minor themes in

Plate 49   *Opposite*
WILLIAM MORRIS (1834–1896)
"St. James," 1881.
Wallpaper; *in situ,* the Ascot Stairs, St. James's Palace, London, 1900. Benjamin Stone Collection; City of Birmingham Public Libraries, Birmingham, England.

Plate 50
WILLIAM MORRIS (1834–1896)
"St. James," 1881.
Wallpaper, block printed, Jeffrey and Co.; for St. James's Palace, London. From *The Art of William Morris* by Aymer Vallance (London: G. Bell and Sons, 1897). Boston Athenaeum.

Morris designs, a combination that makes them interestingly rich. In many the primary pattern is superimposed on a secondary pattern, which is in some designs almost major, as in the background flowers and foliage of "Jasmine" (plate 52). In some patterns a major decorative device—such as an ornamental diagonal band inspired by the Renaissance textiles that Morris admired and studied in the Victoria and Albert Museum—and even second and third major floral forms are superimposed on small patterns of foliage, as in the 1887 "Bruges" wallpaper. There is great variety in Morris's designs, from the deceptive simplicity of "Daisy" to the inspired baroque of "Acanthus," but most designs have as well a serene dignity and refinement.

Morris's art has become widely loved, and his wallpapers are extremely popular today; certain of his patterns have remained in production for over a century. Furthermore, his moral and aesthetic principles have had great influence on other artists of his time and after. Some gave up their easels for the sake of the decorative arts, which could be made more widely available. The Arts and Crafts movement that Morris engendered was one of the finest periods of English design. His influence extended to the Continent and America through the years of Art Nouveau, to the beginnings of Art Deco in Austria and France after the turn of the century, and even to the Bauhaus. But his immediate influence was on the English artists and architects who allied themselves with him in some way. Many of these artists, true to the Morris spirit, designed wallpapers.

Morris would never allow any criticism of Edward Burne-Jones, who was a founding member of the Morris firm. At one time the two were so close that Morris planned a new wing of Red House for his friend. However, Morris's health soon forced him to live closer to the firm in London, and the Burne-Jones family eventually chose to live both in London (breakfast with Morris every Sunday) and in a country retreat at Rottingdean, near Brighton. Morris and Burne-Jones are thought to have collaborated on a wallpaper design for the tavern room that Burne-Jones added to his country house and named the Merry Mermaid (plate 53). Burne-Jones described the Mermaid as a "pot-house parlour, where men can drink and smoke and be vulgar. . . . The most delightful room it is, and I have wanted such a one all my life."[16] The large wallpaper design shows two blue mermaids in roundels of acanthus in gold and tan. Martin Harrison and William Waters suggest that Morris drew the acanthus foliage and Burne-Jones the figures, which show a resemblance to the mermaid in the Burne-Jones painting *The Sea Nymph* (1878–81).[17] The figure in this painting is in the exact pose of the upper mermaid in the wallpaper drawing. The painting itself makes a strong decorative assertion in the dramatic swirls of the fish and the sea, not unlike the wallpaper. Although Burne-Jones produced many decorative works for Morris, there is only one other wallpaper design by him, a filling and frieze of willowy peacocks, in his notebook, "Book of Designs," at the British Museum.

Burne-Jones's dreamy and romantic canvases were greatly influenced by his mentor, Dante Gabriel Rossetti. The charismatic Rossetti, who was also an original partner in the Morris firm, left an account of designing just one wallpaper. In 1861, just as the firm was being organized, the new

Plate 51 *Opposite*
WILLIAM MORRIS (1834–1896)
Wallpaper, block printed, Jeffrey and Co., 1887;
for Balmoral Castle. Reprinted from the original
blocks by Arthur Sanderson and Sons, Ltd.,
Middlesex, England. By courtesy of the Board of
Trustees of the Victoria and Albert Museum,
London.

Plate 52
WILLIAM MORRIS (1834–1896)
"Jasmine," 1872.
Wallpaper, block printed, Jeffrey and Co.; *in
situ,* dining room of "The Grange" (Edward
Burne-Jones's house in London, now
demolished). Royal Commission on the
Historical Monuments of England, London.

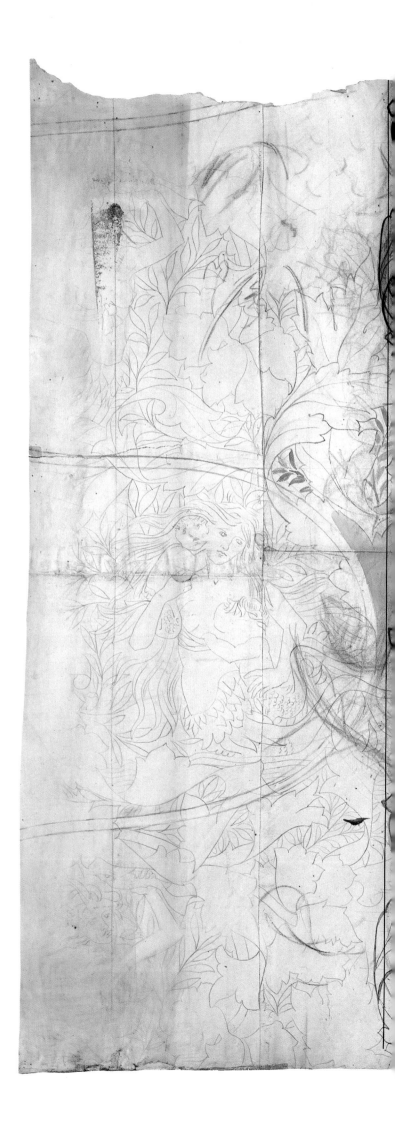

bridegroom Rossetti wrote with zest about a wallpaper design (plate 54) he was sketching for his flat:

> We have got our rooms quite jolly now. Our drawing room is a beauty, I assure you, already, and on the first country trip we make, we shall have it newly papered from a design of mine. . . . I shall have it printed on common brown packing-paper and on blue grocer's paper to try which is best. The trees are to stand the whole height of the room so that the effect will be slighter and quieter than in the sketch, where the tops look too large. Of course they will be wholly conventional; the stems and fruit will be Venetian Red, the leaves black—the fruit, however, will have a line of yellow to indicate roundness to distinguish it from the stem; the lines of the ground black, and the stars yellow with a white ring round them. The red and black will be in the same key as the brown or blue of the ground, so that the effect of the whole will be rather sombre, but I think rich also. When we get the paper up, we shall have the doors and wainscotting painted summerhouse green.[18]

Later in the same letter Rossetti announced the founding of the Morris firm: "We are organizing a company for the production of furniture and decoration of all kinds, for the sale of which we are going to open an actual shop!"

Rossetti approached wallpaper designing in a spirit of excitement quite typical of him. The project was a game; wallpaper was definitely a lesser art. But in 1861, long before the advent of Art Nouveau, he had carefully considered aspects of a pattern for a wall, and allowed his own design of trees to grow from the wainscotting to a "crown" effect of treetops at the ceiling—a device unknown in Rossetti's time, but commonly used three decades later in the 1890s.

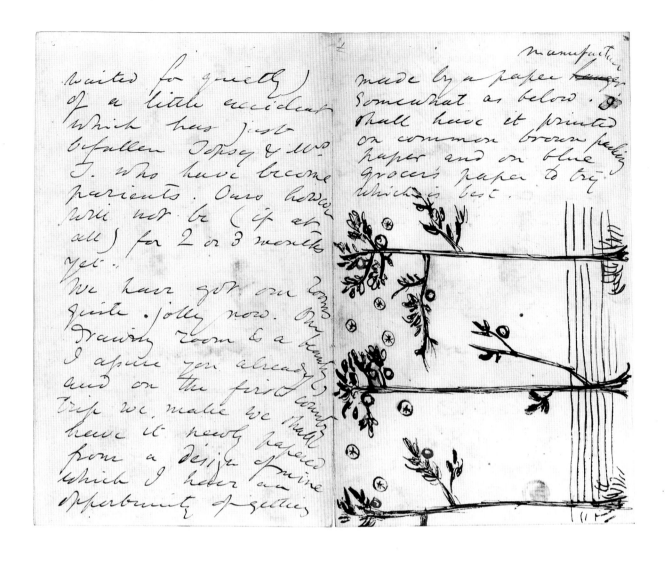

Plate 54 *Above*

DANTE GABRIEL ROSSETTI (1828–1882)

Wallpaper design in a letter, January 1861. From *Letters of Dante Gabriel Rossetti to W. Allingham,* ed. G. B. Hill (London: Unwin, 1897). The Pierpont Morgan Library, New York.

Plate 55 *Left*

DANTE GABRIEL ROSSETTI (1828–1882)

Dantis Amor, 1859.

Oil on wood panel, 29½ x 32 in. (74.9 x 81.3 cm); for the settle now at Red House, Kent, England. The Tate Gallery, London.

Plate 56 *Opposite*

WALTER CRANE (1845–1915)

"Peacocks and Amorini," 1878.

Design for wallpaper. This watercolor drawing shows the design for both flat paper and embossed leather. By courtesy of the Board of Trustees of the Victoria and Albert Museum, London.

Although we have Rossetti's sketch, we do not know if his wallpaper was actually produced, and he appears to have designed no others. However, his description and sketch are very useful in giving us his own ideas of a drawing room wallpaper: it should be somber and rich but quiet, the motifs should be from nature but rendered "conventionally," or in a stylized way. Although Rossetti was a founding member of the Pre-Raphaelite Brotherhood, their symbolic, detailed naturalism became in his paintings a kind of mystic romanticism closer to William Blake. The soaring line and the patterning that appear in the wallpaper sketch may have been inherited from Blake; Rossetti revered a Blake note-

book he owned that was patterned with angels, swirling flames, and clouds.[19] For both Rossetti and Blake, patterning, as in rows of angels' heads, could be done less than meticulously (unlike fellow Pre-Raphaelite John Everett Millais, who could spend a day painting an area "no larger than a five shilling piece") and was intended for emotional effect. Even the device of the crowning trees in Rossetti's wallpaper design may have been derived from Blake.

The wallpaper's crisscrossed star pattern has parallels in other work by Rossetti at this time. It resembles the simple shorthand pattern for stars appearing in some of Rossetti's Froissartian watercolors of around 1860, as well as the title-

Plate 57
WALTER CRANE (1845–1915)
"Deer and Rabbits," 1887.
Frieze for "Woodnotes" wallpaper, Jeffrey and Co. The
Whitworth Art Gallery, University of Manchester, England.

Plate 58 *Opposite*
WALTER CRANE (1845–1915)
"Woodnotes," 1886.
Wallpaper, block printed, Jeffrey and Co. The Whitworth Art
Gallery, University of Manchester, England.

page stars in the drawing for his sister Christina's book of poems *Goblin Market* of 1862. These stars also appear in *Dantis Amor* (1859; plate 55), a Rossetti oil painting on wood of Dante's Beatrice that was once a panel in the settle now at Morris's Red House. The diagonal section of the painting representing night is dotted with Rossetti's crisscrossed stars.

Walter Crane, a younger disciple of Morris and a socialist, was a leader in two Morris-inspired societies, the Art Workers' Guild and the Arts and Crafts Exhibition Society. Although Crane's decorative and graphic art is widely regarded as superior to his fine art, he was a precocious painter and was allowed to exhibit at the Royal Academy as a very young man. A leading spokesman for Morris's ideas of art as a universal human right, Crane was an accomplished wallpaper artist with a fluent and flowing line, and his wallpapers won prizes. Wallpaper, reasonably inexpensive and available to many, must have appealed to his socialist nature. In his decorations at St. James's Palace in 1880, Morris used Crane's "Peacocks and Amorini" wallpaper (plate 56), designed, in the fashion of the times, with separate patterns for frieze, dado, and filling. This design had won a gold medal at the International Exhibition in Paris in 1878. Crane wrote about it in his idealistic way: "The arabesque . . . and interlacing branches may figure the constant growth of an ideal life, like a tree bearing flowers and living fruit. Amorini suspend its festal garlands and light the flame of its thoughts or play with the masks of grief and gladness overhung by the bow and quiver of Love."[20] He further personified each of the creatures in the pattern, citing "the craft of the serpent" overruled by "the benign wings of the dove," and the "pride and splendor" of the peacock among the boughs of the tree of life. Other Crane wallpapers bore similar descriptions.

As an artist Crane believed in a powerful line and wrote that it was "the difference between the quick and the dead." He asked his students to study Greek vases to understand purity of line.[21] Of the many elaborate wallpapers that exhibit his entwining and arabesque line, "Corona Vitae" (1890), "Fig and Peacock" (1895), "Woodnotes" (1886; plates 57; 58), "The Golden Age" (1887; plate 60), and "Peacock Garden" (1889) are among the most densely organized and

most interesting. They are rhythmic and covered with well-drawn symbolic forms; the colors are generally subdued. Many allow figures (humans, birds, animals) to entwine ingeniously in restless linear foliage that forms an interlocking pattern. They are indeed characteristic of the sinuous Art Nouveau of the 1890s. Crane himself, however, rejected the idea that his work might have Art Nouveau characteristics and referred to the style disapprovingly as "that strange decorative disease."[22]

Crane greatly admired Japanese art for its flat shapes, daring use of solid blacks along with color, and authoritative line. These qualities, as well as the academic, classical forms of his early training and his love of Renaissance formality, are all to be found in his children's books and in his wallpapers, which appear to have been created with Crane's total energies and gifts—hardly as a lesser art (plate 59; for Crane's children's wallpapers see appendix A).

Plate 59
WALTER CRANE (1845–1915)
"Four Winds," 1890.
Ceiling paper, block printed, Jeffrey and Co. Crane intended this ceiling paper to be used with his "Corona Vitae" (1890), a wallpaper inspired by Sicilian silk brocade wall hangings. By courtesy of the Board of Trustees of the Victoria and Albert Museum, London.

Plate 60   *Opposite*
WALTER CRANE (1845–1915)
"The Golden Age," 1887.
Wallpaper, Jeffrey and Co. The Whitworth Art Gallery, University of Manchester, England.

Plate 61 *Opposite*
WALTER CRANE (1845–1915)
"Macaw," 1908.
Wallpaper, Jeffrey and Co. Courtesy of Arthur
Sanderson and Sons, Ltd., Middlesex, England.

Plate 62
C.F.A. VOYSEY (1857–1941)
"Tulip and Bird," 1896.
Wallpaper, Essex and Co. William Morris Gallery,
Walthamstow, London.

One of his last designs, "Macaw" (1908; plate 61), is brilliant in color, freshly naturalistic, and has freed itself from line. It was praised as "the most delightful paper produced by the famous English firm that William Morris founded. . . . Walter Crane stands at the head of all modern designers of wallpaper in the opinion of many."[23] The firm referred to was not Morris's but Jeffrey and Co., the firm that *printed* wallpapers by Morris, Crane, and other distinguished artists. Metford Warner, the guiding spirit of this company, once stated in an address that he deliberately sought out artists "in order to bring wallpaper up to the level of the Arts."[24]

Many of the artists who designed for Warner were followers of Morris, among them the architect Charles Francis Annesley Voysey. Voysey's much admired English-vernacular-style houses, with their simple forms, enveloping roofs, low-slung gables, and clear, bright trim colors, have almost all survived intact and are increasingly respected. Although Voysey's architecture was understated, his wallpaper style was intrepid and eclectic. While awaiting later fame as an architect, he learned the art of designing wallpapers and textiles from another Morris associate and friend, Arthur Heygate Mackmurdo. From the first Voysey was a successful designer and a master of flat ornament, and his long wallpaper-designing career spanned the years of the Arts and Crafts movement and lyrically embraced curvilinear Art Nouveau (although Voysey denied this, calling the style "distinctly unhealthy").[25] During these nearly five decades he produced some two hundred patterns for wallpaper alone, from the early, Mackmurdo-inspired, seaweedlike "Pentacrinus" (1886), to luxuriant florals that were admired on the Continent, such as "Isis" (1893; see plate 71), with single flowers twelve inches across, to restrained, flat, stylized designs like "Tulip and Bird" (1896; plate 62), with its charm-

ing hidden bird-and-flower motif, typically Voysey. The crisp, flat forms of his most distinctive designs are uniquely his own and startling; the bold, stylized birds and leaves of "Grategus" (plate 63), for example, appeared in 1901.

Two Belgian architects were strong admirers of the Voysey wallpapers at the turn of the century. Henry van de Velde, an early leader of the school that became the Bauhaus, wrote of seeing Voysey's wallpapers in an exhibition: "It was as if Spring had come all of a sudden."[26] Victor Horta, the architect perhaps closest to the spirit of Art Nouveau, used Voysey's wallpapers in some of his celebrated houses (see chapter 4).

Voysey's eclectic style *absorbed* design; he once declared that he dared not enter Morris's showroom in London for fear of copying the master. He lectured and wrote on design, stressing simplicity and spiritual values. In spite of his many successful patterns, he was not enthusiastic about wallpaper: "A wallpaper is of course only a background and were your furniture good in form and colour a very simple or quite undecorated treatment of the walls would be preferable, but as most modern furniture is vulgar or bad in every way, elaborate papers of many colours help to disguise its ugliness . . . if you have but enough confusion the ugliness of modern life becomes bearable."[27] Voysey, like many of Morris's followers, was a reformer zealous for change, and some of his pronouncements have an endearing, curmudgeonly ring. He once seriously admonished, "Cold vegetables are less harmful than ugly dish-covers; one affects the body and the other affects the soul."[28] On another occasion he likened too many badly designed textiles and wallpapers

Plate 63 *Top*
C.F.A. VOYSEY (1857–1941)
"Grategus," 1901.
Wallpaper, machine printed, Essex and Co.
The Whitworth Art Gallery, University of
Manchester, England.

Plate 64 *Bottom*
C.F.A. VOYSEY (1857–1941)
"The Demon," c. 1893.
Wallpaper drawing. British Architectural Library,
Royal Institute of British Architects, London.

to the "sensation of a drunken brawl," and deplored what he called the din of "a thousand ornaments bawling."[29] "We cannot be too simple," he said, "we are too apt to furnish our rooms as if we regarded our wallpapers, furniture and fabrics as far more attractive than our friends."[30] "Simplicity in decoration . . . without which no true richness is possible" was to Voysey a maxim, however puzzling in the context of his elaborate wallpapers but pristine architecture.[31] A complex man, Voysey appears to have considered "richness" a component of simplicity. He was deeply concerned with the spiritual in art, and in this light his startling motifs—including wooden silhouettes of the client worked into a porch overhang, or a wallpaper frieze on which figures hud-dle in small circular spaces under trees, or the self-portrait in his "Demon" wallpaper (c. 1893; plate 64)—have been explained as symbols "of his love of living things—birds flying or nesting in treetops, huntsmen, lilies, roses, demons and dragons."[32] Duncan Simpson sees Voysey's "discordant" Gothic figures and demons as "a reminder of ephemerality, [and] human vanity," bringing warmth and humanity to his work.[33] There is no doubt that Voysey was one of the great pattern designers, and that he managed in his work to be uniquely himself, as well as a devout believer in the ideals of Morris. Most importantly, his moral fervor for simplicity led to his compellingly fresh architecture and equally new flat, stylized patterns.

Plate 65
Arthur Heygate Mackmurdo (1851–1942)
"Swirling Leaf," 1884.
Wallpaper, block printed, Jeffrey and Co.; for the Century
Guild. By courtesy of the Board of Trustees of the Victoria and
Albert Museum, London.

Voysey's mentor, the architect and reformer Arthur Heygate Mackmurdo, had a short designing life, but his designs thrust the Arts and Crafts movement unquestionably into Art Nouveau, with forms that are almost flamelike in their swirling patterns. Mackmurdo's most famous wallpaper, "Swirling Leaf" (1884; plate 65), is characteristic of these designs, having pale outlines on a dark background of off-center forms in which a leaf is never symmetrical. In 1882, inspired by Morris's example, Mackmurdo and his partner Herbert Horne set up the short-lived Century Guild, "to render all branches of art the sphere no longer of the tradesman but of the artist."[34] Their magazine, the *Hobby Horse,* may have inspired Morris's interest in book publishing. The guild was a creative workshop for arts and crafts (plate 66), which lasted only until 1888, when its several members began dispersing to make their own contributions to society. Horne, for instance, went to Florence, where he wrote a biography of Botticelli and left the city a museum, the Museo Horne. True to the Morris spirit, Mackmurdo was by 1904 most interested in economics and monetary reform and in 1926 published his treatise, *The Human Hive,* which proposed to pay everyone the same hourly fee for work, based on the price of wheat.

The artist Heywood Sumner was a mural painter and book illustrator who also worked for a time for Mackmurdo's Century Guild. His wallpapers for Jeffrey and Co. were noted in a Brussels exhibition, and his wallpaper design "Tulip" may have been used by Victor Horta in the Tassel House. It was said of him that he put nature before ornament, and his dense and intricate designs for wallpaper most characteristically use wrapped ornamental bands as frames for carefully observed plant forms (plate 67). Sumner was an outdoorsman; he spent the last forty years of his life as a serious amateur archeologist, carefully recording in beautiful calligraphy and watercolors his studies of New Forest earthworks, most notably Roman pottery sites.

Mackmurdo also somehow managed to be a friend to those two opposites John Ruskin and James McNeill Whistler. He had visited shrines in Italy with Ruskin as a young man and was influenced by Ruskin's teachings, teachings that had also been important to Morris, both aesthetically and morally. Ruskin believed that God-given nature was the only source of all great art, and thus art was

Plate 67
GEORGE HEYWOOD SUMNER (1863–1940)
"The Oak, the Ash, and the Bonnie Ivy Tree," 1896.
Wallpaper, block printed, Jeffrey and Co. Winchester Museum Service Collection, Winchester, England.

Plate 66   *Opposite*
ARTHUR HEYGATE MACKMURDO (1851–1942)
"Rose and Butterfly," c. 1884.
Wallpaper, Jeffrey and Co.; for the Century Guild.
William Morris Gallery, Walthamstow, London.

a source of morality, and finally of a great society. To Ruskin, the worker as artist was not autonomous, but must be a force for good. Whistler's work, according to Ruskin, provided no "moral intention"; it was detached and, unforgivably, verging on the abstract.

Whistler, on the other hand, saw art and morality as quite separate, and totally rejected Ruskin's philosophy. He refused to copy nature as the only source of art; indeed, he considered that view an abuse of nature portrayed in art: "To say to the painter, that Nature is to be taken as she is, is to say to the player, that he may sit on the piano."[35] He was also deeply influenced by Japanese restraint and asymmetry both in his paintings and in what he called his "decorations," which he declared as important as his paintings.[36] His decorations were often based on esoteric color alone, but sometimes enlivened with a hint of almost abstract pattern, as in his "petaled" stairway panels for his London patron, Frederick Leyland. His masterful decorations for Leyland's Peacock Room (now at the Freer Gallery, Washington, D.C.) are of vividly stylized peacocks and near-abstract patterns from them (plate 68). The Peacock Room's existing ancient and costly brown leather wallpaper with regular small red flowers, which Whistler did not like, was translated into a glowing deep blue-green and gold work of art. Whistler's painted patterns in this glorious room are constantly varied, and the entire composition is treated very asymmetrically, in the Japanese manner.[37]

·Leyland was furious when he saw his wallpaper "ruined." Whistler's art was indeed deplored on many sides. After an exhibition, Ruskin called the artist a "coxcomb" who dared "ask two hundred guineas for flinging a pot of paint in the public's face."[38] Whistler sued Ruskin for libel, and in the ensuing trial Burne-Jones supported Ruskin. One of the critics who testified for Ruskin described Whistler's art as merely "one step nearer pictures than a delicately tinted

Plate 68

James McNeill Whistler (1834–1903)
The Peacock Room (south wall), 1876–77. The leather wallpaper underneath Whistler's paint shows a design of flowers and ribbons. Courtesy of the Freer Gallery of Art, Smithsonian Institution, Washington, D.C.

wall-paper."[39] A *Punch* cartoon portrayed the members of the jury as tubes of Winsor-Newton paint. In the end Whistler won the court battle but was awarded only one farthing, which he defiantly wore on his watchchain.

As a result of the trial Whistler was ruined financially and lost the house he had designed for himself in collaboration with a fellow spirit, the architect E. W. Godwin. Godwin, whom Max Beerbohm called "the greatest aesthete of them all,"[40] approached design and wallpapers with some of Whistler's aesthetic principles. For a drawing room based on Chaucer's *Romance of the Rose,* he instructed his decorators to refer to the poem for help on how to proceed.[41] He was obsessed with Japanese art, as can be seen in "Sparrow and Bamboo" (1872; plate 69). He provided Japanese prints for

Plate 69
EDWARD WILLIAM GODWIN (1833–1886)
"Sparrow and Bamboo," 1872.
Wallpaper design, pencil on tracing paper. A second design by Godwin of the same year has the plural title "Sparrows and Bamboo." By courtesy of the Board of Trustees of the Victoria and Albert Museum, London.

Plate 70

EDWARD WILLIAM GODWIN (1833–1886)

"Bamboo," 1872.

Wallpaper, block printed, Jeffrey and Co.; *in situ,* the Major
James Goodwin House in Hartford, Connecticut, now demolished. Stowe-Day Foundation, Hartford, Connecticut.

his children's nursery, dressed them in small kimonos, and
created Japanese-inspired wallpapers. His "Bamboo" wallpaper, in fact, was popular enough in the 1870s to decorate the
dining room of Major James Goodwin's house in Hartford,
Connecticut (plate 70). His "Sparrows and Bamboo" wallpaper, a design with Japanese branches and small sparrows,
though shockingly asymmetrical to contemporary eyes, is
refreshing to ours. Returning from a trip and expecting to
find his own wallpaper hung in his absence, Godwin was
greeted by his worried housekeeper saying, "Well, did
y'ever see such a thing? Why, of course I wasn't going to
have it hung until ye'd seen it."[42]

In his final rebuttal to Ruskin after the trial, Whistler
insisted that only the chosen artist could produce art, certainly not the common man: "The people have been
harassed with art . . . their homes have been invaded, their
walls covered with paper, their very dress taken to task. . . .
Alas! ladies and gentlemen, Art has been maligned. She has
naught in common with such practices."[43] Whistler believed
the chosen artist had responsibility only to a personal art-
goddess. His was an art that would call forth a new kind of
decoration: more abstract, asymmetrical, lyrical—and
prophetic of the forms if not the purposes of Art Nouveau,
although he too would have rejected the idea.

THE ART NOUVEAU STYLE

The Force of Nature in Line and Form (1890–1905)

rt Nouveau is the term generally used for defining the style of art which, around 1900, had as its main theme a long, sensitive, sinuous line that reminds us of seaweed or of creeping plants."[1] Robert Schmutzler here echoes the definition of Nikolaus Pevsner, who describes the leitmotif of Art Nouveau as "the long, sensitive curve, reminiscent of the lily's stem, an insect's feeler, the filament of a blossom or occasionally a slender flame, the curve undulating, flowing and interplaying with others, sprouting from corners and covering asymmetrically all available surfaces."[2] Artists' wallpapers of the end of the nineteenth century that demonstrate these characteristics will be examined in this chapter; more geometric, and somewhat more restrained wallpapers of the period and after will appear in the following chapter.

One wonders if any of the present-day tenants at 14–16 rue la Fontaine, Paris—the location of Hector Guimard's Castel Béranger (c. 1894–98)—have kept on their walls some of the unique wallpapers the famous architect designed for each of the interiors. In pastel colors, these wallpaper images are composed of vigorous swirls and bold abstractions (plate 72). The patterns are similar, yet there are major and minor themes and variations in size and shape and color. Guimard's wallpaper palette is muted, but not quite pale; in some patterns he uses a silver or gold accent. In these interesting wallpapers, we recognize the Guimard signature that is best known in his Paris Métro entrances, with their twisted cast-iron vines and buds (those strange growths were at one time referred to as the eyes of frogs). Happily, Guimard published an album, *Le Castel Béranger* (1896), showing each of the wallpapers, as well as all the architectural detailing of this building, down to the last doorknob, a *gesamtkunstwerk,* or total work of art.[3] Each item is the essence of the flowing, undulating Art Nouveau style of natural forms allowed wild and luxuriant growth into abstraction and asymmetry. There were many names for this style, some derogatory. In Germany the style was known as Jugendstil, or youth style. In France it was sometimes known as *style nouille* (noodle style) or even *style de bouche de Métro* after Guimard's Métro entrances.[4] In the case of the wallpapers at the Castel Béranger, the natural forms

Plate 73

ARCHIBALD KNOX (1864–1933)

Entrelac design for textile or wallpaper, c. 1900.
Courtesy of the Manx National Heritage,
Isle of Man, England.

Plate 74 *Opposite*

EUGENE-EMMANUEL VIOLLET-LE-DUC (1814–1879)
Design for canvas wall hanging. The gap in the design allows
for a repetition of the flowering vines. From *Histoire d'une
maison* (Paris: J. Hetzel, 1873). Bibliothèque Forney, Paris.

upon which the patterns are based are so abstracted as to be
virtually unrecognizable, yet they are undoubtedly from
nature. Perhaps they are water patterns, or reflections?
Guimard was at the epicenter of the flamboyant Art
Nouveau style during its brief lifetime (1890–1905). Yet soon
he also participated in its rejection: about 1905 his architecture began to move toward a more restrained and rational
geometric style.

Although Art Nouveau was short-lived, it had a long
buildup. The style was centered in Paris and Brussels but

grew as well out of developments in England. The Gothic
Revival, so formidable in the nineteenth century, was itself a
powerful ornamental force. Adapted from early Renaissance
textiles, Pugin's meandering pomegranate bands in the wallpaper of the Queen's Robing Room at the Palace of
Westminster were harbingers of the style, as were the bands
and curves in Morris's wallpapers inspired by similar
Renaissance textiles in the new South Kensington Museum.
These, Morris said, he used "as much as any man alive." On
the side of new art, the pattern theorist and architect Owen
Jones had helped to liberate the decorative artist's sub-
servience to the past in decoration, urging an understanding
of historic styles in order to build on them, not to imitate.
He proposed that "the principles discoverable in the works
of the past belong to us; not so the results," thus defying the
literal historicism that characterized the first half of the century.[5] Eugène Grasset, the revered and widely influential
French artist and teacher, advocated a careful study and
understanding of natural forms, followed by free and new
interpretation of those forms, and many artists who created
wallpapers during the last decades of the century heeded his
advice to produce designs of organic growth and movement,
sometimes bordering on abstraction. But the Japanese were
perhaps the most important influence on this new art. Since
the 1860s, Japanese art—with its linear and stylized depiction of nature, its elegant use of semiabstract symbols, and
its dramatic sense of diagonals, asymmetry, and flat color—
had intensely interested artists both in England and on the
Continent. All these factors were integral elements of the
"noodle style."

As early as 1873 Eugène-Emmanuel Viollet-le-Duc, the
architect of medieval restoration in France, included his
designs for painted canvas wall hangings in a book entitled
Histoire d'une maison, pointing out that these cost scarcely
more than wallpapers and less than fabric.[6] Viollet-le-Duc
was an advocate of advanced architecture, at an early date
proposing iron as a light structural framework for architecture "hitherto unattempted."[7] In this he had important followers, notably the Belgian Art Nouveau architect Victor
Horta, whose work with twisted and decorative but structural iron in his buildings still amazes us. To our eyes
Viollet-le-Duc's drawings for wall hangings are also surprising—they are historicist, yet early manifestations of the Art

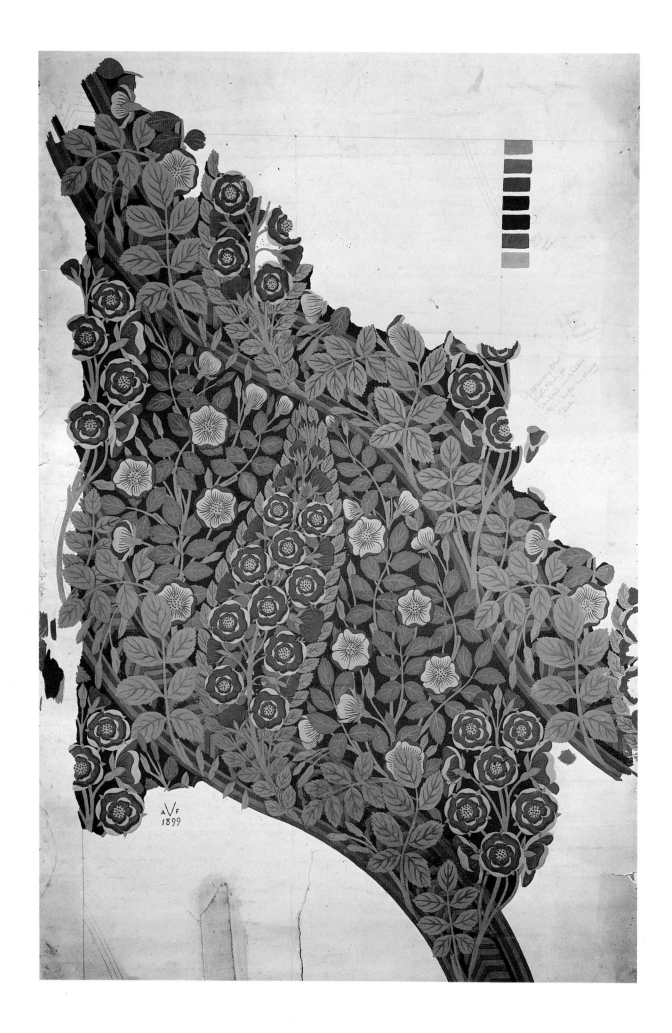

Nouveau style. The wall hanging for the dining room of the house pictures a heron, a pheasant, and crisp, flowering trees that would reach the ceiling. It is like Chinese wallpaper in its precise plant forms and its spacing; it resembles Japanese prints in its linear, stylized birds; and it is proto-Art Nouveau in the moving, growing line of the trees and the drooping poppies. The wall hanging for the salon (plate 74) is curvilinear Art Nouveau inspired by Gothic: reaching plant forms and a medieval manuscript border crown the room, and the dado contains a formal lily and organically curling morning glory. Viollet-le-Duc's decorations here embody the same decorative freedom that Stuart Durant finds in his schemes for the side chapels at Notre Dame; both reflect Viollet-le-Duc's "more than common sympathy for the essential vitality of organic form."[8]

Morris's followers had tendencies toward the undulating line of Art Nouveau; even Morris himself was not exempt. Walter Crane's curvilinear grandeur was emphatically of the style, in spite of the fact that he objected to what he called its "wild and whirligig squirms."[9] Mackmurdo designed almost nothing that didn't ring of freedom of line and asymmetry, and Voysey's fertile design mind could handle the sinuous curve effortlessly. Consider his writhing "Water Snakes" wallpaper, in which he seems to have accepted Grasset's challenge to use a serpent or other "hideous" animal in design.

Archibald Knox and Allan Vigers were also impressive artist-designers of wallpapers in the Art Nouveau style. Knox's ingenious textile and wallpaper designs for Liberty were natural forms interwoven with Celtic *entrelac* from his native Isle of Man (plate 73). Vigers's detailed designs were sometimes naturalistic, sometimes stylized, always vital multiflorals, beloved by wallpaper historians (plate 75).

Wallpapers by English artists were important in Continental interiors. In Brussels in 1893 Henry van de Velde saw an exhibition of English "artistic wallpapers" and wrote two significant articles in which he gave them the highest praise, citing in particular wallpapers by Voysey (plate 71) and Crane.[10] Van de Velde had given up painting at thirty—he had read Morris and embraced the concept of a more egalitarian art, which he believed would arise through the decorative arts. As a member of the important Brussels group Les Vingt, he worked to bring about a new art in

which ornament would be intrinsic to structure.[11] To that end the group exhibited not only major avant-garde artists, but also decorative art starting in 1891 and Morris wallpapers in 1894.[12] Van de Velde himself designed several wallpapers, the most interesting a repeated stem motif with a diagonal pattern, which he used in the atelier in his own Haus Bloemenwerf at Uccle, Belgium (plate 76). This sweep-

Plate 75 *Opposite*
ALLAN FRANCIS VIGERS (1858–1921)
"Japanese Rose," 1899.
Wallpaper design, produced by Jeffrey and Co., 1901.
By courtesy of the Board of Trustees of the Victoria and Albert Museum, London.

Plate 76
HENRI VAN DE VELDE (1863–1957)
Wallpaper, c. 1898; for the atelier at Uccle, Belgium.
Bibliothèque de l'Ecole Nationale Superieure des Arts Visuels, Brussels.

ing design somewhat resembles traditional Javanese batik, and van de Velde may have been influenced by the work of his contemporary, the Dutch painter Jan Toorop, who spent his childhood in Java. There is some evidence that Toorop himself designed wallpapers.

Victor Horta, then a young Belgian architect, was also enamoured of the curving stem as a motif for his designs and used many English wallpapers in his quintessential Art Nouveau houses of soaring imaginative forms and space. In the spectacularly original Tassel House in Brussels (1892–93), Horta used Voysey's "Elaine" (plate 77), a large stylized flower design of soft colors, soft flowing shapes.[13] Today the house, its unforgettable painted stem-form wall decoration rising and interlacing amid the decorative steel of the stairwell, is hung with Morris's relatively subdued "Marigold" (1875) and "Larkspur" (1874) wallpapers. In a bedroom of his Solvay House (1894) Horta used a Voysey wallpaper—"Flight" or "Savaric" (plate 78), one of this artist's joyous, flat, precise groups of birds and foliage, a daring contrast to most Art Nouveau wallpapers.[14] For the

Plate 77
C.F.A. VOYSEY (1857–1941)
"Elaine," 1895.
Wallpaper; *in situ,* the dining room of Victor Horta's
Tassel House, Brussels. Musée Horta, Brussels.

Plate 78

C.F.A. Voysey (1857–1941)

"Flight" ("Savaric"), c. 1896.

Wallpaper; *in situ,* a bedroom in Victor Horta's Solvay House,

Brussels. Courtesy of L. Wittamer–de Camps, Brussels.

Plate 79
C.F.A. VOYSEY (1857–1941)
"Tokyo," 1893.
Wallpaper, machine printed, Essex and Co.
By courtesy of the Board of Trustees of the
Victoria and Albert Museum, London.

Château de la Hulpe of the Solvays, Horta used Voysey's "Tokyo" (1893) pattern, perhaps the most compelling of all Art Nouveau wallpapers, a large all-over design of great poppies with drooping heads (plate 79).[15] At the Winssinger House in 1894, Horta used Morris's "Acanthus," a design of subtle color and vigorous movement, yet very stately presence (see plate 46). Horta must have believed that the vitality of these wallpapers enhanced his new architecture. He became internationally famous; then, after a decade of pioneering forms and celebrated houses, and with the demise

of Art Nouveau, he moved toward more austere and rectilinear forms.

In the meantime, after a visit to Belgium to see van de Velde's Haus Bloemenwerf, Samuel Bing asked him to design the interior of his shop the Maison de l'Art Nouveau, which opened in Paris in 1895. Significantly, Bing from the outset offered for sale wallpapers by Morris, Crane, and Voysey. Dedicated to art and artists, Bing was an important dealer in Oriental art and had earlier run a shop, La Porte Chinoise, devoted only to it. Vincent van Gogh and other artists often went there to study Japanese prints.[16] Bing had also published the monthly *Artistic Japan* from 1888 to 1891. He appreciated that the Japanese aesthetic embraced the smallest things of life and encouraged young painters to study Japanese art. "Nothing exists in creation," he said, "be it only a blade of grass, that is not worthy of a place in the loftiest conceptions of Art."[17] A genius at finding new art and artists, Bing considered himself fortunate to serve as "a sponsor to the new life," and the name of his shop became synonymous with the movement.[18]

The painter Maurice Denis was one of Samuel Bing's chosen artists. In 1893 Bing asked Denis and other young artists to prepare decorative ensembles for his new shop, ensembles to be chosen or designed by the artists themselves. Many of the young artists were members of a group they called the Nabis, who considered themselves prophets for art. Their goals were to restore morality to art, all art, and to reunite the fine arts with the decorative arts. As one of the Nabis, Jan Verkade, reported: "About the beginning of the year 1890, a war cry was issued from one studio to the other. No more easel paintings! Down with these useless objects! Painting must not usurp the freedom which isolates it from the other arts. . . . Walls, walls to decorate. . . . There are no paintings, there are only decorations."[19] Paul Gauguin, a member of the group for a time, declared: "All art is decoration."[20] Denis, the acknowledged spokesman for the group, stated: "A painting should be an ornament."[21] And Nabi Pierre Bonnard, when asked what he had most admired and used from Japanese art, exclaimed: "The lovely patterns!"[22]

In this spirit Denis designed for Bing an elaborate frieze on paper for a bedroom. Entitled "History of a Woman" (1896), the work became a part of the painter's own bedroom and can be seen in his painting *Visit in the Mauve Bedroom* (1907). Denis, however, was pondering wallpaper patterns. While on his honeymoon in Brittany in 1893 he wrote dreamily in his diary of ideas for *papiers peints* as "meanders and reflections of water, green and white . . . brambles by a stream. Wheat tones somber on a background of white and blue . . . the buds of the chestnut, rose and cream and gray-green. . . . For a ceiling . . . *harpistes,*

belles attitudes."[23] Certainly some of this musing entered the artist's eventual designs for wallpaper, mostly created in the years before 1895. His "Harpistes" pattern is very close to the diary description in palette, motif, and mood, and in addition has the flowing, undulating curves of Art Nouveau (plate 80). It is also remarkably surreal, entwining women's torsos and the harps in swirling white mists of Japanese-inspired line.

Plate 80
MAURICE DENIS (1870–1932)
"Harpistes," 1893.
Ceiling paper design. Private collection, Paris.

Only one of Denis's wallpaper designs is known to have been produced. André Marty, the publisher of *L'Estampe Originale,* lithographed "Les Bateaux Roses" (plate 81) in 1895. It was printed on small sheets to be fitted together, and was in fact advertised as an "art" wallpaper. The pattern is a simple diaper arrangement of small Breton fishing boats, with a background of swirled lines for the water. The boats are a very pale apricot; the background, two shades of tan. In a gouache drawing, Denis made another version of Breton boats in yellow, with an interesting foam motif for the

sea (plate 82), but most of his wallpaper designs (c. 1893; also in gouache drawings) were derived from nature. All except one exhibit a rather somber palette. The simple florals "Les Couronnes de Fleurs" and "Bouquets" use a palette of gray-green and pale yellow; others use gray-blue. "Les Poissons," however, uses a sumptuous gold for the fish against a deep rose background with golden swirls and circles, in a pattern much like the background of Denis's painting *Madame Ranson au chat* (1892). Several patterns use the traditional Japanese water motif of swirled lines in the back-

Plate 81
MAURICE DENIS (1870–1932)
"Les Bateaux Roses," 1893.
Wallpaper design, lithographed by *L'Estampe Originale.*
Musée départemental du Prieuré, Saint-Germain-en-Laye,
France.

Plate 82
MAURICE DENIS (1870–1932)
"Bateaux Jaunes," c. 1893.
Wallpaper design, gouache on paper on
cardboard. Musée départemental du Prieuré,
Saint-Germain-en-Laye, France.

Plate 83

MAURICE DENIS (1870–1932)

Les Régates à Perros, 1892.

Oil on canvas, 16⅛ x 13 in. (41 x 33 cm).

Private collection.

Plate 84

MAURICE DENIS (1870–1932)

"Les Biches," c. 1893.

Wallpaper design, gouache on paper on board.

Private collection, Paris.

Plate 85
MAURICE DENIS (1870–1932)
"Les Colombes," c. 1893.
Wallpaper design. Private collection, Paris.

Plate 86
MAURICE DENIS (1870–1932)
"Trains," c. 1893.
Wallpaper design. Private collection, Paris.

ground. However, in the wallpaper "Les Biches" ("The Deer"), these swirls could be mountain pastures (plate 84), and in "Les Colombes" ("The Doves") they could be fields (plate 85). Resembling caterpillars, "Trains" (plate 86) is an affectionate wallpaper tribute to the small train from Paris to Saint-Germain-en-Laye, where Denis lived. The Japanese swirls in the background of this design are railroad tracks. Denis gives his wallpapers a special, gentle rendering typical of his symbolic and tranquil paintings of his family and subjects from the French life dear to him. They recall the happy vacations in Brittany, his wife and children in a meditative mood, the French countryside. Denis believed that all ornament should have meaning and be an essential part of life; his wallpapers have simple, direct messages and are less

complex than his paintings. A work of art, according to Denis, was an "impassioned equivalent of a sensation experienced."[24] And all art, he contended, was capable through its line, color, and form of stimulating ideas and emotions beyond the objects pictured.[25] Denis's meditative and often trancelike paintings are clearly more impassioned than the simple motifs of the wallpapers. The charming "Bateaux Roses" pattern may recall "a sensation experienced," but the image of Breton women waiting on a pier with the same boats in the distance in the painting *Les Régates à Perros* (1892; plate 83) arouses more complex feelings and ideas, and is infinitely more moving. Since both works are decorative and both are art, it is like comparing a rhyming couplet with a sonnet.

Dominique Maurice-Denis, son of the painter, remembers the "Bateaux Roses" wallpaper in the dining room of their first home in Saint-Germain-en-Laye.[26] Maurice Denis painted the family against this background in 1902; the painting proudly shows the wallpaper behind the happy group. The romance of such a menage must have appealed to Denis's friend and fellow Nabi Edouard Vuillard, whose painting *Intérieur chez Maurice Denis* shows members of the Denis family with the "Bateaux Roses" wallpaper in the far background and Gauguin's *Yellow Christ* in the foreground.

In May 1899, when some of Denis's wallpaper motifs were published in *L'Art Décoratif,* he included "Les Fillettes" (c. 1893; plate 88), a wallpaper pattern of small girls somewhat resembling angels, trustingly holding hands. A 1912 painting, *Au Paradis,* had a similar motif, this time of angels

with small girls (plate 87). The following year Denis purchased a kind of paradise, an ancient priory in Saint-Germain-en-Laye that he knew well and had painted; it gave him spacious and even symbolic quarters, acres of trees and gardens, and a brook for his large family. The children were free to go in and out of his studio as they pleased.

It was quite appropriate that Denis lived in a priory. His strong religious convictions entered into most of his paintings. He believed that painting must restore morality to art as fervently as did his friend Verkade, who became a monk. Judging from the entries in his diary, one senses that Denis was well aware of the fragility of life and of its blessings. All of this is reflected in his wallpaper art, not only in its motifs of angels, harpists, and angelic little girls but in the serene and meditative images it shares with his other art.

Plate 87
MAURICE DENIS (1870–1932)
Au Paradis, 1912.
Oil on wood, 19⅝ x 29½ in. (50 x 75 cm).
Musée d'Orsay, Paris.

Plate 88   *Opposite*
MAURICE DENIS (1870–1932)
"Les Fillettes," c. 1893.
Wallpaper design, gouache on paper on board. Musée départemental du Prieuré, Saint-Germain-en-Laye, France.

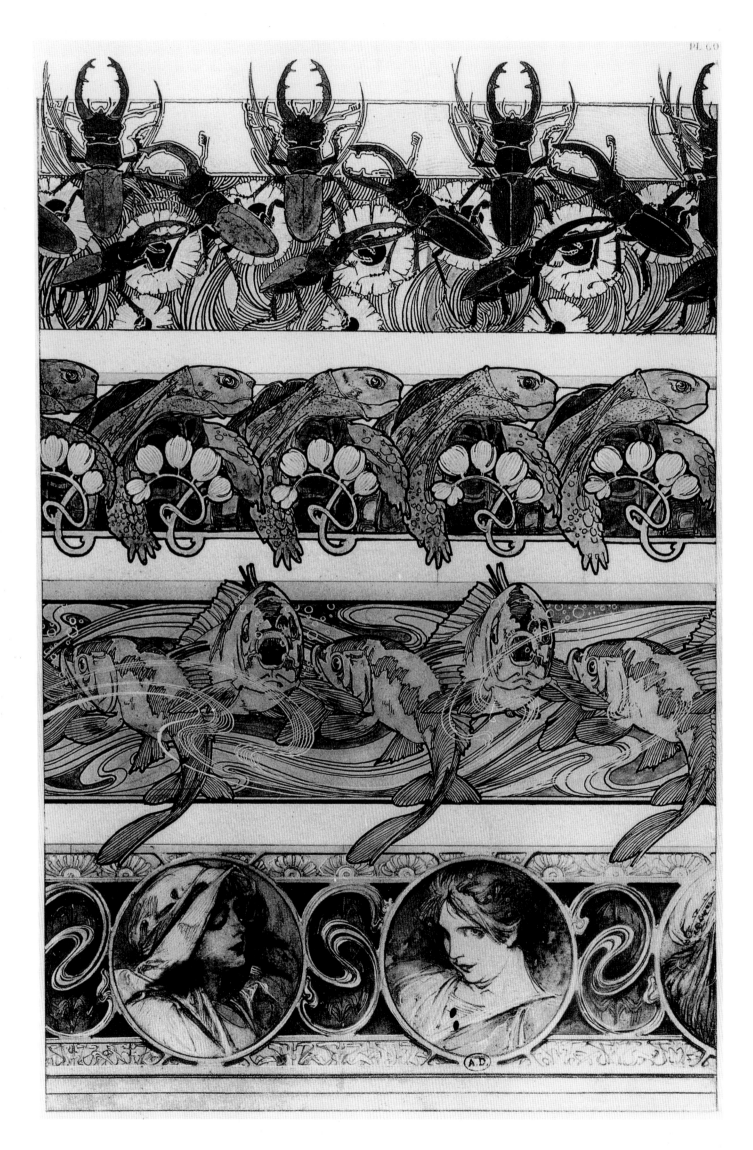

Also working in Paris at the turn of the century was Alphonse Maria Mucha, a Czech who was the embodiment of the Art Nouveau artist, although he denied it on the grounds that art is eternal, never "new."[27] Mucha became a celebrated artist, but spent much of his career designing posters and advertisements. He made several trips to the United States, where he was lionized, but he did not find the wealthy sponsor he dreamed of to enable him to paint seriously. Late in his career, having at last found an American sponsor, he returned to his home in Moravia and was able to produce some large paintings on Slavic history, but he is remembered for his work in the decorative arts and graphic design.

Mucha's handsome wallpapers were published in his album of designs, *Documents Décoratifs* (1902). This album, describing Mucha as "a teacher of design," included his patterns for furniture, silver, carpets, and china in addition to wallpaper, and was meant to be a teaching resource as well as a catalog of his designs for production. Mucha had hoped to be able to devote his life to serious painting after *Documents Décoratifs* was published, but since the album was successful he was commissioned to do another book of designs on the subject of the human figure.

Mucha, like many of his contemporaries, gave some studied attention to Japanese art. The floral wallpapers in *Documents Décoratifs* enclose an agile Art Nouveau line. The full plant of flowers, stems, and roots is used quite effectively in two designs and examined with Japanese sensitivity and stylization (plate 90). These wallpapers have the unique pale colors that in Mucha's time attracted great attention, and the flat, dramatically outlined forms characteristic of him. The drawing is invariably masterful and free. Above all, Mucha followed Eugène Grasset's teachings for his wallpaper patterns and practiced the rearrangement of natural forms that Grasset expounded as well as his exhortation to use animals in design. Grasset had said, "There is no serpent or hideous monster which, *well interpreted,* could not please the eye."[28] Mucha's astonishing naturalistic wallpaper borders of dogs or turtles or gaping-mouthed fish were his literal, serious interpretation of Grasset (plate 89). In our own more sardonic age, they would be considered an amusing spoof of wallpaper.

Plate 90
ALPHONSE MARIA MUCHA (1860–1939)
"Poppies with Roots," 1902.
Wallpaper design. From *Documents Décoratifs.* By courtesy of the Board of Trustees of the Victoria and Albert Museum, London.

Plate 89   *Opposite*
ALPHONSE MARIA MUCHA (1860–1939)
Animal wallpaper borders. From *Documents Décoratifs,* 1902.
Musée des Arts Décoratifs, Paris.

In the wallpapers and in his other art, Mucha was an idealist who believed that art uplifts the human spirit. He idealized womanhood. He portrayed Sarah Bernhardt as an empress in the remarkable posters he designed for her. By comparing his photographs of the professional models who sat for him with his paintings—in which he portrayed them with haloes and backgrounds of stars—one can see how he

Plate 91
WILL BRADLEY (1868–1962)
"Silverbrook"
Wallpaper design. From *Bradley: His Book,* July 1896.
By permission of the Houghton Library, Harvard University, Cambridge, Massachusetts.

romanticized them.[29] In his wallpapers it is the natural world that he glorifies—plants, animals, fish, even insects. One critic has seen his searching line, the embodiment of the Art Nouveau line, as representing infinity and thus immortality.[30]

Outside of France and Belgium a number of artists in several countries created wallpapers in the curving Art Nouveau style. Through Louis Comfort Tiffany, Americans had close ties with France and the Maison Bing. In his wallpaper years Tiffany, a student of George Inness and a lifelong painter, was head of a prestigious New York decorating firm. This firm, Associated Artists, was given the honor in 1881 of decorating the White House State Rooms for President Chester A. Arthur. Unfortunately, archival records do not show wallpapers used.[31] There are a few known wallpapers by Tiffany, including two designed for the wallpaper company Warren and Fuller.[32] One of these is a filigreed black on gold design of a snowflake for a ceiling; the other is a delicate repeat pattern of silver cobwebs and gold clematis on a very pale yellow background, showing that Tiffany was as capable as anyone else of rising to the challenge of designing with animals, insects, and spiders (plate 92).[33]

Tiffany's associate, the American decorative artist Candace Wheeler, became director of Associated Artists in 1883 after Tiffany withdrew from the firm. She won Warren and Fuller's first prize for wallpapers that year with her wallpaper theme of the bee: this scheme included a dado of the hive in gold; the filling of the honeycomb in silver, ringed with golden clover and bees in black and yellow; and a frieze of bees and clover.[34] Wheeler once whimsically designed a pattern of gold coins for a millionaire.[35]

In 1889 Tiffany began designing stained-glass windows for Samuel Bing. By 1895 his firm was asked to make all the windows, designed almost entirely by Nabi artists, for the opening of the Maison de l'Art Nouveau. Tiffany had long put wallpaper behind him. He compared the relative power of form and color of "shaded flowers" in "hideous" wallpaper with the glowlike "embers" of flowers in stained glass, where color was paramount and form was "distinctly a secondary consideration."[36] His remark on form was indicative of an urge toward abstraction and spiritual essences, which were widely sought at the turn of the century.

Another American, the printer and illustrator Will Bradley, worked staunchly for the unity of the arts; in 1896, after con-

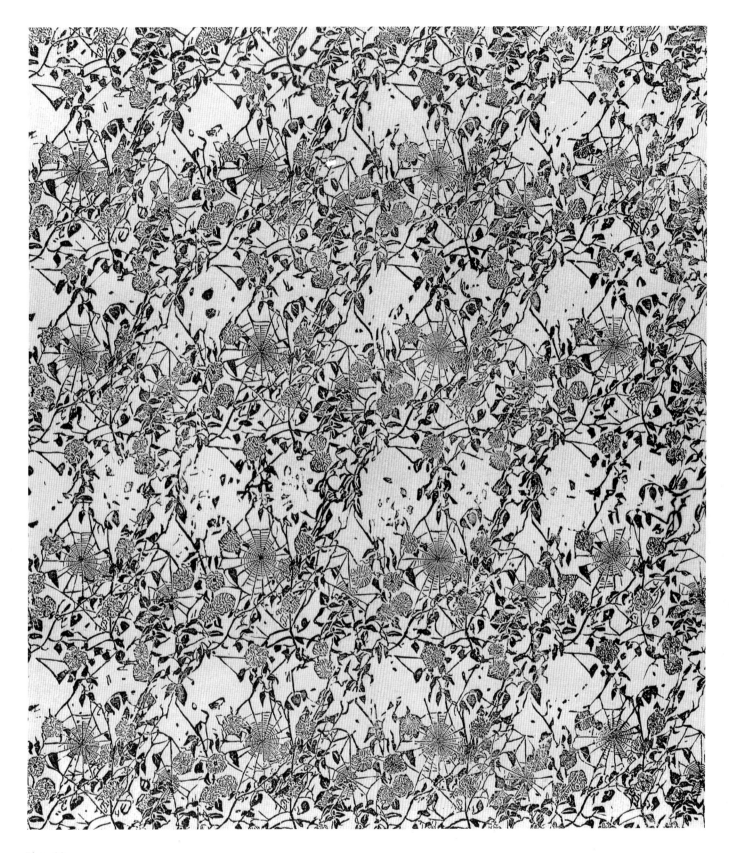

Plate 92

Louis Comfort Tiffany (1848–1933)

"Cobweb," 1880.

Wallpaper. From Clarence Cook, *What Shall We Do
With Our Walls* (New York: Warren, Fuller and Co., 1880).

Stowe-Day Foundation, Hartford, Connecticut.

siderable success as an illustrator, he began to think about designing wallpapers and fabrics as well as other home furnishings. In his own magazine, *Bradley: His Book,* the July 1896 issue (which he called "a woman's issue") shows two wallpaper designs, which were probably never produced.[37] They are flat and decoratively linear, much like Bradley's graphic art. One, "Silverbrook," has Japanese movement in line and mass and uses the traditional line swirl for water (plate 91). The other is a linear nursery pattern, "The Babies' Garden," of cherubs' heads among foliage. In addition to his Japanese bent, Bradley was strongly drawn to the striking graphic art of the English artist Aubrey Beardsley, whose massed blacks, rippling curves, and daring stylizations seen in the art magazine the *Yellow Book* attracted a whole gener-

Plate 93
WILL BRADLEY (1868–1962)
"Design for a Bedroom," 1901.
The Metropolitan Museum of Art;
Gift of Fern Bradley Dunfer, 1952.

ation of artists. The nineties were the age of the little art magazine and the poster, possibly because they were widely accessible art forms.[38] But toward the end of the century Beardsley's art (and Bradley's because his style was similar) was labeled decadent. By this time Oscar Wilde, whose *Salomé* (1893) Beardsley had illustrated, had been tried and convicted of "degenerate" crimes. Americans were being urged by their new president, Theodore Roosevelt, to practice "the strenuous life" and not to emulate "cultivated, ineffective men with a taste for bric-a-brac."[39] Bradley discontinued his magazine in 1897 after a physical breakdown and found refuge in "wholesome" early American art: Colonial typography and woodcut. By the turn of the century, when he was asked to design interiors, his decorative designs for "A Bradley House" in the *Ladies' Home Journal* show that he was well aware of the simple, "American" lines of the new Craftsman movement and of Frank Lloyd Wright's first prairie houses. His patterns for most of these rooms are flat and bold. Nevertheless, in his design for a boudoir in this house, Bradley drew an overornamented but straight-lined interior and dared a peacock wallpaper in silhouette with trailing tail, stylized and spare. The peacock was of course a much-loved image of Art Nouveau (plate 93).[40] These are Bradley's only wallpapers; his long, successful career after the turn of the century was in graphic art and typography.

As Germany was slow to use wallpapers in preference to sturdier wall coverings, wallpaper in the Art Nouveau style arrived late. Here the major artists creating wallpapers were the Jugendstil painters Otto Eckmann and Walter Leistikow. By 1894 Eckmann, like van de Velde, had given up painting and turned to the decorative arts. He became a professor of decorative arts in Berlin and designed a series of wallpapers about 1900 to be machine-printed, declaring: "We must convince the manufacturer that business and good taste do not have to be enemies."[41] All of Eckmann's wallpapers are named after things in nature but are often evocative, even abstract: "Fasan" for instance, named after the call of a pheasant, is a scrolling linear design with wing shapes in the frieze, free yet formal (plate 97). Eckmann's more naturalistic wallpaper of placid eddies in water surmounted by a serene swan border is a witty, even poetic

Plate 94

<small>CHARLES DANA GIBSON (1867–1944)</small>
"A Gentleman's Wallpaper" ("Gibson Girl"), 1902. Machine printed, the Birge Company, Buffalo. Described as suitable for a bachelor's apartment, the "Gibson Girl" faces in this wallpaper are powdered in chalky white; the blue hair in the design provides flowing Art Nouveau lines. Courtesy of Cooper-Hewitt, National Museum of Design, Smithsonian Institution/Art Resource, New York.

design (plate 96). For the pattern "Wild Vine" the accent of the vertical vine is as important as the drooping foliage and flowers; all are surmounted by a sinuous horizontal frieze of leaves and berries (plate 98). Although it is difficult to believe that he imagined his wallpapers could fade into the background of a room unnoticed, Eckmann once pronounced that "the aim of wallpaper patterns is to lead the eye pleasantly from one piece of furniture to the next."[42]

Leistikow, a noted Russian landscape artist who lived in Berlin, was a leader of artists and, along with Louis Corinth

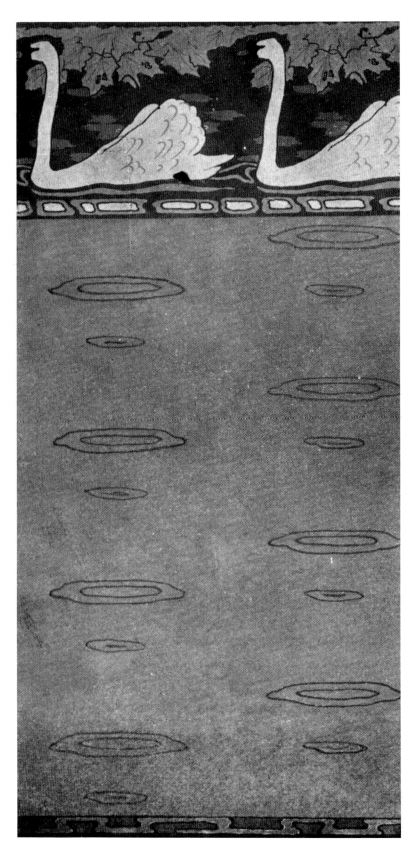

Plate 95
WALTER LEISTIKOW (1865–1908)
"Wild Swans," c. 1900.
Wallpaper. Bibliothèque Forney, Paris.

Plate 96
OTTO ECKMANN (1865–1902)
"Swan," 1900.
Wallpaper. Bibliothèque Forney, Paris.

Plate 97
OTTO ECKMANN (1865–1902)
"Fasan," 1900.
Wallpaper, machine printed, H. Engelhard, Mannheim,
Germany. Deutsches Tapetenmuseum, Kassel, Germany.

Plate 98
OTTO ECKMANN (1865–1902)
"Wild Vine," 1902.
Wallpaper, machine printed. Deutsches
Tapetenmuseum, Kassel, Germany.

Plate 99
JOSEPH MARIA OLBRICH (1867–1908)
"Tulips," 1902.
Wallpaper. Deutsches Tapetenmuseum,
Kassel, Germany.

Plate 100 *Opposite*
JOSEPH MARIA OLBRICH (1867–1908)
Drawing for bedroom in the David Berl
House, Vienna, 1899. Staatliche Museen
Preussischer Kulturbesitz, Berlin.

and Max Liebermann, a founder of the Berlin Secession in 1898. This group of artists, rebelling against the art establishment as the Vienna Secessionists had done the year before, wished to create a new art for their times. Although he admired Edvard Munch and defended him from critical attacks, Leistikow was a much more conservative painter himself. His canvases are of somber scenes and colors, but his wallpapers are lively and imaginative, using friezes as a strong contrast to the wallpaper filling. He, like Eckmann, produced a swan wallpaper, of stylized, flat, flying swans against shorthand Japanese lines of water or sky, with a memorable frieze of decorative swans split in silhouette (plate 95), quite reminiscent of Bradley's bold wallpaper forms. He also designed more conservative, floral Jugendstil patterns of undulating line and a remarkable "Segelschiffe" ("Sailboat") wallpaper with a filling of abstract-line marine shapes in a diamond trellis, the Japanese-inspired frieze of boats silhouetted against meandering lines of sky and clouds.

In Austria as in Germany, curvilinear Art Nouveau arrived late and in both countries departed early, making way for a new, more restrained decorative mode. In the late nineteenth century, Joseph Maria Olbrich, the brilliant Austrian architect and painter, was a transitional figure. From the beginning the artists of the Vienna Secession valued the decorative arts and gave an entire room to the wallpapers of Olbrich and Koloman Moser at the second exhibition of the Secession, in 1898. Olbrich himself designed the domed Secession building in a new, pure rectilinear style, but he decorated the golden dome profusely with laurel leaves. Olbrich's wallpapers were also closer to Jugendstil forms than to the new, more controlled, geometric, architectural art that he was helping to bring to life. His "Tulips" design is a dazzling, rippling bouquet of flowers with ribbonlike foliage undulating up the wall (plate 99). If one were to visualize it in a bedroom, the thundering words of Adolf Loos, the Viennese architect and enemy of ornament, might echo around it: "Imagine the moment of birth and death, the screams of an injured son, a mother's death, the last thoughts of a dying daughter—and then imagine all this going on in one of Olbrich's bedrooms."[43] Olbrich's undeniable genius did not allow him to relinquish these curving natural forms (plate 100), even though taste was turning toward restraint.

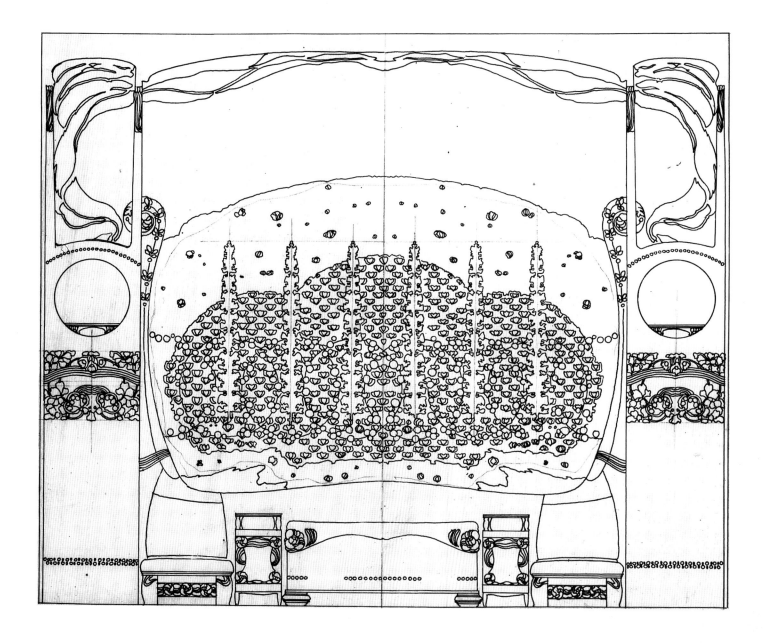

Art Nouveau has been accused by many of having a frailer moral purpose than the Arts and Crafts movement that preceded it. Yet many artists, van de Velde and Denis among them, believed it was possible to work for a new art for a new age and also be a fervent follower of Morris, bringing art to everyone. There was idealism in the precept that "every object was to be animated by the organic flow of life."[44] There was idealism in creating wallpapers as art, along with easel paintings. And there was idealism in the belief that an abstraction could be portrayed visually, and thus the belief that searching and longing could be expressed in line, or even infinity and immortality.

The Art Nouveau years for all the major artists who cre-

ated wallpaper were short, perhaps because decorative art in those years truly did become—or because its detractors insisted it had become—undisciplined ornament, exaggerated in form, overburdened with line, florid. Denis wrote that Art Nouveau "became only a display of pretentious facility, lacking in the aesthetic and moral meaning it should have had."[45] The reaction to these excesses, which triumphed three decades later as Bauhaus design, was in a pendulum swing extremely anti-ornament. Henri van de Velde, fervent Art Nouveau artist and theorist, had said rightly about Art Nouveau: "Ornamentation seems to have determined the form."[46] But he also continued to call persistently for truth in structure, a position that led quite directly to the Bauhaus.[47]

MOVEMENTS TOWARD RESTRAINT

(1900–1960)

In the first half of the twentieth century, the decorative as well as the fine arts were full of complex and often contradictory tendencies. Diverse movements came into prominence then gave way to others as the first grew stale or provoked countermovements. Or a movement, as it developed, came to encompass styles that ran counter to its original characteristics. These complexities were reflected in the artists' wallpapers of this period. If one looks primarily to the styles of the wallpapers themselves, some clarifying patterns may be discerned.

Quite early in the twentieth century a reaction set in against the decorative excesses of Art Nouveau. Movements in this direction began with the Austrian Wiener Werkstätte just after the turn of the century; Scottish architect Charles Rennie Mackintosh was a forerunner a few years earlier. Somewhat later came the artists and architects of the Deutscher Werkbund, founded in Munich, of the De Stijl group in the Netherlands, and of the Bauhaus in Weimar, Germany, just before, during, and after World War I. For most of the first half of the century, Le Corbusier in France and Frank Lloyd Wright in the United States were the spokesmen for these extremely powerful artistic currents toward a controlled (or banished) ornament—an aesthetic that continues, much abated, today.

These movements can be characterized by their relative restraint, geometry, rectilinearity, belief in truth in structure, and, in the most extreme manifestations, by their urge toward purity in design. The straight line, the square, and the cube, and most often black and white or primary colors were honored. Artist-architects like Mackintosh, Josef Hoffmann, Walter Gropius, Le Corbusier, and Wright believed in a totally designed environment for living, more structured and often more machine-produced than they could see around them. As the century progressed, European and American interiors became less and less ornamented and more and more pristine, until wallpaper in most people's houses, if it existed at all, was "oatmeal"—a flat and neutral, slightly textured color on the wall.

Mackintosh's work has frequently been regarded as having Art Nouveau characteristics and certainly there are ele-

Plate 101   *Preceding pages*
KOLOMAN MOSER (1868–1918)
"Mermaids"
Wallpaper for a bathroom. From *Flachenschmuck,* 1901.
Fine Arts Library, Fogg Art Museum, Harvard
University, Cambridge, Massachusetts.

Plate 102   *Opposite*
JOSEF HOFFMANN (1866–1956)
"Jagdfalke" (on the right), designed 1910–11,
produced 1913. Wallpaper. On the left is Maria
Friedmann's wallpaper "Strohblumen" ("Dried
Flowers"), designed before 1913. Austrian
Museum of Applied Arts, Vienna.

Plate 103

CHARLES RENNIE MACKINTOSH (1868–1928)
Stenciled wallpaper; *in situ,* the sitting room, Derngate,
Northampton, England, 1916. In 1920 this wallpaper was
replaced at the client's wish with a more subdued Mackintosh
design (see plate 106). Hunterian Art Gallery, University of
Glasgow; Mackintosh Collection.

ments of that style in the decorative medallions on his furniture, in some of his walls and glass, and in the lines of the twisted-twig bouquets he liked to arrange for his exhibitions. But the Mackintosh line and form in the furniture, and in most of the exteriors and interiors of the famous buildings, are restrained, geometric, and austere. Ludwig Mies van der Rohe, extolling powerful, simplified forms, saw Mackintosh as a "purifier of architecture."[1] To late-nineteenth-century eyes, however, the Mackintosh buildings and interiors were gaunt. Consequently, in Scotland and England, this architect and his Glasgow group were known as the Spook School. Hermann Muthesius, who wrote of the beauty and comfort of English domestic architecture in *The English House* (1904), and who greatly admired Mackintosh's work, nevertheless pointed out that his perfect "severe and subtle" interiors were intolerant of everyday life: "an unsuitably bound book on the table would be a disturbance."[2]

Mackintosh's work was appreciated by the Austrian Secessionists, in particular Josef Hoffmann and Koloman Moser, who were forging a new "Austrian" aesthetic in Vienna that embraced both decorative and fine arts.

Mackintosh was referred to as the Scottish Secessionist and was invited to join an early Secession exhibit in Vienna in 1900, where his lean and ordered interiors met with acclaim, although there were also jeers. More than a decade later, just before World War I, Mackintosh planned to live in Austria, when it became apparent he would be unable to make a living as an architect in Britain. During the war, having chosen to stay in England, he was at one point regarded as a possible spy, because he had friends in Austria. His most memorable wallpapers, most often wall stencils on paper, were designed just after this difficult period. A stencil design for the sitting room of 78 Derngate (plate 103), W. J. Bassett-Lowke's house in Northampton, England, recalls a Moser motif in the Secessionist art journal *Ver Sacrum,* and may have been inspired by memories of Vienna.[3] The wallpaper pattern is composed of geometric columns surmounted with rectangles composed of brilliantly colored triangles on a black background (plate 104). The Derngate sitting room was small, and Mackintosh sought to achieve spaciousness and mystery with the black walls.[4] Mackintosh changed this spectacular design in 1920, at the client's wish, to a more subdued horizontal stenciled frieze on a gray background, a design the same client later requested for a second house (plate 106). In 1919, for the guest bedroom at Derngate, Mackintosh used a crisp, black-and-white-striped wallpaper with a braided edging of bright blue, the wallpaper wrapping onto the ceiling. In the Derngate master bedroom he used a restrained gray wallpaper with narrow borders of abstract-patterned mauve and a mauve carpet. Similarly, for another Northampton client in 1917 he designed brown wallpapered walls with vertical bands of red and blue geometrical stenciled forms as accents, sparingly placed. This architect's precise but imaginative wallpapers appeal to us today as art; they were startling in England in 1917, their forms controlled, their color an authoritative statement, their handling innovative and fresh.

With Mackintosh's blessing, the Wiener Werkstätte was formed in 1903 by Hoffmann, Moser, and Fritz Wärndorfer. Mackintosh wrote his Secession friends: "Begin today! If I were in Vienna, I would assist with a great strong shovel!"—undoubtedly meaning that in his view much of flamboyant Art Nouveau and Jugendstil needed to be jettisoned.[5] Hoffmann, Moser, Gustav Klimt, and other Secession artists

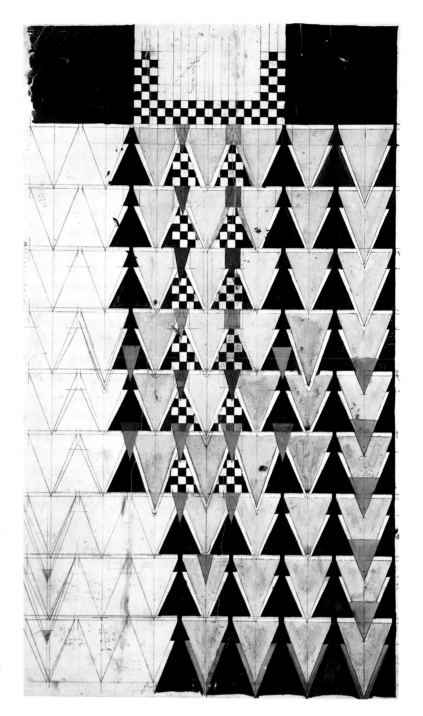

Plate 104
CHARLES RENNIE MACKINTOSH (1868–1928)
Stencil design, 1916; for the sitting room wallpaper at Derngate, Northampton, England. Hunterian Art Gallery, University of Glasgow; Mackintosh Collection.

Plate 105 *Left*
JOSEF HOFFMANN (1866–1956)
Primavesi Villa, Winkelsdorf, Czechoslovakia; bedroom
of daughter, Mäda Primavesi, c. 1913–14. Wallpaper,
"Mauerblumchen," by Lotte Frommel-Fochler, 1910–13.
Library of Congress, Washington, D.C.

Plate 106 *Below*
CHARLES RENNIE MACKINTOSH (1868–1928)
Wallpaper; *in situ,* New Ways, Northampton, England, 1923.
The Derngate wallpaper substitute of 1920 was used by the
client both at Derngate and in this second house designed by
Peter Behrens. Hunterian Art Gallery, University of Glasgow;
Mackintosh Collection.

Plate 107 *Opposite*
KOLOMAN MOSER (1868–1918)
"Goldene Schmetterlinge"
Wallpaper. From *Flachenschmuck,* 1901. Fine
Arts Library, Fogg Art Museum, Harvard
University, Cambridge, Massachusetts.

had rebelled against the status quo in 1897, and called for an art that expressed the age. The inscription on the portal of their building proclaimed: "To the age its art; to art its freedom," and the building itself, designed in a new reserved, rectilinear style by the gifted architect Joseph Maria Olbrich (see chapter 4), embodied this proclamation. Conceived as a temple of art (and called the Golden Cabbage by the irreverent), it featured a golden dome of laurel leaves and bas-reliefs of owls by Moser on one side. It has been noted that the owls may have been inspired by a similar motif in a Voysey wallpaper exhibited in Vienna in March 1898, the year the building was completed.[6] The Secession style in general has been described as "a newly rigid ordering of the viscous curvilinearity of Jugendstil."[7] The early Werkstätte designs were to make an even more remarkable "shift to simplification."[8] The Werkstätte's aims were no less ambitious than those of Ruskin and Morris: to give art to daily human life and to do so by fashioning works in the decorative arts as important and artist-created as those in the fine arts. Josef Hoffmann wrote of his dream: "a center of gravity surrounded by the happy noise of handicraft production and welcomed by everybody who truly believes in Ruskin and Morris."[9] He imagined the striking of the hour when "the wallpaper, the ceiling painting, as well as furniture and utensils will be ordered not from the dealer but from the artist."[10]

In its first years Werkstätte design was to be deliberately restrained and controlled. Hoffmann and Moser, the artistic directors, were both professors of art at the Kunstgewerbeschule, the state school of design in Vienna. They strongly believed that their artists' superb work in the decorative arts could unify the arts. The dramatic new style could be partly described by the words Hoffmann in later years chose to describe his own: "The pure square and use of black and white as dominant colors specially interested me, because these clear elements had not appeared in former styles."[11] From the beginning the Werkstätte style was successful with the rich Viennese, but its expensive—and, later, even extravagantly fanciful—productions were never affordable to the less affluent. Hoffmann at first calmly expected approval of the new Austrian art to trickle down from the upper classes to the lower. He had said: "Above all, give joy."[12] Later, disillusioned but sanguine, he had to concede: "It is absolutely no longer possible to convert the masses . . .

but then it is all the more our duty to make happy those few who turn to us."[13]

Most of Hoffmann's own designs for wallpapers are geometric and precise; one classic Hoffmann pattern, "Prism," repeats the shafts of a column as vertical fluting. The same fluting softened the reinforced concrete facade of Hoffmann's famous Ast House in 1911. Reflecting Austrian nationalism, his designs often include a nostalgic return to peasant art, made more sophisticated with a controlled geometric framework (plate 102). For the Primavesi country house in its magnificent mountain setting in Winkelsdorf, Czechoslovakia, Hoffmann used many peasant motifs in an urbane mode. The house was much decorated; Eduard Sekler, Hoffmann's biographer, relates that Hoffmann himself liked to stay in a guest room of simple black and white, but that the Primavesis' daughter, Mäda, remembered that the flickering vertical wallpaper chevrons in two shades of blue in her suite (plate 105) sometimes drove her to the woodshed![14] Abroad, Hoffmann's black-and-white wallpapers were greatly admired by Elsie De Wolfe, the American doyenne of interior design.[15]

In addition to wallpapers, many decorative art objects were created by Werkstätte artists: textiles, bookbindings, furniture, ceramics, silver, even hatpins. The most outstand-

ing Werkstätte artist was undoubtedly Koloman Moser, who did few Werkstätte wallpapers, but whose earlier Secession "reciprocal" wallpaper designs are totally surprising and inventive, and whimsically lyrical. Their interlocking forms, providing a negative space that is as important in the design as the positive space, anticipate the work of M. C. Escher. They were shown in the second exhibition of the Secession in 1898, and published in the album *Flachenschmuck* (*Flat Ornament*) in 1901. "Goldene Schmetterlinge" ("Golden Butterfly") is characteristic of these wallpapers: the color subdued, the darks intense, the meandering band boldly checkered, the pattern startlingly beautiful and new (plate 107). With a special sense of fun, Moser included in this album another design, a wallpaper for a bathroom, in which interlocking mermaids cavort under billowing waves (plate 101). There also exists an enchanting wallpaper drawing by Moser of white rabbits on a dark ground in the checkerboard pattern he favored (c. 1903; plate 108). With great restraint yet solidity the "negative" flat rabbits appear like paper chess pieces. Hoffmann did his own version of this pattern, which he titled "Long Ears" (c. 1902; plate 109). Hoffmann and Moser worked closely together, each inspiring the other; both were known for using in their designs the square and the cube—Hoffmann was affectionately nicknamed Quadrat.

It was Moser's daring black-and-white motif "Plentiful Catch," originally a design in *Flachenschmuck* (plate 110), that was singled out for attack by the architect Adolf Loos. When this motif of positive and negative interlocked fish was used on a chest acquired by the Viennese minister of

Plate 108   *Top*
KOLOMAN MOSER (1868–1918)
"Rabbits," c. 1903.
Wallpaper design. Courtesy of
Julius Hummel, Vienna.

Plate 109   *Bottom*
JOSEF HOFFMANN (1866–1956)
"Long Ears," c. 1902.
Design. Backhausen and Son, Vienna.

instruction, Loos was incensed by what he saw as vulgarity: a design, on furniture, of fish with their mouths gaping. He wrote his denunciatory essay "Ornament and Crime" in 1908 and continued to wage a bitter vendetta against the Werkstätte until its end.[16] He particularly disliked the idea of equating arts and crafts in a *gesamtkunstwerk,* a total art environment. "Whoever goes to [Beethoven's] Ninth Symphony and then sits down to design a wallpaper pattern is either a rogue or a degenerate," he wrote.[17]

Loos attacked Hoffmann's dramatic Palais Stoclet—built in 1905–11 in Brussels for the industrialist Adolf Stoclet—which was decorated as a total work of art by Werkstätte artists. Eventually, even dresses for Mrs. Stoclet were made to complement the design. Loos found such an arrangement ludicrous and related an admonitory tale of the man in the totally designed house who was scolded by his architect for wearing the slippers designed for his *bedroom* in his living room![18]

Plate 110
KOLOMAN MOSER (1868–1918)
"Plentiful Catch"
Design. From *Flachenschmuck,* 1901. Fine Arts Library, Fogg Art Museum, Harvard University, Cambridge, Massachusetts.

Plate 111 *Opposite*
CARL OTTO CZESCHKA (1878–1960)
Wallpaper; *in situ,* Haus Pickler, Budapest,
designed by Josef Hoffmann, 1909–10.
Austrian Museum of Applied Arts, Vienna.

Plate 112
JOSEF HOFFMANN (1866–1956)
Installation for Wiener Werkstätte exhibition, Mannheim,
Germany, 1907. Courtesy of Galerie St. Etienne, New York.

Two sets of artist-designed wallpapers were created for the Palais Stoclet nursery (see appendix A). For the Stoclet building and others, the wallpapers of Werkstätte artists Carl Czeschka, Ludwig Heinrich Jungnickel, and Franz von Zulow often used bright peasant motifs in a sophisticated balance of color, black, white, and lively patterning, which still have excitement today, as do the Werkstätte publicity photographs of various exhibitions, seen against their wallpaper backgrounds (plate 112). A lively wallpaper of birds by Czeschka in a squared interior by Hoffmann appeared in a 1909–10 issue of *Deutsche Kunst und Dekoration* (plate 111). This beautiful and livable room was designed by Hoffmann for the Pickler house in Budapest (1909–10).[19]

The Wiener Werkstätte changed fundamentally after

Plate 113

DAGOBERT PECHE (1886–1923)

"Spitze," c. 1920.

Wallpaper. Deutsches Tapetenmuseum, Kassel, Germany.

Plate 114   *Opposite*

DAGOBERT PECHE (1886–1923)

"Summer," 1921.

Wallpaper, Flammersheim und Steinmann, Cologne, Germany.

Deutsches Tapetenmuseum, Kassel, Germany.

Koloman Moser left it in 1907. Moser's heiress wife had been asked to support the always financially shaky Werkstätte and did so; he was not consulted. He was deeply unhappy that the workshop was, in his opinion, catering too much to public taste. "The public," he stated, "usually had no idea what it actually wanted."[20] He returned to painting, but his paintings seem now much less impressive than his brilliant decorative work.

The advent of Dagobert Peche in 1915 added a new note of gaiety, lightness, and often frivolity to Werkstätte designs. Peche had been an architecture student; his work in a special exhibition of art wallpapers in Vienna in 1913 was outstanding.[21] Hoffmann had for some years admired Peche; after he invited the young artist to join the artistic direction of the Werkstätte, Peche set to work industriously and very soon was recognized by all as a master of many crafts. Hoffmann recalled that "we always waited impatiently for him to come up with new ideas."[22] Peche created dozens of original and memorable wallpaper patterns, as well as silver, textiles, furniture, and ceramics, primarily in his own fanciful design style aptly described as "spiky baroque." His exuberant work pointed the Werkstätte toward Art Deco, and may well have been one of that style's pioneer forces.[23] Peche had a playful nature; he liked to design expensive ornaments and toys, items others sometimes referred to ruefully as extravagant extravaganzas. Elaborate and delicate lace creations appealed to him: one of his wallpapers is titled "Spitze" ("Lace"; plate 113). This is a pale and delicate linear design of containers, fernlike foliage, and small flowers scratched against a darker background of two-toned fluted space. There are quite liberated imaginative forms in this wallpaper, as is often true with Peche's designs, and the whole is like etched glass. "Summer" also has lighter forms on dark, with spiky light-and-dark foliage and brittle tulips that are simple yet totally fresh, with their surprising, almost metallic, petals (plate 114). Peche's wallpaper "Schilf" ("Reed") features waving blades of grass, their rhythms so ingeniously presented that no other motifs are needed (plate 115). In 1925 *Deutsche Kunst und Dekoration* recognized the wonder of this artist's "tender, almost brittle charm."[24] A display case (c. 1920) designed by Peche, lined with his "Laube" ("Arbor") wallpaper, is an example of his daring: the oversized rococo of the cabinet complements the utterly fanciful

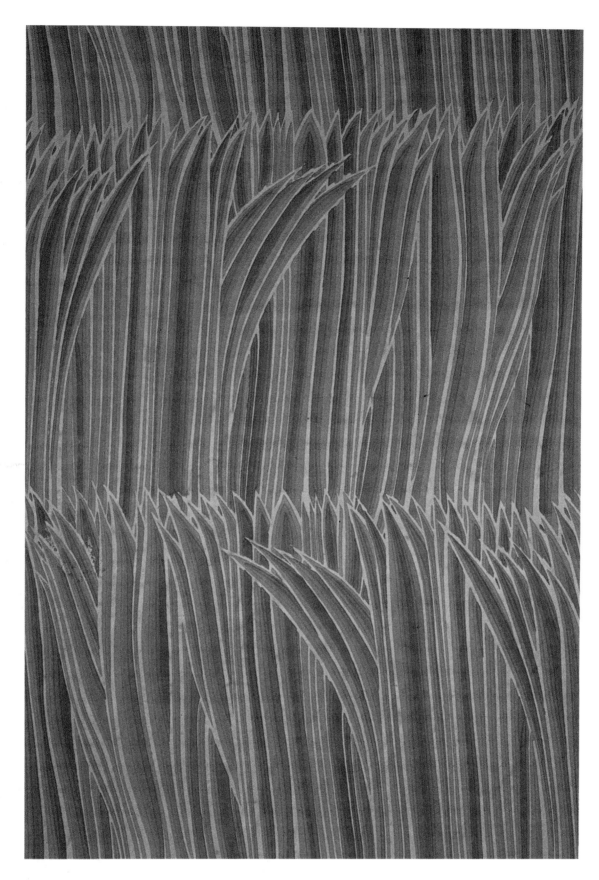

Plate 115

DAGOBERT PECHE (1886–1923)

"Schilf," 1921.

Wallpaper, Flammersheim und Steinmann, Cologne, Germany.

Deutsches Tapetenmuseum, Kassel, Germany.

spiky plant forms of the wallpaper inside (plate 117). Peche directed the Werkstätte's branch in Zurich in 1917–18, but returned to Vienna ill and died in 1923 at only thirty-seven. One of his boldest designs is "Semiramis," a cornucopia of floral imagination in stark light and dark (plate 116). This appeared in his 1919 solo album by Max Schmidt of Vienna.

Several Wiener Werkstätte wallpaper albums were published. A second collection by Peche was produced by Flammersheim and Steinmann of Cologne in 1922; after his death, the same firm produced a solo album for Werkstätte artist Maria Likarz in 1925. This collection included her pattern "Siam," which, strongly influenced by Cubism, is a geometric adventure, as playful as children's blocks (plate 118). The fourth Wiener Werkstätte pattern book was by Mathilde Flögl for the Swiss firm of Salubra, published in 1929. Flögl's wallpapers, of isolated objects like draped pearls, fans, and teapots, were examples of late Art Deco and appeared just before the Werkstätte closed in 1932.

Plate 116
DAGOBERT PECHE (1886–1923)
"Semiramis," 1913.
Wallpaper. Deutsches Tapetenmuseum, Kassel, Germany.

Plate 117   *Right*
DAGOBERT PECHE (1886–1923)
"Laube" cabinet, c. 1920.
Austrian Museum of Applied Arts, Vienna.

Plate 118
MARIA LIKARZ (b. 1893)
"Siam," 1925.
Wallpaper, Flammersheim und Steinmann, Cologne, Germany.
Austrian Museum of Applied Arts, Vienna.

Major European and even American forces, however, ran counter to the Werkstätte's later developments and paralleled its earlier impulses toward restraint. The Werkstätte itself was a founding member of the Deutscher Werkbund, formed in Munich in 1907. The Werkbund wished to promote cooperation between art and industry and did not accept a concentration on handicrafts—Morris's solution to a better life for the masses. From the beginning its members recognized that the unfettered freedoms of Jugendstil were not compatible with a machine age. Members of the group disagreed about the degree of free-

Plate 119
RICHARD RIEMERSCHMID (1868–1957)
Floral wallpaper, Erismann et Cie., Breisach, Germany.
Courtesy of the Deutsches Tapetenmuseum, Kassel, Germany.

Plate 120   *Opposite*
PETER BEHRENS (1868–1940)
"Peacock," c. 1900.
Wallpaper. From *L'Art Décoratif,* April 1900.
Bibliothèque Forney, Paris.

dom to allow the artist who designed for industry. Van de Velde was in favor of total freedom; Muthesius advocated standardization. But they were all concerned with quality, including quality of life for the worker, and thus a degree of standardization was necessary. Peter Behrens, a painter who was one of the first industrial artists, was a leading member of the Werkbund. He became artistic director of the important electrical firm AEG in Berlin and designed widely and brilliantly for industry, remarking that "even . . . a specialist buys from the external appearance. A motor ought to look like a birthday present."[25] His wallpapers, though designed around 1900, are tinged with traces of a Jugendstil neatly trimmed and ordered and then further abstracted. The peacock feathers in Behrens's "Peacock" wallpaper are almost Mayan in their rigid, stylized handling (plate 120). It was Behrens who first said *"Wenig ist mehr"* ("Less is more"), not Mies van der Rohe, as is commonly thought.[26]

The artist Richard Riemerschmid was an important member of the Werkbund and for many years director of the Munich School of Arts and Crafts. His pronouncements on art and industry had, in 1907, the ring of the Bauhaus, which would not come into existence until 1919. Riemerschmid admired forms that were "taut, austere, confident and unpretentious." Like English design theorist W. R. Lethaby, he believed contemporary design could be found in dockyards and factories, and that life itself creates style. Everyday objects should be designed "as a ship is designed": to function harmoniously.[27] Riemerschmid's wallpapers are shipshape, cheerful, and semiabstract, shown in attractively trimmed interiors, although he also designed some wallpapers that reflect traces of ornamental and curvilinear Jugendstil (plate 119). His designs often have a vestige of bright peasant art; this interest in the peasant motif was shared by the Werkstätte and Werkbund, but ignored by the Bauhaus and De Stijl groups, which were to follow them.

No one would ordinarily think of the impersonal abstractions of the De Stijl group as being at all involved with wallpaper, and the artists themselves would have denied it; their colorful, geometric interiors were designed for purity and objectivity, set against *painted* walls. But De Stijl artist Piet Mondrian used squares and rectangles

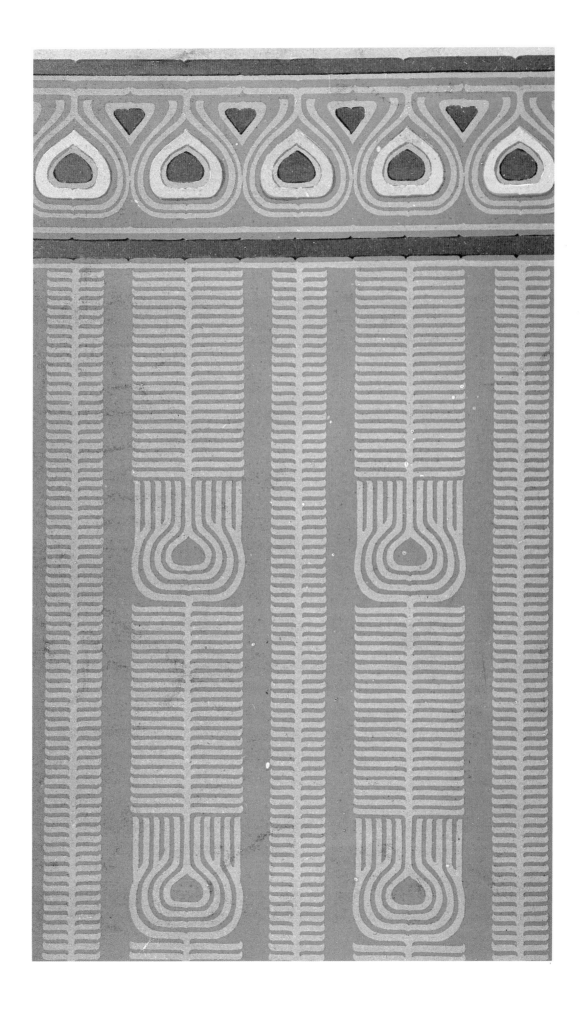

of colored cardboard on the walls of his Paris studio, sometimes precisely positioning his easel paintings as part of a total wall composition (plate 121). Both Alexander Calder and Ben Nicholson testified to the power of the resulting environment, Calder saying the visit to Mondrian's studio gave him "a shock that started things"; Nicholson feeling that he was in "one of those hermit's caves where lions used to go to have thorns taken out of their paws."[28] Mondrian himself described the repose he was striving for, insisting: "Instead of being superficially decorative, the entire wall gives the impression of the objective, universal, spiritual condition that comes to the fore in the most severe style forms."[29] Mondrian claimed to make no distinction between easel painting (which he called condensed innerness) and "the decorative wall," and criticized fellow painter Fernand Léger for his willingness in certain circumstances to do so.[30] He believed that "all art becomes 'decoration' when depth of expression is lacking."[31] Art was for life, part of "the general search for clarity and purity in everything."[32]

Even in his last studio in New York, Mondrian arranged his walls with the cardboard "wallpaper," which he continually studied and changed; its rectangles, however, were always parallel with the lines of floor and ceiling. Pictures of this room show his famous painting *Victory Boogie-Woogie* in a diamond shape, although the painting itself has no diagonals. The Dutch painter objected to his De Stijl colleague Theo van Doesburg's diagonal emphasis *inside* a painting, on grounds that thus the repose of vertical and horizontal in a room would be broken. The artist César Domela, who visited Mondrian's studio, remarked that a box of matches

Plate 121
PIET MONDRIAN (1872–1944)
Easel painting as part of cardboard "wallpaper," Paris, c. 1931.
Courtesy of the Haags Gemeentemuseum, The Hague.

picked up and put down in a different place would be carefully returned to its exact former position by the master. "Otherwise the composition of the atelier wouldn't work anymore."[33] Domela eventually decided to change his own austere, Mondrianesque interior, saying one "really can't live in a painting."[34]

Van Doesburg, the most commanding voice of De Stijl, attempted to bring some of the De Stijl aesthetic to the Bauhaus, which he visited in Weimar. Yet although he had student followers he was never appointed to the faculty. The fabled Bauhaus was above all a school, one that pulsated with ideas. Its history began when Henry van de Velde, as the leading theorist of Art Nouveau in Belgium, was invited by English-educated Grand Duke Wilhelm Ernst to head an art school in Weimar in 1902. In time van de Velde became a leading member of the Deutscher Werkbund. Just after the start of World War I in 1914, van de Velde resigned from the school as an enemy alien and recommended Walter Gropius, a young Werkbund member already respected as an architect, to head the institution. Gropius accepted in 1919 and in due course named the school the Bauhaus, from the word *bau,* which means both building and growing. In his manifesto of 1919, Gropius asserted: "There is no essential difference between the artist and the craftsman."[35] In 1924 he wrote of Ruskin's and Morris's legacy to the Bauhaus.[36]

In the short space of time between the two world wars this amazing provincial school with its star-studded faculty (including Lyonel Feininger, Wassily Kandinsky, Paul Klee, and Oskar Schlemmer) was to influence both design and fine art immeasurably. However, not until after 1927 did the Bauhaus design wallpapers, in response to a request from the brother of a student in the school who had inherited a wallpaper factory.[37] The school's mural-painting department then set to work to create something very new: finely textured abstract wallpaper patterns with discreet, virtually monotone colors, for printing rolls. They were designed to be affordable and available to all. The Bauhaus had no experience with wallpaper, but to everyone's surprise these patterns were highly successful (plate 122). Royalties from the wallpapers became an important source of income for the institute. In the first year, four-and-a-half million rolls were produced.[38] Three wallpaper pattern books of Bauhaus wall-

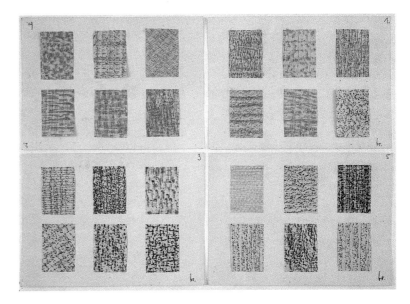

Plate 122
Bauhaus wallpapers, designed 1928, produced by Gebruder Rasch and Co., 1929. These were the earliest Bauhaus wallpapers; in the following years these very successful wallpapers used more complex textures and colors. Courtesy of Gebruder Rasch and Co., Bramsche, Germany.

papers were published between 1929 and 1932 by the original firm of Emil Rasch in Bramsche, Germany. Today this firm makes similar wallpapers, including some recently produced designs from drawings by Gropius found in the Bauhaus archives, which are now in Berlin. Bearing instructions in faint pencil, these drawings reveal that two or more printing rolls were to be printed over each other to make an intricate and extremely small textured pattern. With textures and subtly blended colors, the Bauhaus wallpapers project a richness that a plain color on the wall cannot have. They are the most subdued of all art wallpapers.

Unlike the Bauhaus wallpapers, Le Corbusier's wallpapers project large-scale drama. Although a Swiss, Le Corbusier (Charles-Edouard Jeanneret) was involved with the Deutscher Werkbund as a young man and worked for a time for Peter Behrens as an industrial artist. (In 1910 Mies van der Rohe, Le Corbusier and Gropius all worked in Behrens's office in Berlin.) Le Corbusier's earlier independent architectural work in the area of his boyhood home of La Chaux-de-Fonds, however, was influenced by the Arts and Crafts movement and the French artist and teacher

THE SECOND LE CORBUSIER SERIES

Note concerning the creation for the Salubra Company of a Le Corbusier Collection 1959

-A/ Plain papers
-B/ „Wall" series
-C/ „MARBLE I" series
-D/ „MARBLE II" series

This collection contains, for the plain papers, twenty basic colours prepared by Le Corbusier with the Salubra colours on Salubra paper. These colours are powerful (dark or light).

Each of the papers of the series is of a pure tone mixed with white, according to circumstances.

The texture (the nature of the coloured surface) is almost smooth in accordance with one of the Salubra processes.

1 st
PLAIN PAPERS

An album has been composed in the following way:

1. Twenty plates 18/37 centimetres, bound on the left, without any systematical order.

2. These twenty plates are enclosed in a double cover 25 x 40 cm.

3. The inner surface of the back of the cover contains small samples (10 x 3 cm) of each of the twenty colours of the series, each one pasted close to the other and grouped by ten like the keys of a piano, forming a „keyboard of colours". The distance of these keys from top to bottom is 22½ cm, allowing these two keys to appear above and below the twenty plain coloured plates 18/37 cm. The two series of coloured keys are separated by a median white horizontal band, on which are indicated the reference numbers of each colour.

4. This album permits to compare twenty times successively the twenty colours of the „Le Corbusier series 1959" offering in this way to the architect, the decorator or the client, four hundred colour-schemes.

5. The consumer will recognize amongst these 400 colour-schemes the colour equilibriums which correspond to his real nature (his temperament, his tastes, his psycho-physiology of sensations).

6. A window of bristol cardboard run over the coloured keys permits to separate 3 or 4 colours in colour equilibrium. It will then be possible to assign these 3 or 4 colours (or more) to one wall, or to two or three or four walls; to a carpet; to curtains, to seats, etc. . . . .

7. The strips of the „Le Corbusier plain papers" are 80 centimetres in width.

8. It is advisable to hang the strips horizontally (with butt joints). Nothing is less noble than the sight of vertical joints).

At other times, the ceiling will be covered with a „WALL" paper or a „MARBLE I" paper (sketch d/).

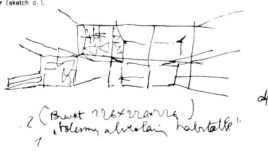

3 rd
Application of the „PLAIN PAPERS"

The twenty colours of the series find their stability in the two extremes: withe and black.

For instance:

A bedroom rue Nungesser et Coli Paris 1932:

governing colour: white (walls, vault and floor)

walls: red   )
blue   ) around the bed
yellow)   (sketch e/)

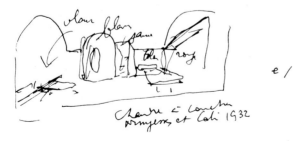

2 nd
„WALL"
„MARBLE I"
„MARBLE II"

This series: „WALL", „MARBLE", is suitable to certain particularly original colour-schemes (but rather delicate!).

The application of these designs (very powerful) can be limited to an isolated element of a room (of a premises) or to the connection of several rooms (or premises) in the case of a „plan libre".

For example:

Application localized to one wall only
or to two walls, etc, etc . . . .
or to fragmentary elements such as ceiling, vertical columns, etc

For this series „WALL" and „MARBLE I" — „MARBLE II", the strips of Salubra can be hung horizontally or vertically according to the architect's choice (sketch a/, b/ and c/).

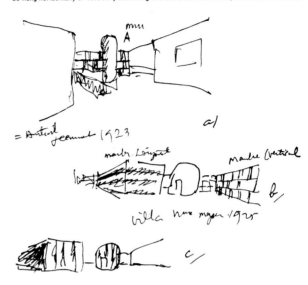

At the Museum of Modern Art in Paris: „Permanent Le Corbusier Room" (Paintings)

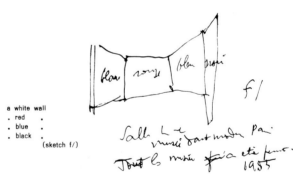

a white wall
. red   .
. blue   .
. black   .
          (sketch f/)

At the Cité Universitaire in Paris:
The Swiss and the Brazil Pavilion

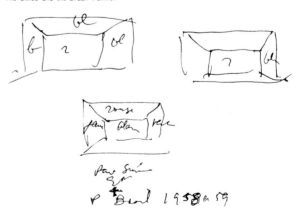

Eugène Grasset.[39] After studying Owen Jones's *Grammar of Ornament,* Le Corbusier tried to develop forms based on Jones's studies; he was, for instance, inspired by the ornament of the columns at the Egyptian temples of Karnak and Luxor representing a grove of papyrus.[40] For his parents' villa in 1912 he chose a floral wallpaper.[41] Even his drawings for the famous Villa Schwob of 1917 show traditional wallpapers in the salon, dining room, and bedroom.[42] As early as 1914, however, Le Corbusier had begun his crusade against decoration, declaring: "Ornament . . . is a synthesis; it is decoration that is debatable."[43] He referred to Hoffmann's panels of architectural ornament as "doilies."

Le Corbusier was a lifetime painter and in 1918, with his friend the artist Amédée Ozenfant, he coined his pen name for their publication *Après le cubisme.* In this manifesto the two accused Cubist painters of turning Cubism into a decorative art, the lowest art (they believed) in the hierarchy of arts.[44] By 1923 Le Corbusier proposed the home as a *machine à habiter:* a machine for living. He was beginning a moral crusade for purity in architecture: "Why do we have the enormous and useless roofs on pretty suburban villas? . . . Why the damasked wallpapers . . . with their motley design?"[45] He espoused simplicity: "Today," he wrote, "we seem to realize that however rich we are, we cannot eat a whole chicken each."[46] He urged severe restraint: "Demand bare walls in your bedrooms, your living room, and your

Plate 123 *Opposite*
LE CORBUSIER (1887–1965)
Drawings for plain wallpapers, 1932; for Salubra. Courtesy of Forbo-Salubra, Grenzach-Wyhlen, Germany.

Plate 124
LE CORBUSIER (1887–1965)
A scheme showing variations for the "Mauer" wallpaper; for Salubra, 1959. Courtesy of Forbo-Salubra, Grenzach-Wyhlen, Germany.

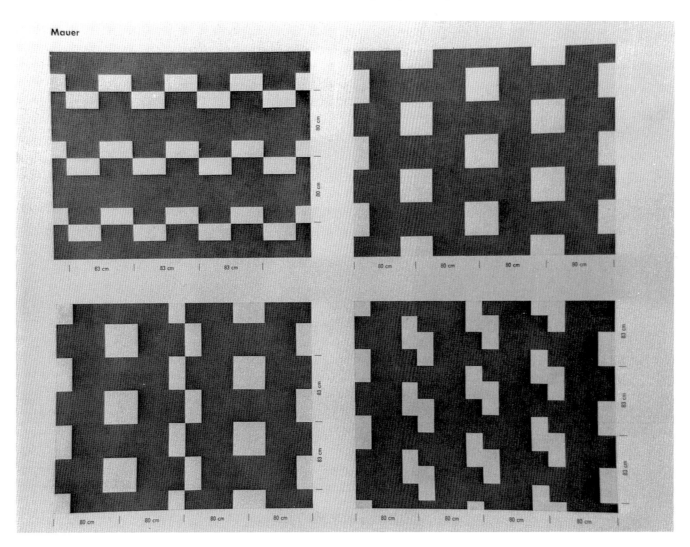

dining room."[47] In 1925, the year of his astonishing and beautiful Pavillon de l'Esprit Nouveau at the Exposition des Arts Décoratifs in Paris, he continued in this vein: "If some Solon imposed the following two laws: Enamel Paint and Whitewash, we would make a declaration of moral principle to 'love purity' and 'be discriminating'! Such a declaration would lead to pleasure and the pursuit of perfection. Consider the effects of the Enamel Paint law. Every citizen would be required to replace his stencils, wall hangings, wallpapers, and damasks with a layer of pure white enamel paint . . . then our inner selves would all be cleaned up."[48]

Salvador Dalí once referred to Le Corbusier as "the inventor of the architecture of self-punishment."[49] Nonetheless, Le Corbusier believed in decorative art, with the provision that it must obey its task of "serving us politely and helpfully. After that, it is to thrill us, let there be no mistake."[50] He called works of decorative art "tools, beautiful tools,"[51] but remarked that *modern* decorative art "is not decorated."[52] The machine aesthetic, streamlined and unencumbered, was to him closest to the spirit of the times.[53] In 1922 Le Corbusier designed his sleek and inexpensive Citrohan houses for the urban dweller. In 1932 he designed a series of wallpapers for the Swiss firm Salubra. These he called the Color Keyboard. The presentation allowed the client to choose his own colors out of the four hundred combinations possible. All the wallpapers were solid colors, and, as Le Corbusier's drawings show, they were to be used on the ceiling as well as the walls (plate 123). Indeed, some ceilings might be papered in two or three plain colors, the walls remaining white. Or one or two walls might be white, with several colors used for the other walls and the ceiling. These colors were to be chosen by the client to "accord with his inner feelings."[54] Anni Albers once remarked that Le Corbusier used textiles on walls architecturally; his drawings show that he used wallpapers similarly. Le Corbusier thought of his plain colors in wallpaper as oil paint in rolls, at once more convenient and more consistent than oil paint, and referred to his wallpaper as machine-prepared painting.[55] Again for Salubra in 1959 Le Corbusier devised two very bold-patterned wallpapers of grand size, rich texture, and ingenious geometric possibilities, to be used in varied ways. The colors were his favorites, the primaries, white, and black (plates 124; 125; 126). One of them, "Mauer" ("Wall") could be hung horizon-

Plate 125 *Opposite*
LE CORBUSIER (1887–1965)
"Mauer", c. 1959.
Wallpaper, Salubra. Courtesy of Forbo-Salubra,
Grenzach-Wyhlen, Germany.

Plate 126
LE CORBUSIER (1887–1965)
"Mauer," c. 1959.
Wallpaper; *in situ.* Courtesy of Forbo-Salubra,
Grenzach-Wyhlen, Germany.

tally or vertically, but Le Corbusier characteristically cautioned against vertical hanging, advising: "Nothing is less noble than the sight of vertical joints."[56]

Frank Lloyd Wright shared much common ground on architectural principles with Le Corbusier—each designed wallpapers and inexpensive houses, and each believed profoundly that his own architecture could enhance human life—but these two most important architects of the twentieth century never met.

Wright's career began in the late nineteenth century. He had early ties with the English Arts and Crafts movement through his close friendship with the craftsman C. R.

Ashbee, who founded the Morris-inspired Guild of Handicraft in London in 1880. In a prophetic lecture of 1901, however, Wright powerfully envisioned the usefulness of the machine over handicraft.[57] But even in this lecture Wright praised Morris's contributions to the "new art" declaring: "All artists love and honor William Morris."[58] He urged that the machine be mastered with proper design—with the artist as the master.[59] Wright's views were particularly noted by rising young architects—Gropius in Germany, for example, and van Doesburg in Holland. They were deeply impressed with his architecture when drawings and photographs appeared in the famous Wasmuth editions, published in Europe in 1910 and 1911.[60] However, unlike

Plate 127

FRANK LLOYD WRIGHT (1869–1959)

#105, 1957.

Wallpaper, F. Schumacher and Co., New York; *in situ*.

Schumacher Archives, New York.

these architects of pristine forms, Wright the iconoclast did not hesitate to incorporate ornament, even handcrafted ornament, into his architecture, and his thousands of drawings made throughout his career exhibit an obsession with a restrained ornamentation as well as with total design.

The series of wallpapers Wright made for Schumacher in 1955, late in his life, shows that he never abandoned precise geometric ornament. Because he believed he could not draw, in his early days in Louis Sullivan's office he created ornament in his "own rectilinear way . . . condemned to square and triangle," but unable to attain "the sensuous expressions the master [Sullivan] so much loved."[61] He grew to favor this geometric ornament and always considered it an integral part of his architecture, not "applied art." He was, however, against "decorations" as early as 1910: "There are no 'decorations' as such, nor is there any place for their application."[62] Indeed, according to Wright's theory of "organic" architecture, all the furnishings of a house are a part of the whole. "In Organic Architecture then, it is quite impossible to consider the building as one thing, its furnishings another and its setting and environment still another. . . . The very chairs and tables . . . are of the building itself, never fixtures upon it."[63] Even for his inexpensive Usonian houses, Wright designed handsome furnishings, beginning in about 1937. Yet his wallpapers are less architectural and integral than Le Corbusier's. They are ingenious, using geometry with detailed and rich variations, as well as optical excitement. Some are almost like electronic diagrams; others are like Op art (plates 127; 128; 129), their colors Wright's favored grayed earth tones or the primaries. These crisp, clean patterns are not grand in scale but are quite vivid, even intrusive, on the wall, totally unlike the subdued Bauhaus designs or Le Corbusier's dramatic extended wallpaper spaces.

With patterned wallpapers these two great architects, Wright and Le Corbusier, at midcentury were trying to make a contribution to art for the people. Ironically, the taste of the ordinary man was for undecorated surfaces. Although by the 1960s the anti-ornament movement had become somewhat less powerful, it had persuaded mass opinion to opt for pure, plain walls, a preference that was to change very slowly in the decades leading up to the end of the century.

Plate 128   *Top*
FRANK LLOYD WRIGHT (1869–1959)
#103, 1956.
Wallpaper, screen printed, F. Schumacher and Co., New York.
By courtesy of the Board of Trustees of the Victoria and Albert Museum, London.

Plate 129   *Bottom*
FRANK LLOYD WRIGHT (1869–1959)
#706, 1956.
Wallpaper, screen printed, F. Schumacher and Co., New York.
By courtesy of the Board of Trustees of the Victoria and Albert Museum, London.

THE
ART DECO
YEARS

From Elegance
to Exuberance
(1910–1940)

Plate 130 *Preceding pages*
JEAN LURÇAT (1892–1966)
"Les Fusées," c. 1924.
Wallpaper, produced by Pierre Chareau.
Musée des Arts Décoratifs, Paris.

Plate 131 *Opposite*
MARTINE
"Les Eucalyptus," 1912.
Wallpaper, cylinder printed, Paul Dumas.
Bibliothèque Forney, Paris.

Although there were important Austrian precursors of the style that would long after the fact be dubbed Art Deco, its development was primarily a French phenomenon, stretching from the halcyon years just before World War I, through the determinedly mad and glittering period of the twenties to the despondent days of world depression and the threat of Hitler in the thirties. The times reflected themselves in the decorative arts. Art Deco's early period, which reached its high point just before the 1925 Exposition des Arts Décoratifs in Paris, was exuberant, confidently classical or playfully Oriental, and often deliriously colorful; it believed in decoration and exulted in ornament. This outburst of joie de vivre contrasted in the same years with the restraint of Mackintosh, the earlier Wiener Werkstätte, and De Stijl. In later years, influenced by Cubism and Futurist obsessions, the Art Deco style became more streamlined, abstract, and geometrical, yet still zestful, thus reversing the pattern of the Wiener Werkstätte, which under Hoffmann and Moser had been restrained, then under Hoffmann and Peche became almost flamboyant. Meanwhile the forces that led to the Bauhaus were moving inexorably toward curbing any irreverence in either Deco or Werkstätte and eclipsing both. Much of the wallpaper by important artists of the period participated in these trends. In the last years of the style, wallpaper was abandoned altogether, or enjoyed as a Dada art form, provocatively meaningless.

The Art Deco style began to take shape in a surprising school, the Ecole Martine, in which the "spontaneous and ardent genius" was the painter Raoul Dufy.[1] The school was founded by Paul Poiret, a swaggeringly individualistic painter and couturier. In 1911, after a visit to the Wiener Werkstätte and members of the Deutscher Werkbund, he determined to found a school of design and brought back to Paris hundreds of yards of fabrics from the Wiener Werkstätte as inspiration. He hired teenage girls, whom he named the Martines, to design for him; they may well have been inspired by those vivid, urbane yet folkloric designs. Within six months the school's bright, fresh art was exciting Parisians. Its wallpaper patterns were typically very large, the colors exotically bold, and the style spontaneous and

often naive (plate 131). Not everyone was pleased, however. The duchesse de Gramont was heard to remark sternly that some furnishings of Martine were "a night of bad dreams after eating potted hare."[2] Nevertheless, in 1912 after only a year of production the Martines were given the artistic accolade of exhibiting in two rooms of the Salon d'Automne. Poiret abhorred the rigid discipline he had seen imposed on the students at the Wiener Werkstätte and believed that his methods accounted for the Martines' immediate success: he took them to zoos, the seashore, the country, and museums, and allowed them to create freely. Their designs were then adapted, as Poiret put it, "with industrial courage . . . at heavy cost."[3]

The Martines worked very closely with Dufy, who took a great interest in their spontaneous child-art. In 1910 Poiret had befriended Dufy, who was then an impoverished Fauve painter. Together they enthusiastically set up the "Petite Usine" (little factory), to block print Dufy's designs. The Dufy patterns, recalling his woodcuts for Guillaume Apollinaire's *Le Bestiaire,* became spectacular textiles, in part with the Martines' help (plates 132; 133). It is unclear if any Dufy designs were printed as wallpapers. René Simon Lévy states that "some blocks . . . were used in fact on both cloth and paper" and reminds us that the block-printing process is the same for both.[4] Sarah Wilson suggests that Dufy may have "created deliberately naive designs for the Martine shop," such as the juvenile purple-and-yellow tulip design with green dots on a black ground.[5] What is certain is that in this exhilarating environment the Martines' work may well

Plate 132   *Top*
RAOUL DUFY (1877–1953)
"The Mouse"
Woodcut. From *Le Bestiaire* by Guillaume Apollinaire
(Paris, 1911). By permission of the Houghton Library,
Harvard University, Cambridge, Massachusetts.

Plate 133   *Bottom*
RAOUL DUFY (1877–1953)
"Blé et Oiseaux" ("Les Fruits"), c. 1925.
Toile de Tournon. Musée de l'Impression sur Etoffes,
Mulhouse, France; courtesy of Bianchini-Férier, Lyons, France.

have been as much a stimulus for Dufy as his was for them. Palmer White, Poiret's biographer, relates that "frequently Poiret arrived in the [Martine] atelier with an embroiderer, a wallpaper manufacturer, or a curtain manufacturer, sometimes with Matisse, Dufy, Segonzac, or Van Dongen."[6] According to White, "Dufy produced his famous series of four hand-blocked hangings—printed from blocks carved from sketches by the Martines."[7] Paul Dumas published many wallpapers marked "Martine" on the selvage, and some may have been adapted or created by Dufy. This surmise is supported by the fact that at least one design Poiret notes as being by the Martines is now credited to Dufy. Poiret describes it as "fields of ripe corn, starred with marguerites, poppies, and cornflowers."[8] A design by Dufy fitting this description exists at Maison Bianchini-Ferier, Lyons. In 1912 this large fabric house offered Dufy a designing contract, and Poiret generously allowed all the Dufy blocks to go to them. He continued to employ Dufy for other purposes, however, and the artist may have designed or consulted on some wallpapers for the shop Maison Martine. For instance the Martine pattern "Les Gazelles," shown in a 1923 dining room (plate 134), is an artist's wall pattern that fits into the Dufy oeuvre. Of great, green, boldly textured foliage harboring vermilion gazelles against gray, spotted areas, it is breathtakingly daring in concept and color, but far from gaudy. It is very reminiscent of Dufy's textile style, which often has elements of naiveté surmounted with sophistication, and here too the animal figure is much like other Dufy animal motifs, placed to give a diagonal and vital sweep in the pattern. Because of their stylized forms and the fascinating flora that surround them, Dufy's animal designs are often singularly successful.

Plate 134
MARTINE
"Les Gazelles," c. 1923.
Wallpaper; *in situ.* Bibliothèque Forney, Paris.

Dufy once remarked that painters, especially Fauves, through their love of pure colors and arabesques had extended their pictures "beyond the frame, on to our clothes and our walls."[9] By hanging in his atelier a lily wallpaper in the design of his fabric "L'Arums" (plate 135), Dufy devised a background that appears in many of his paintings. Dufy's biographer Dora Perez-Tibi believes the two walls shown in the paintings were hung with cloth and that any Dufy designs on paper were made for fabric tests.[10] The flower in the pattern, a calla lily, was Dufy's favorite; the rosy color that often appears in the paintings must have been symbolic of his joyous view of life. The most famous painting of

Plate 135

RAOUL DUFY (1877–1953)

"L'Arums," c. 1920.

Toile. Collection Raoul Dufy; courtesy of Bianchini-Férier, Lyons, France.

Plate 136
RAOUL DUFY (1877–1953)
30 ans ou la vie en rose, 1931.
Oil on canvas, 38⅝ x 50⅜ in. (98 x 128 cm). Musée d'Art
Moderne de la Ville de Paris/Cliché Musées de la Ville de Paris.

these wallpapered corners is *30 ans ou la vie en rose* (1931; plate 136), a painting Dufy kept until his death. In it he celebrates thirty years as an artist; there are flowers in the wallpaper, flowers in a painting mounted on the wallpaper, and flowers on a table in front of the wallpaper. The predominant colors are rose and pink, although Lévy reports that Dufy's assistant Fournier remembered the "Arum" wallpaper in this room as being ivory.[11] In *L'Atelier de l'impasse*

Guelma (1935–52), Dufy presents an almost transparent montage description of these patterned walls from indoors and outdoors. Another painting with this patterned background, *Hommage à Mozart,* was once owned by Poiret, and other Dufy paintings dedicated to composers share the setting. In the composer paintings the wallpaper with the bell-shaped flowers is often shown in tones of blue, but the design remains the same.

In 1925 an article by Georges Remon pictured as *papiers peints* (wallpapers) three of Dufy's extraordinary fabric designs that we know as his toiles de Tournon.[12] Toiles are commonly used as wall coverings in France; it is not surprising that there is a 1925 photograph showing a Dufy toile, "L'Afrique," hung in a dining room (plate 137). Dufy followed toile de Jouy tradition by presenting in his toiles aspects of daily life decoratively surrounded by foliage, fruits, and flowers, and using only one rich color on a background of cream or white (plate 139). The Jouy toiles were manufactured in France by the legendary Christophe-Philippe Oberkampf in the eighteenth century and were designed by gifted artists, among them Jean-Baptiste Huet

Plate 138
JEAN-BAPTISTE HUET (1761–1811)
"L'Hommage de l'Amérique à la France," 1783–89.
Toile de Jouy. Courtesy of Musée de l'Impression sur Etoffes, Mulhouse, France.

Plate 137
RAOUL DUFY (1877–1953)
"L'Afrique," c. 1925.
Toile; *in situ.* Bibliothèque Forney, Paris.

Plate 139

RAOUL DUFY (1877–1953)

"L'Afrique," c. 1920.

Toile de Tournon. Musée de l'Impression sur Etoffes,

Mulhouse, France; courtesy of Bianchini-Férier, Lyons, France.

(plate 138), who also designed wallpapers for Réveillon. Many of Dufy's splendid toiles of the twenties are again closely related to his *Bestiaire* illustrations for Apollinaire, cut in 1910 by Dufy himself in wood block (plate 133). The many motifs from the woodcuts for the poem are beautiful and strong as wall textiles: the wheat, the pumpkin, the birds, the grapes, the elephant, the hairy mountain goat, the strongly incised human figures. Enveloping them all are the memorable, fanciful flowers and foliage. "I can give you only half the joy I feel," said Dufy. His direct, spontaneous love of life as well as his love of fantasy pervades these toiles. They are twentieth-century craft fused into art, their

patterns as fine as Morris's from the nineteenth century. In 1927 masses of Dufy's toiles were used to decorate the French president's residence, the Elysée Palace.[13]

Jean-Emile Laboureur, a contemporary of Dufy, was one of the finest graphic artists of the Art Deco period, and a scholar of printmaking. His little-known graphic work has, in the words of André Dunoyer de Segonzac, a pervading "elegance of spirit."[14] Instructed in lithography by Toulouse-Lautrec, Laboureur also worked in etching and woodcut, commenting keenly and often ironically on his life as a visitor in Pittsburgh, as an interpreter in the trenches during

World War I, or as an observer in his native Brittany. His etchings are particularly radiant, with a surprisingly even, silvery gray light. Several of his wallpaper designs have been preserved. One, "Le Marin" ("The Sailor," 1912–20; plate 140) is like a Dufy toile with foliage and figures. It was produced as a fabric as well as a wallpaper, in somewhat garish colors of rose and blue on a white ground, or in orange and brown. It depicts a sailor on an island of palms confronting a native woman in a grass skirt. Laboureur's 1921 etching *Les Trois Marins* (*The Three Sailors;* plate 141) is an interesting contrast. The angular geometric Laboureur style is the same: the sailors in both etching and wallpaper have small heads, extremely brawny shoulders, and assertive stances. Their anatomies are in fact Cubist, but as Robert Allen points out,

Plate 140   *Opposite*
JEAN-EMILE LABOUREUR (1877–1943)
"Le Marin," 1912–20.
Wallpaper, block printed, André Groult. Courtesy of Cooper-Hewitt, National Museum of Design, Smithsonian Institution; Gift of Frankl Galleries/Art Resource, New York.

Plate 141
JEAN-EMILE LABOUREUR (1877–1943)
Les Trois Marins, 1921.
Etching, 8⅞ x 11¾ in. (22.5 x 29.7 cm).
Courtesy, Museum of Fine Arts, Boston; Gift of Mr. and Mrs. Peter A. Wick.

3565

Laboureur's Cubism is frankly decorative rather than analytical.[15] The wallpaper sailor is clearly on shore leave; the Brittany sailors are on home leave; with their Breton sabots and jaunty postures, they are bent on pleasure. The refined technique and even grays of the etching are gentle but incisive in their satire, and the village background is serene. The wallpaper's very aggressive, heavy block-printed masses and exotic locale are in jolting and expressive contrast.

Other Laboureur wallpaper designs show an equal intelligence and wit, but are less intense than "Le Marin." One is a large and inviting beribboned ogival trellis design entitled "Bouquet de Mariée," ("Wedding Bouquet"), in soft blues and grays (plate 142). Another, "Escargots," is of meandering strawberry plants dotted with snails, which are as interesting as the strawberries. A third is of very thorny vertical raspberry plants in Deco colors of black and gray on a gold background; there is a bee in the design that manages to be both urbane and naturalistic. Laboureur's wallpapers present the natural world with an air of sophisticated well-being.

Laboureur admired the graphic work of Daumier and Rowlandson and of his great friend Marie Laurencin, who also designed wallpapers (plate 143). A member of the Bateau-Lavoir group, Laurencin was admired by many painters. Most of them were devoted to African sculpture, which she disliked, and Cubism, which she said she could not master; her wispy painting style was dramatically different. Yet she was the only woman painter at the center of this painters' world for two decades, painting her unique, soft, peopled domains, filmy and pastel. Much of her soft-focused style may stem from the fact that she was myopic. Her paintings are often a hazy stage setting of humans with animals, a kind of peaceable kingdom. Her life, her painting, and even her wallpapers all project a sense of fantasy, unreality, even theatricality. Two of Laurencin's wallpapers survive, although some of her blocks were reportedly used for flooring in the forties when wallpaper was no longer fashionable.[16] "Les Singes" ("The Monkeys"), a delicate Dada design in which playful monkeys with draperies perch on sprays of plum blossoms (plate 144), reminds one of Laurencin's special fondness for animals. Its playfulness is also in the tradition of *singerie* (see chapter 2), in which monkeys act as people. Her painting *La Femme au singe* (*Woman*

Plate 143
JEAN-EMILE LABOUREUR (1877–1943)
Portrait of Marie Laurencin, 1914.
Woodcut, 9¾ x 8⅝ in. (25 x 22 cm). Cabinet des Estampes, Bibliothèque Nationale, Paris.

Plate 142   *Opposite*
JEAN-EMILE LABOUREUR (1877–1943)
"Bouquet de Mariée," c. 1912–20.
Wallpaper, block printed, André Groult.
Bibliothèque Forney, Paris.

with a Monkey, 1915) is Goya-inspired and probably a self-portrait. It was painted during Laurencin's exile in Spain with her German husband during World War I. Her wallpapers for the decorator André Groult probably date from the difficult years just after the war that saw her return to Paris after separating from her husband.

Laurencin's second known wallpaper, "Apollinaire" (c. 1912–20; plate 145), has been named for her lover, the poet Guillaume Apollinaire, because in it he appears as she often

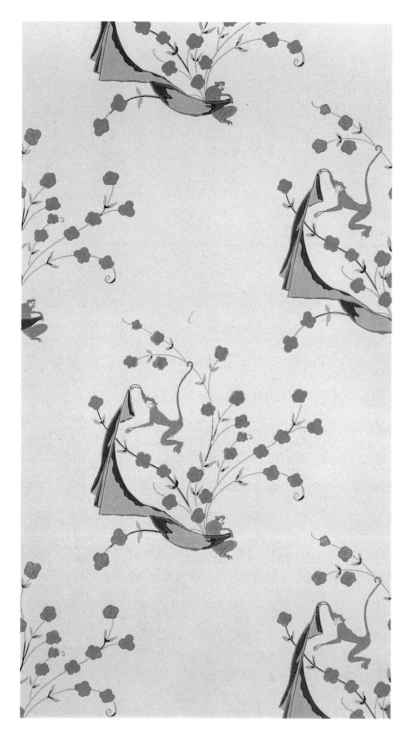

Plate 144
MARIE LAURENCIN (1883–1956)
"Les Singes," c. 1912–20.
Wallpaper, block printed, André Groult.
Musée des Arts Décoratifs, Paris.

Plate 145 *Opposite*
MARIE LAURENCIN (1883–1956)
"Apollinaire" ("Isis"), c. 1912–20.
Wallpaper, block printed, André Groult.
Bibliothèque Forney, Paris.

drew him, a strange being with a pointed head or hat. Fernande Olivier, Picasso's mistress, apparently concurred, remarking that Apollinaire had a head shaped like a pear.[17] After Picasso introduced Apollinaire to Laurencin in 1907, the poet thought of her as his muse; she inspired the Dove in his *Bestiaire*.[18] In 1909 Henri Rousseau painted them together in *The Muse Inspiring the Poet*. In Laurencin's wallpaper, Apollinaire is shown blowing a horn, and small animals run alertly about on a plum-blossom background. This wallpaper has at times been titled "Isis" for the Egyptian goddess with a horned helmet who in myth continually seeks her husband. Typical of both Laurencin wallpapers are miniature forms and a delicate line, as well as wit and charm, and no doubt very personal meanings. Their total freedom is in the Dada tradition.

By 1925 the Art Deco pendulum was swinging toward a more machinelike precision. The architect Jean Badovici proclaimed it in 1924: "Behold the completely new sobriety of line in all the decorative arts! The soul of this geometry must have something to say to modern man!"[19] Le Corbusier went further and remarked on "buffoons who believe in decorative art."[20]

The important artist-designer Emile-Jacques Ruhlmann respected both decorative art and wallpaper. Ruhlmann, who had studied painting, was an artist in interiors at the peak of his career in 1925, a career that managed to combine the decoration Le Corbusier loathed with a harmonious classic restraint. Ruhlmann's highly decorative furniture was at the same time polished geometric perfection, most often handmade and luxurious. Although he genuinely believed that the luxury object helped to improve the standard of mass-produced objects, he created as well some inexpensive furniture for the Cité Universitaire in Paris. Ruhlmann began his career by designing wallpapers, which were shown in the Salon des Artistes Décorateurs of 1910. Of these wallpapers nothing more is known. However, his Hôtel du Collectionneur with its dominant wall pattern by Henri Stéphany in the salon was admired by countless visitors to the 1925 Exposition, while Le Corbusier's Pavillon de l'Esprit Nouveau, chaste and pristine, was virtually ignored. The Ruhlmann pavilion was classic Art Deco. The massive scale of the violet and white silk *lamas,* with its symbolic

doves, ropes of pearls, urns, and foliage, enhanced the glossy, classic curves of the Ruhlmann furniture. In 1928 it was repeated for the Salon des Artistes Décorateurs.

Ruhlmann's masterpieces were his interiors in *Harmonies of Ruhlmann,* a 1924 album assembled by Jean Badovici, showing the artist's wallpapers to be both lively and intuitively impeccable (plate 147). For instance, his familiar quivering line with random dots, used often in his wallpapers, appears in the album on the walls of a sumptuous red library-boudoir (plate 146). Ruhlmann's all-over "Roses" pattern in a bedroom uses the same quivering line in opulent Art Deco colors of black, violet, and white on a mustard ground (plate 148). In this album Ruhlmann is at once classic, fearless, and elegant.

Plate 146   *Opposite*
EMILE-JACQUES RUHLMANN (1879–1933)
"The Red Library-Boudoir"
From *Harmonies of Ruhlmann,* edited by Jean Badovici
(Paris, 1924). Bibliothèque Forney, Paris.

Plate 147
EMILE-JACQUES RUHLMANN (1879–1933)
"Les Fruits de Mer," c. 1923–24.
Wallpaper. Bibliothèque Forney, Paris.

Plate 148
EMILE-JACQUES RUHLMANN (1879–1933)
"Roses," 1925.
Wallpaper. Bibliothèque Forney, Paris.

markets, seen in the stylized but naturalistic forms of those early friezes, was later abstracted into concentric circular forms for paintings. Resettled in Paris in 1919 after the war, she and her husband, the painter Robert Delaunay, were suddenly without funds. The revolution in Russia meant the end of her inheritance, an event she said she welcomed: "We were left penniless but we wept for joy."[21] However, it was necessary for the practical Delaunay to begin to earn a living. She proceeded to design scarves and then fabrics in geometrics of fluid movement, rhythm, and color that have never been equaled. In 1925 she used one of these fabrics on the walls of her apartment in Paris. It was a beige harlequin check hung in a near-diagonal (plate 150). It would be dramatic today, and it makes a strong contrast with an earlier family photograph showing the formal, conventional wallpapers of Delaunay's living room walls in 1911, which Arthur Cohen, Delaunay's biographer, describes as "Empire-figured papers and solemn stainings."[22] From 1925 on, Delaunay's inspired geometrics of masterful color eclipsed simple figured patterns. In her best work there is a flow instead of a repeat and the colors seem to have belonged to the sun. Delaunay thought of color as "the poetry, the mystery of an interior life which breaks loose, radiates, and communicates itself."[23] She saw her own times as the age of the dynamic machine, and her rhythmic art and decoration express those years more poetically than repeated motifs in patterns could. Designs, possibly for wallpapers, that demonstrate her genius for pattern are seen in her 1930 pochoir album, *Compositions, couleurs, idées.* Delaunay insisted that crafts and arts are the same, and that "decoration" must be, like architecture, a construction.[24]

For her 1929 pochoir album, *Tapis et tissus,* Delaunay included two Constructivist wallpapers of her Russian women compatriots Lyubov Popova and Varvara Stepanova. Both artists had changed their careers in 1923, when *Pravda* urged artists to work in industry. Their strong and handsome geometric designs are shown in the album in red, gold-orange, and black (plate 151). Both women worked together with Stepanova's husband, artist Alexander Rodchenko, as designers at the First State Textile Factory in Moscow in the early twenties.

In *Compositions, couleurs, idées,* Delaunay was continuing the tradition of the pochoir album in France, often in the

Henri Stéphany, Ruhlmann's associate, became strongly Cubist in his own independent wallpaper designs, using prisms of flowers or geometric Moroccan architecture. He also designed some engaging Art Deco mural scenes for wallpapers and a charming Deco-chinoiserie wallpaper (plate 149).

The ultimate geometrics in wall patterns were Sonia Delaunay's. Delaunay had brought Russian peasant-art exuberance to her early wall friezes, created in Spain and Portugal during World War I. Her fascination with the local

Plate 149   *Opposite*
HENRI STÉPHANY
Chinoiserie wallpaper, produced by Societé Française des
Papiers Peints, 1929. Bibliothèque Forney, Paris.

Plate 150   *Above*
SONIA DELAUNAY (1885–1979)
Fabric on walls of the Delaunay family salon,
19 blvd. Malesherbes, Paris, 1925. Bibliothèque
Nationale, Paris; Sonia Delaunay Bequest.

Plate 151   *Right*
VARVARA STEPANOVA (1894–1958) and
LYUBOV POPOVA (1889–1924)
"Papiers Peints"
From Sonia Delaunay's *Tapis et tissus,* 1929.
Bibliothèque Forney, Paris.

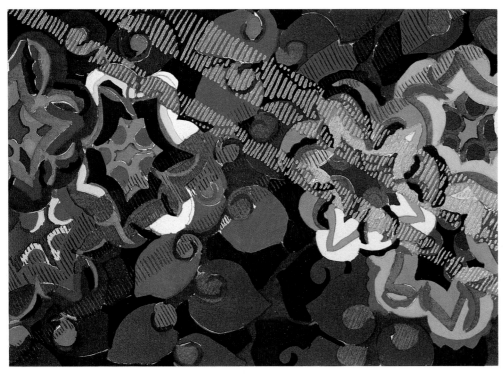
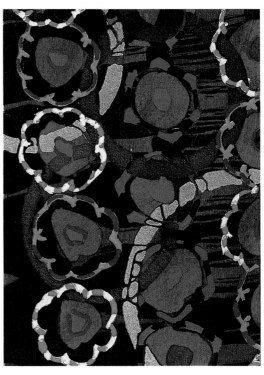

form of pattern books for designers of wallpapers, textiles, and borders. Inherently French, pochoir is an intricate, time-consuming stencil process that was perfected in the Art Deco period by the printer Jean Saudé. Because each sheet is hand-stenciled and slightly different, and because the surface is velvety with as many as twenty layers of color, a pochoir is a singular work of art. Saudé produced many albums of patterns, including patterns for wallpapers, of the artists Emile-Alain Seguy and Edouard Bénédictus. Seguy, who was a disciple of Eugène Grasset, was most prolific, producing eleven albums of designs, beginning with an Art Nouveau–inspired album, *Les Fleurs,* in 1901. His Art Deco masterpieces were *Floréal* (1914) and *Samarkande* (1920; plate 153). Intoxicated by the palettes of the Fauves and by the exoticism of Leon Bakst's set and costume designs for the Ballets Russes productions of *Cleopatra* and *Scheherazade,* this artist designed wall patterns and borders that could grace an Arabian night. Little of the sinuosity of Nouveau remains; the work is exuberant Deco, with controlled forms and flamboyant color. A few Seguy wallpaper designs and fabrics were produced. His last, more restrained album of patterns, *Prismes* (1931), is strongly Cubist. In his long career Seguy exemplified the changes in Art Deco style from the ornamental, colorful, almost florid years through the more geometric and precise post-1925 decoration.

Almost unknown today, Edouard Bénédictus was also a gifted Art Deco designer whose art changed to mirror the decades. In 1986, an exhibition at the Musée des Arts Décoratifs in Paris introduced his brilliant style to a new public. His early work at the beginning of the century was tinged with Art Nouveau, but by the time of his death in 1930 he had created the ultimate Art Deco patterns: stunning in color, complex and intricate in form, courageously affirmative about design for a machine age. Along with many patterns for textiles and some for wallpapers that were produced by Follot, Bénédictus created three pochoir albums of designs for both. In *Variations* (1924), *Nouvelles Variations* (1928), and the more abstract and Cubist *Relais* (1930), there is kaleidoscopic form and an explosion of color and light, often a glowing variation of Cubism (plate 152). Awarded the Legion of Honor as head of the wallpapers division of the 1925 exposition, Bénédictus described the exhibited wallpaper designs as "a new ornamental graphic,"

Plate 153
E. A. Seguy (active c. 1900–1933)
Wallpaper design. From *Samarkande,* 1920.
Musée des Arts Décoratifs, Paris.

Plate 152   *Opposite*
Edouard Bénédictus (1878–1930)
Designs. From *Variations,* 1924.
Bibliothèque Forney, Paris.

with "their pure colors [that] seem to disappear in favor of a general harmony."[25] These are terms that well describe his own work.

Bénédictus also praised wallpapers that were "outside the rules of logic," a description that fits the cheerful Dada

Plate 154
JEAN LURÇAT (1892–1966)
"Celui qui aime ecrit sur les murs," c. 1924.
Wallpaper, produced by Pierre Chareau.
Musée des Arts Décoratifs, Paris.

Plate 155
JEAN LURÇAT (1892–1966)
Design for a girl's bedroom, 1924. Musée
des Arts Décoratifs, Paris.

Plate 156 *Opposite*
JEAN LURÇAT (1892–1966)
"Les Mazeraies," c. 1924.
Wallpaper, produced by Pierre Chareau.
Musée des Arts Décoratifs, Paris.

papiers peints of the painter Jean Lurçat. Although several Lurçat wallpapers consist of geometrical elements, a deliberate Dadaesque amiable madness is the basic element of most. Lurçat is not known for his wallpapers but primarily for his surreal, colorful tapestries and for his efforts to restore artists' understanding of ancient tapestry techniques. Lurçat studied medicine, was a member of the Picasso circle after being wounded in World War I, and joined the Surrealists in the 1930s. He traveled and lived in desert countries and his work bears images and colors of arid landscapes, explosive light, and hard, precise, mosaic forms. He

served in the Resistance in World War II and for many years after the war labored on his masterpiece, the great tapestry series Le Chant du Monde, an apocalyptic view of the universe.

In 1986 at the retrospective of Lurçat's works in the new Musée Jean Lurçat at Angers, France, five of his wallpapers were exhibited. They date from 1924, when he collaborated with architect Pierre Chareau in their boutique for the Salon d'Automne. Lurçat created all the wallpapers, among them one titled "Celui qui aime écrit sur les murs" ("One Who Loves Writes on the Walls"; plate 154), a Dada message inscribed on an upside-down musical composition, surrounded by flying birds, leaves, and plaid squares. In one version the colors are harsh Deco: green, black, and rust on a cream background. A Lurçat wallpaper pattern shown in 1926, "Les Mazeraies," has playful words on a fan: "Tu es un toréador" and "Tu es un clown." The motifs include a toy horn, playing cards, and exotic foliage against a regularly hatched, checked background; the colors are soft blues and browns (plates 155; 156). A third pattern, "Les Fusées," is

exotically Art Deco in color and surreal in spirit with its deep pink background and bright red, green, and black birds (plate 130). Toy pistols, roses, and champagne with alphabet bubbles are motifs, as is an observing eye, a mute Dada signal. Lurçat's wallpapers appeared *in situ* in the art and decoration magazines of the times. But by 1931 greater restraint was evident in his collaboration with Chareau on the Maison de Verre for their friends the Dalsace family. The unpatterned walls of the major rooms in this important house rival Le Corbusier's undecorated surfaces.

In his long career of painting and tapestry design, Lurçat attempted to "sound the very depths of passion, hope, sorrow, or the aspirations of man."[26] The lighthearted wallpaper designs of his youthful past must have been for him nostalgic reminders of the Dada spirit of the twenties.

Plate 157
ROGER FRY (1866–1934)
"Amenophis," 1913.
Textile design for the Omega Workshops. By courtesy of the Board of Trustees of the Victoria and Albert Museum, London.

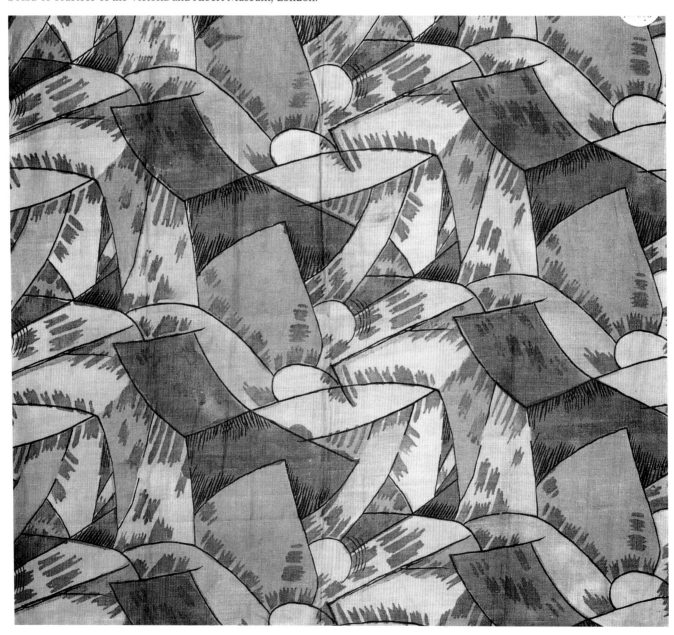

The Art Deco style failed to have a deep effect on the British. To the extent it did cross the Channel it followed the French pattern from exuberant to Cubist and even to Dada. Roger Fry—theorist, art critic, painter, Renaissance scholar, and Francophile—brought the message almost single-handedly. Impressed by the Wiener Werkstätte and Paul Poiret's Ecole Martine, Fry determined to bring something of their lively decorative art to Britain. He believed that the applied arts were important because on them depended the state of the fine arts. He was also deeply stirred by the Post-Impressionist art he saw in France and was convinced that the expressive aims of Post-Impressionism could be applied to the decorative arts. The Omega, as he named his workshop, was to have an organizational structure that would allow artists to work in the crafts for their livelihoods, and as fine artists bring respect to this work. Ultimately he hoped to free his artists' color and form in fine art through their work in decorative art. In 1912 he appealed to George Bernard Shaw for funds, saying: "The Post-Impressionist movement is quite as definitely decorative in its methods as was the Pre-Raphaelite, and its influence on general design is destined to be as marked. Already in France, Poiret's Ecole Martine shows what added gaiety and charm their products give to an interior. . . . Since the complete decadence of the Morris movement, nothing has been done in England but pastiche and more or less unscrupulous imitation of old work."[27] Shaw responded handsomely with 250 pounds. In 1913 after considerable further effort and funding, Fry launched his small group as the Omega Workshops, Bloomsbury, at a sumptuous dinner party proposed and arranged by Vanessa Bell, one of the artists. She had written to Fry: "We should get all your disreputable and some of your aristocratic friends to come. . . . We should all get drunk and dance and kiss. Orders would flow in."[28]

Bell and the others were serious artists, but the Omega was exceedingly casual. Cartoonists enjoyed caricaturing them. All designs were anonymous, and if the artists did not know a craft to begin with, they learned as they went along. When they had problems with wax resist, Fry considered but then rejected the idea that "one of us might offer ourselves up and go to the Central School of Art and learn how to do it."[29] Bell once reflected in a letter: "It's rather fun [easel] painting again after doing all those patterns. Duncan

Plate 158
ROGER FRY (1866–1934)
Still Life, Jug and Eggs, 1911.
Oil on board, 12 x 14 in. (30.5 x 35.6 cm).
Courtesy Anthony d'Offay Gallery, London.

[Grant] has been trying to do a pattern but gets even more muddled than I do, in fact I don't think he'll ever master repeats."[30] Among the best of the known patterns of the Omega are six extraordinary textile designs, shown in several publicity photographs on the Omega's walls. In May 1913 Roger Fry wrote of a "big American firm" that wanted to "buy some textiles with the right to use them as wallpapers which I don't mean to let them have."[31] On at least one occasion one of these patterns, "Amenophis" (plate 157), was abstracted by Fry from a still-life painting, his own *Still Life, Jug and Eggs* (plate 158), an example of Omega decorative art derived from fine art.[32] In this case the colors become more intense, the shapes flatten despite the hatchmarks, and the rhythm of the forms becomes more pronounced because of the repeat. In short, the textile is far more complex and interesting than the painting.

Artists were allowed only three half-days a week at the Omega, in order to give them time for their own painting or

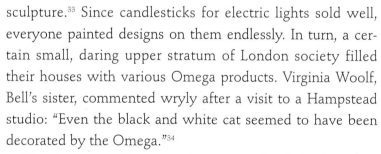

Plate 159
DUNCAN GRANT (1885–1978) and VANESSA BELL (1879–1961)
Wallpaper, cardboard stenciled, c. 1938; *in situ,* Charleston
Farmhouse, East Sussex, England. Courtesy of the Charleston
Trust, London.

Plate 160
DUNCAN GRANT (1885–1978)
The Kitchen, 1902.
Oil on canvas, 20 x 16 in. (50.8 x 30.5 cm). The Tate Gallery,
London/Art Resource, New York.

sculpture.[33] Since candlesticks for electric lights sold well, everyone painted designs on them endlessly. In turn, a certain small, daring upper stratum of London society filled their houses with various Omega products. Virginia Woolf, Bell's sister, commented wryly after a visit to a Hampstead studio: "Even the black and white cat seemed to have been decorated by the Omega."[34]

The Omega wallpaper technique as sketchily described on various occasions seems to have been deliberately undemanding. Fry wrote of decorating with paper panels in a 1917 article for *Colour* magazine, "The Artist as Decorator":

"The paper was first painted in size by artists roughly and rapidly, with no attempt to get a dead even surface. Each panel therefore differs very slightly, but still distinctly in quality from the next, and the whole surface has a play and vivacity which are essential to the effect of richness and solidity. The panel borders in this case were very roughly printed in size colours with a hand block."[35] The instance Fry describes may be one of the few in which wallpaper was created by the Omega in this way, probably for Lalla Vandervelde, a very good client of the workshops. The Omega often treated walls with large painted murals, as they did when they decorated the London Cadena Cafe with Cubist friezes. Bell and Grant decorated Charleston, their country home in Sussex, with expansive hand-painted decorations on the papered walls, as well as some dramatic stenciled small geometrics (plate 159). Similar wallpapers are seen in Grant's 1902 painting *The Kitchen* (plate 160). Another painting with the same title was done by Grant at Wisset Lodge in Suffolk, where he and Bell lived in 1916 during the war—they were obliged to paint over their considerable wall decorations when they left after a short stay.

In "The Artist as Decorator" Fry mentions "marblings of papers made by pressing one coloured paper on another different colour, while both were wet," and suggests this method, even taking into account the artist's more expensive time, as actually less costly than "an elaborately printed wallpaper."[36] After the war Fry decorated his house in Camden with similar hand-printed wallpaper, its solid-color rectangles printed with vivid dots: "ultramarine on yellow-ochre base, or . . . brilliant red on pale green—with the result that the colors buzzed and vibrated."[37]

Plate 161

Omega Workshops

Dado and other wall decorations, c. 1913; *in situ,* an antechamber, site unknown. University of East Anglia, Norwich, England.

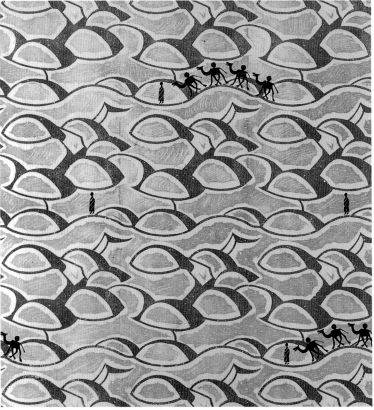

Before its demise the Omega included several other distinguished artists, at least for short periods of time. The sculptor Henri Gaudier-Brzeska contributed briefly to the Omega before his sad early death in the trenches of World War I. In his native France he had designed textiles for a year before coming to England in 1910. In 1912 he wrote of painting friezes for wallpaper, and from this period there is "Cockatoo," a half-drop design of rather vulturelike birds for wallpaper or textile (plate 162). Gaudier-Brzeska wrote in his letters of going to zoos and bird markets and this strange design may have been in part a jest directed at repeated-motif conventions in wallpaper.

The artist Paul Nash was also an Omega artist for a short time. He was not won over, wryly writing to his fiancée: "Now I must go and paint my next candlestick."[38] A month later he wrote: "The Omega can go to the devil, I shan't be there."[39] However, in his *Room and Book* of 1932 Nash showed an Omega interior decorated with an interesting dado pattern of meandering line segments (plate 161). Omega scholar Judith Collins believes this pattern is the Omega version of marble dadoes in Italian churches the artists had observed.[40]

The bold new forms and colors of Art Deco in Britain failed to attract the public, and Fry closed the Omega in the summer of 1919 with some bitterness: "People have the world the average man likes. I don't understand the animal and can't hope to manage him."[41] In her biography of Fry, Virginia Woolf quoted one of the "press gossips" as speculating: "Perhaps he can't live with his own wallpapers."[42]

Plate 162   *Top*
HENRI GAUDIER-BRZESKA (1891–1915)
"Cockatoo," 1911.
Wallpaper or textile design, colored inks, 19⅞ x 15 in.
(50.5 x 38 cm). By courtesy of the Board of Trustees
of the Victoria and Albert Museum, London.

Plate 163   *Bottom*
EDWARD BAWDEN (1903–1989)
"Sahara" ("Desert and Camels"), c. 1930.
Wallpaper, lithographed, Curwen Press. By courtesy of the
Board of Trustees of the Victoria and Albert Museum, London.

Except for a bit of trompe l'oeil chinoiserie—a wallpaper frame by Rex Whistler[43]—and some lithographed wallpapers by the Curwen Press artists around 1930, no further work was done in wallpaper design by the major artists in England in the Art Deco period. One Curwen artist, Edward Bawden, as amused by the wallpaper format as Gaudier-Brzeska appears to have been, designed some witty patterns. In his design "Sahara" or "Desert and Camels" (1930; plate 163) a tiny desert caravan winds its way around a room across vast sand dunes, never seeing all the other small caravans on the same quest. The wallpaper was a souvenir of Bawden's work as a war artist in Saudi Arabia, a place he found exotic and fascinating. The art patron Edward James used Bawden wallpaper patterns in his bathrooms at Monkton House, West Sussex, and Italian Futurist Gino Severini's streamlined wave pattern as a wallpaper in his hallway (plate 164). Bawden's wallpapers did not sell well;[44] he used some of them in his own house, recording one of

Plate 164
GINO SEVERINI (1883–1966)
Wall textile; *in situ,* Monkton House, West Sussex, England. Wallpaper in the same pattern, block printed by John Perry, was used for the curved stairwell. By kind permission of Monkton House/IPC Magazine, *Country Life,* London.

Plate 165
EDWARD BAWDEN (1903–1989)
Cat among Pigeons, c. 1986–87.
Watercolor, 19½ x 25¼ in. (49.5 x 64.8 cm). The wallpaper
shown in the background is "Church and Dove" by Bawden,
lithographed by the Curwen Press in 1925. Fine Art Society,
London/copyright the Estate of Edward Bawden.

them, "Church and Dove," in a memorable watercolor of a cat observing the wallpaper (plate 165).

Eric Gill, an artist friend of Fry's whose own art was chiseled and spare, may have had the Omega in mind when he said: "Now here's my trouble. I don't believe the human race is capable of such a sacrifice. I believe it will still demand wallpapers and muck of that sort and patterns on biscuit boxes."[45] By the end of the thirties, however, most of the

avant-garde had capitulated to Le Corbusier's demand for "pure" walls, although they drew the line at total nondecoration. "A fondness for ornament is no more readily acknowledged by refined persons than a fondness for gin," a British Art and Industry official pronounced.[46] To which Martin Battersby, who lived through those years, replied that refined persons "were as unashamed in their preference for ornament as in their fondness for gin, [and they wanted] an original and even slightly outrageous decor."[47] Thus the early thirties ushered in the decadent years of Art Deco. Houses with chaste walls contained blackamoor statues or plaster draperies. The fantastic decorative art of the time included Salvador Dalí's sofa of Mae West lips, Meret Oppenheim's fur cup and saucer, and unpatterned but "unchaste" wall coverings like quilted satin or ivory vellum squares. By the end of the decade wallpaper was out. In the television version of "Mr. and Mrs. Edgehill," a Noel Coward short story set in 1939, Lady Cynthia says candidly of an acquaintance: "I can't help imagining her wallpaper, somehow."

Something of that late, frivolous style and the elegant, bolder versions of Art Deco before it have reappeared. Designers are again delighted with *faux*. Frank Stella's "Protractor" paintings, which have made him recognizable world-wide, are hauntingly Deco; some of Roy Lichtenstein's work is equally so. Deco-inspired architecture is ubiquitous. After the years of the arid world of the Bauhaus, there has been a return to theatricality, bold colors, exaggerated streamlined forms, ornamental exuberance, passion for the exotic, and tongue-in-cheek humor. Even wallpaper has made a comeback.

Plate 166
Donald Deskey (b. 1894)
"Nicotine," 1933.
Wallpaper, aluminum; *in situ,* Men's Smoking Room, Radio City Music Hall. This wallpaper is streamlined and humorous, with brown and yellow nicotine colors. Radio City Music Hall Productions, Inc., New York.

THE WALLPAPERS OF CHARLES BURCHFIELD

(1921–1929)

Plate 167   *Preceding pages*
CHARLES BURCHFIELD (1893–1967)
"Red Birds and Beech Trees," 1924.
Wallpaper, M.H. Birge and Co., Buffalo.
Private collection.

Plate 168   *Opposite*
CHARLES BURCHFIELD (1893–1967)
"Country Life and the Hunt," 1928.
Panoramic wallpaper, twenty-eight panels,
original edition wood-block printed,
M.H. Birge and Co., Buffalo.

harles Burchfield was one of the first outstanding American artists to design wallpapers, and he remains one of the most important. Although his mystical watercolors are far from conventional, Burchfield is the twentieth-century American artist whose wallpapers come closest to traditional ideas of wallpaper design. His best designs, some inspired directly by his earlier watercolor paintings, are rich and densely interesting, often with a secondary background design interwoven with the primary foreground motifs in a formula William Morris perfected in his own wallpapers. Burchfield called his wallpaper designs flat and regretted their necessary simplicity, but in general his patterns have a slight depth, which Morris's designs also have, and a painterly complex of forms and colors that Morris's designs do not have.

Quite possibly Burchfield studied Morris's work after taking a job as a designer at the distinguished wallpaper firm of M. H. Birge and Co. in Buffalo in 1921. All his life Burchfield was a student and admirer of fellow artists. In his last year at the Cleveland School of Art he wrote in his journal, "Ferdinand Hodler combines powerful action and draftsmanship, decoration and expressionism."[1] Burchfield himself retained a unique expressionistic vision that manifests itself in most of his paintings and in some of his wallpapers. It is probable that in addition to Morris's work he knew the wallpaper designs of Dagobert Peche, the brilliant artist who did many wallpaper designs for the Wiener Werkstätte. Some of Burchfield's designs show Peche-like motifs, notably his one Art Deco design, the popular "Modernistic." It seems almost certain that he studied the nineteenth-century French scenic wallpapers and the eighteenth-century Chinese paneled wallpapers before he tackled three enormous projects assigned to him at Birge: "Country Life and the Hunt," a scenic wallpaper with twenty-eight continuous panels (plate 168); "The Riviera," a smaller panorama with ten panels of the Birge home in France; and "Birds and Blossoms," a wallpaper in the traditional Chinese mode, with four panels (plate 169). The styles of all three were derivative, as Burchfield himself was the first to acknowledge. Burchfield also designed his share of wearily conventional designs such as "Rose Bouquet" (1923) and "Flowers in Diagonal" (1927),

Plate 169

CHARLES BURCHFIELD (1893–1967)

"Birds and Blossoms" ("Chinese Garden"), 1929.

Chinoiserie wallpaper, four panels, hand printed, M.H. Birge
and Co., Buffalo. Collection of the Burchfield Art Center,
Buffalo; Gift of Reed Forest Productions, Inc., 1977.

both based on the trellis. Unlike Morris, who directed his own firm, Burchfield had only moderate design freedom until his last years at Birge.

When Burchfield left Birge in 1929, having become chief designer two years earlier but suffering from ill health, he put behind him his experiences in the factory and belittled his considerable accomplishment there. For thirty-eight years, until his death in 1967, he was totally absorbed with being a painter. There was no major retrospective during his lifetime of his wallpapers and the paintings that inspired them, although in 1937–38 his wallpaper work was included in an exhibition of internationally famous historic wallpapers.[2] In 1973 the Burchfield Center in Buffalo, which had been founded the year before the artist's death, mounted an exhibition of nineteen of his wallpapers, as well as relevant

paintings.[3] Since that date, other wallpapers have reappeared, and now some two dozen of his designs are known.

Burchfield thought of his wallpaper years as negative ones during which his painting was severely curtailed and his health jeopardized. Always self-castigating, at one point he wrote guiltily in his journal of how comfortable he had become in his job. He nevertheless took pride in his own and others' craftsmanship. "The artist and the artisan are twin brothers and I believe that the latter puts just as much of his best self, his dreams and aspirations, his honor and his inherent straightness into the work, as the former," he declared.[4] But it was Burchfield the troubled artist who wrote in 1923: "In looking at some pussy-willows today and seeing the infinite variety of highlights on their glossy shells and the infinite variation of color on the stems, I thought how easy it is to limit one's self by doing designs which are limited to 12 colors and which demand flat treatment—I must overcome this tendency to lose the delight in sketching—of myriad accidental effects."[5]

He had interviewed for the job at Birge with a portfolio that included a design of arches: "what I thought wallpaper was all about."[6] Once hired, he set about quite deliberately separating his two lives as designer and artist by painting the urban landscape instead of his beloved bleak but lyrical natural world. But for inspiration in the factory he used some earlier watercolor paintings in his wallpaper designs. His first design was his own eventual favorite wallpaper, "The Birches" (plate 170).[7] This was adapted from *Bluebird and Cottonwoods,* a watercolor of 1917 (plate 171), which the

artist later called his golden year. The "Birches" wallpaper in soft grays and blues is in the Burchfield style, with groups of trees against gray boulders and a surprising ghostly filigree of foliage laced with salmon-pink shoots. These are fanciful images, typical of Burchfield's best paintings and, in a wallpaper, infinitely patterned and interesting. Curiously, in this case the wallpaper seems more daring than the painting. If the *painting* were repeated as a wallpaper, it would show intrusive horizontal bands across the wall: the band for the foreground base of the painting, the band for the trees, and the band for the sky. But the wallpaper presents the scene less realistically, observes less perspective, and conjures the ghostly foliage over the whole design. As a design that must be repeated many times on the wall, this wallpaper would

Plate 170
CHARLES BURCHFIELD (1893–1967)
"The Birches," 1921.
Wallpaper, M.H. Birge and Co., Buffalo.
Collection of the Burchfield Art Center, Buffalo;
Gift of the Burchfield Foundation, 1975.

Plate 171
CHARLES BURCHFIELD (1893–1967)
Bluebird and Cottonwoods, 1917.
Watercolor, 21¾ x 19½ in. (55.2 x 49.5 cm).
Private collection.

have a great deal of verticality, but its density would prevent its repeat from becoming obvious. In "Birches," Burchfield quite knowingly translated an exceptional wallpaper from a painting.

Burchfield's translation of the 1917 watercolor *Song of the Redbird* (plate 172) into the wallpaper "Red Birds and Beech Trees" (1924; plate 167) was not as successful. In this wallpaper there is severe perspective and a vanishing point, which on the wall would read as many vanishing points in small blocks. Moreover, the red birds on the trees are large,

regularly repeated red spots. Burchfield no doubt intended less than total realism and allowed the wallpaper to have a "sky" of Oriental clouds in mauve, a very stylized touch. There is possibly no other wallpaper by Burchfield so closely adapted from a painting. Interestingly, Burchfield used this pattern for his own pantry in his home in West Seneca, New York.

Hazy July Noon, a watercolor of 1916 (plate 173), was the inspiration for a rather traditional, floral wallpaper pattern with a most artful repeat. Entitled "Sunflowers" (1922; plate

Plate 172
CHARLES BURCHFIELD (1893–1967)
Song of the Redbird, 1917.
Watercolor, 36 x 50 in. (91.4 x 127 cm).
Mrs. Harris B. Steinberg, New York.

Plate 173

CHARLES BURCHFIELD (1893–1967)

Hazy July Noon, 1916.

Watercolor, 20 x 14 in. (50.8 x 35.6 cm). Collection of the
Burchfield Art Center, Buffalo; Gift of Tony Sisti, 1979.

Plate 174
CHARLES BURCHFIELD (1893–1967)
"Sunflowers," 1922.
Wallpaper, M.H. Birge and Co., Buffalo.
Private collection.

Plate 175
CHARLES BURCHFIELD (1893–1967)
"Robins and Crocuses," 1923.
Wallpaper, M.H. Birge and Co., Buffalo.
Collection of the Burchfield Art Center, Buffalo.

174), this wallpaper is somewhat Victorian in its heavy, opaque colors, and although its hues are close to the painting, its impact is far removed from the more transparent, sun-drenched, joyous effect of the watercolor. This design might be contrasted with another showing the influence of the Japanese print, the "Robins and Crocuses" wallpaper of 1923 (plate 175). Here Burchfield unhesitatingly used the bold darks of the Japanese print masters in the meandering patches of a stream alight with early lavender and white crocuses, against snowbanks and robins. And he included some typical Burchfield trees: totally fantastic, dripping, gray creations. The robins are an oversized but endearing touch in an utterly fanciful landscape that is very dramatic with its darks and lights in a pattern that offers an interesting repeat.

Burchfield turned dry corn stalks into a harmonious wallpaper study in "Field Corn and Morning Glories" (1927). The simplified brown, gold, and tan stalks interweave vertically, and among them morning glories peer out in pinks and

blues against a dark background. This pattern required ten colors. An intricate and beautiful pattern of about the same date is a little-known design of fanciful spring flowers against a background of hyacinth shoots, with strange, dark, fuchsia-patterned leaves. It is alive with Burchfield's distinctive expressionism—in this case an expression of total kinship with nature in spring.

"Nightfall" is a more mysterious study for wallpaper, a design of Burchfield's middle years at Birge. In it, deep-maroon heart-shaped leaves form circular patterns, pink fuchsias enliven these forms, and fantasy motifs in white and lavender surround the leaves. The background is pink and white and the whole design is rich, lavish, and quite possibly claustrophobic.

One of the wallpapers Burchfield said he "cooked up" on demand was the amazing Art Deco pattern "Modernistic" (1927; plate 176). Brightly colored and rather fragmented, with multiple streamlined forms and a white background that was rare for him, this wallpaper was extremely popular, so much so that "Designed by Burchfield" appeared on all his wallpapers thereafter. Ironically, "Modernistic" is one of the least typical of his designs.

Burchfield wrote of his life at Birge as "work that is directly opposed to my ideals in art,"[8] and with typical self-disparagement commented that the line at Birge "could stand but one or two of my designs a year."[9] Clearly, he did compromise his own design principles in some of his wallpapers. Others are excellent designs, complex and painterly, which manage to say Burchfield whether or not the name is on the selvage. Looking at his designs today, one concludes that they often seem to succeed when they are derived from or recall the paintings and hence are endowed, as are his best watercolors, with complex forms and strong emotion. Burchfield could impart mystical properties to landscape, making profound statements of old stumps, dead corn stalks, and decrepit buildings, to which he gave mysterious window "eyes." Some of this expressiveness, which is akin to Morris's insistence on "meaning" in allowing the viewer to experience life and nature beyond the immediate design, is evident in many of Burchfield's wallpapers. Yet whereas Morris's work has been almost continuously in production since the 1870s, not one of Burchfield's wallpaper designs is being produced today.

Plate 176
CHARLES BURCHFIELD (1893–1967)
"Modernistic," 1927.
Wallpaper, M.H. Birge and Co., Buffalo.
Collection of the Burchfield Art Center, Buffalo;
Gift of the Burchfield Foundation, 1975.

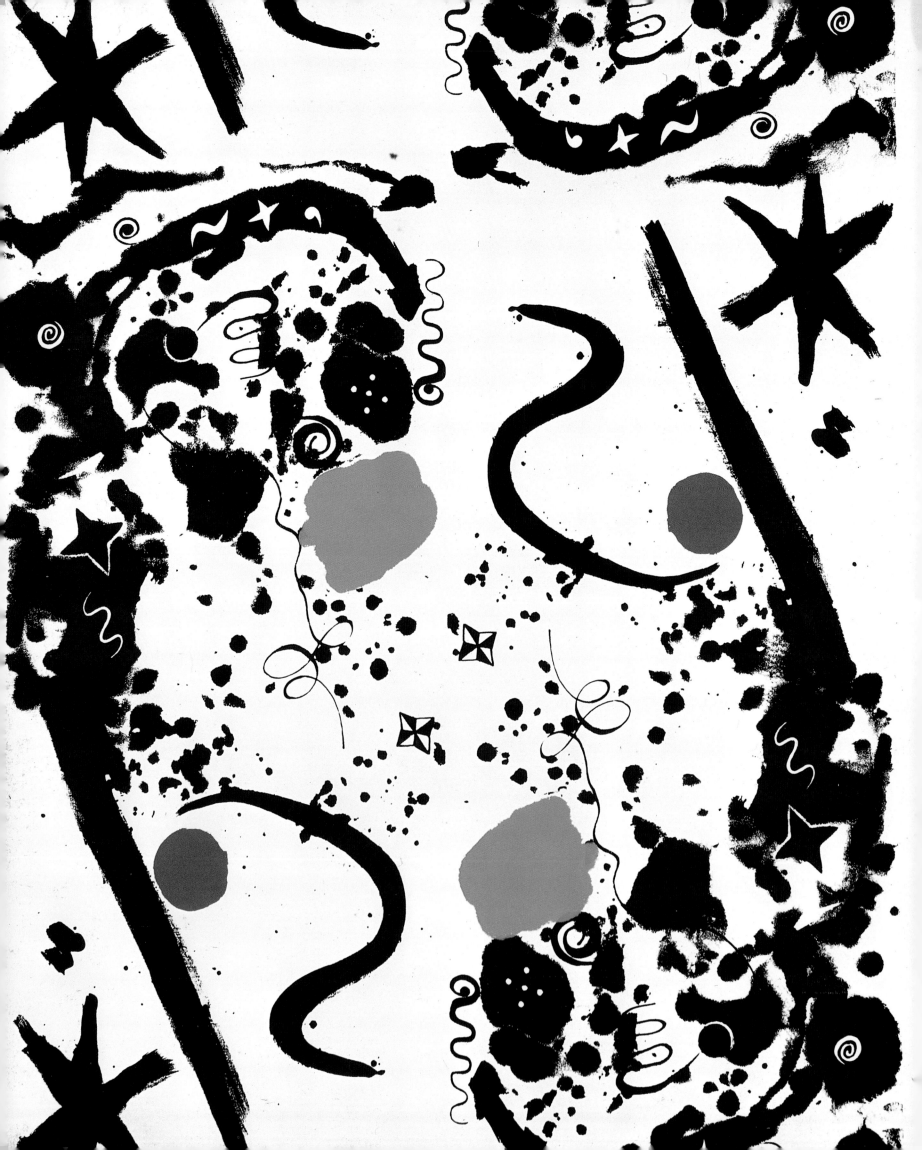

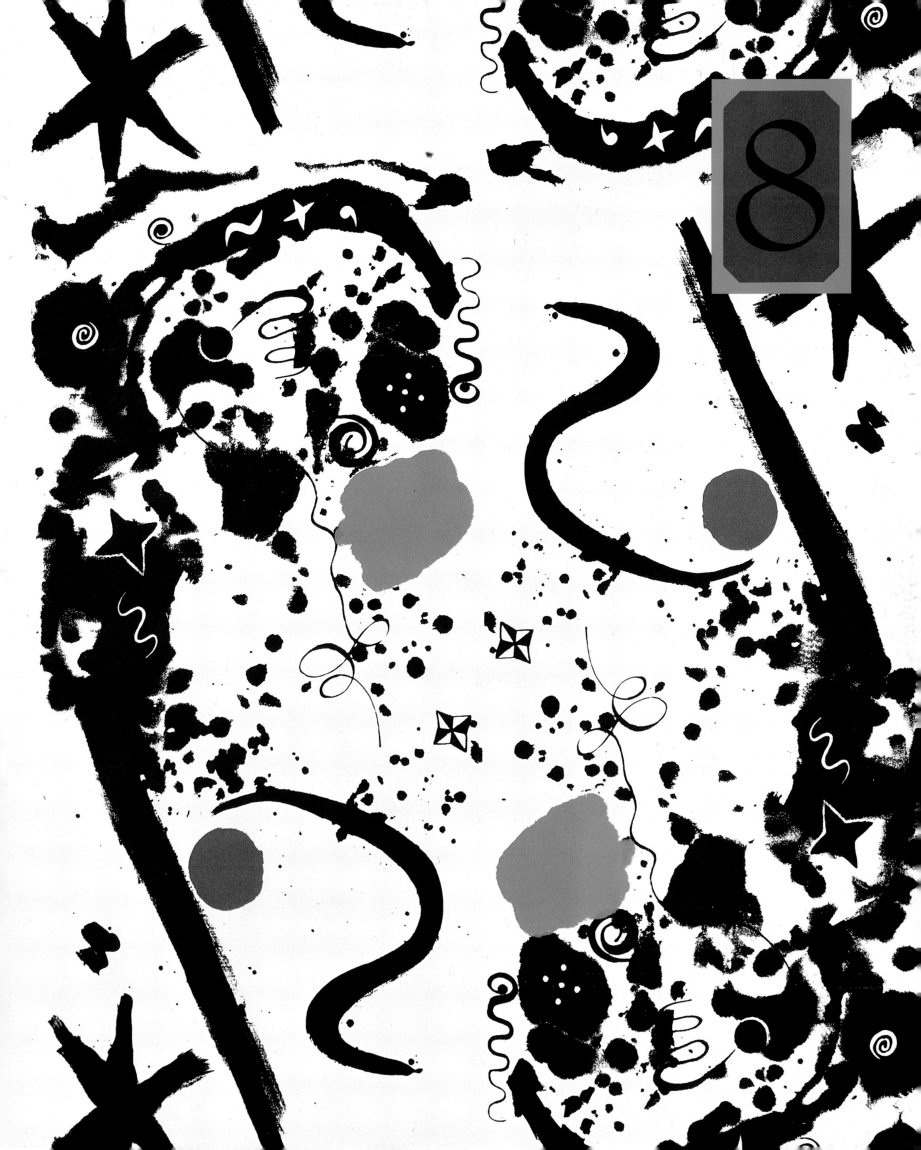

L. MAGRITTE

INDUSTRIEL

Téléphone : BRUXELLES 92 28

BRUXELLES, LE _Dimanche_ 1921.

16, AVENUE DU BOULEVARD

Cher Pierre,

Je suis "au travail" depuis Mardi, et quoique les dessins que j'ai à faire ne sont pas modernes, la besogne est tout de même intéressante, d'autant plus que dans un an on compte ne faire que des papiers peints modern[es]

Il y a une technique spéciale à acquérir pour ce métier, des petites choses que l'on ne soupçonne pas, des règles à connaître, et qui sont des lois d'harmonie bien déterminées,

Par exemple ce premier dessin que j'ai fait n'est pas bon à cause de deux feuilles qui sont presque horizontales – en supprimer une dira-t-on, mais alors il y a un vide. il faut chercher une autre combinaison

Il faut aussi ne pas avoir de mouvement comme dans un dessin comme ceci :

FROM SURREALISM TO SPOOF

Later Twentieth-Century Artists (1950–1980)

Plate 177 *Preceding pages*
ALEXANDER CALDER (1898–1976)
"Splotchy," 1949.
Wallpaper, Laverne Originals, New York. Museum of Art,
Rhode Island School of Design, Providence.

Plate 178 *Opposite*
Letter from René Magritte to Pierre-Louis Flouquet,
describing work at the Peeters-Lacroix wallpaper factory
in Haren, Belgium, 1921. Archives et Musée de la
Littérature, Bibliothèque Royale, Brussels, Belgium.

Most artists of the latter part of the twentieth century have not taken wallpaper very seriously. Indeed, since wallpaper's decline, it is hard to find an important artist who has approached wallpaper design in a conventional way. Although many of the artists of the Deco era were able to consider wallpaper relatively traditionally, most post-Deco artists have treated its conventions lightly.

René Magritte's long career as a Surrealist painter extended past midcentury. It is difficult to know if his wallpaper design work in the Peeters-Lacroix wallpaper factory in Haren, Belgium (1921–22; plate 178) was an influence on his painting. After an enthusiastic start in the factory,[1] followed by a disillusioning year of the work, Magritte left in disgust, declaring in a manifesto written with factory colleague, friend, and fellow painter Victor Servranckx, that the decorative arts for an artist kill "pure" art.[2] Throughout his life, in listing pet hates Magritte more than once included the decorative arts: "I detest my past and anyone else's. I detest resignation, patience, professional heroism, and obligatory beautiful feelings. I also detest the decorative arts."[3] However, in order to make ends meet after he left the wallpaper company, he designed posters and advertisements, and even in the 1930s he was still doing what he referred to as imbecile work. Magritte and one or another of his friends often had grand burnings of the past together: letters, memorabilia, and once, an overcoat.[4] Thus a large sample of Magritte wallpaper seems no longer to exist and the wallpaper pattern books from Peeters-Lacroix show only tiny swatches of Magritte's designs for wallpapers (plate 179). Often his designs are listed as collaborations. Unfortunately it is impossible to visualize a complete pattern from these samples, but some generalizations about color and form can be made. In the swatches, Magritte used the strong heavy colors of his paintings—one might even say De Chirico–like colors—and Art Deco and Cubist forms of simple geometric angles and curves. These forms appear to have been forcefully outlined and often include a flower or fruit motif against a decorative vertical stripe of some width. The designs have none of the smooth, slick style of an extant portion of Servranckx wallpaper (plate 180), although some of Magritte's designs in the pattern books are labeled as collaborations with Servranckx.

Magritte's wallpaper designs appear to have been primarily floral. Suzi Gablik has reported, after an interview-visit that lasted eight months, that Magritte said it was his role in the factory to paint "cabbage roses."[5] Although no solid evidence exists that any of his detested wallpaper work influenced his paintings, Magritte was undoubtedly aware of the potent impact that the repeated images of a wallpaper can have. In his paintings and drawings some vestigial patterns appear surrealistically. One instance is the pattern of disem-

bodied eyes on a drawing of a man's tie; another, a pattern of a nude woman's torso in the background of *Lola de Valence* (1948); another, his pattern of small, bowler-hatted, bureaucratic men with umbrellas, raining down from the sky in *La Golconde* (1953; plate 181). Magritte identified himself with the last image and was photographed more than once in this role: the small and anxious man in the mysterious universe. "I think we are responsible for the universe, but this does not mean that we decide anything," he once said.[6]

One writer has referred to Magritte's "papered" room in the painting *On the Threshold of Liberty,* in which panels of

Plate 179

Rene Magritte (1898–1967)

Wallpaper designs. From a Peeters-Lacroix pattern book
(Haren, Belgium, c. 1922). Musées Royaux des Beaux-Arts
de Belgique, Brussels.

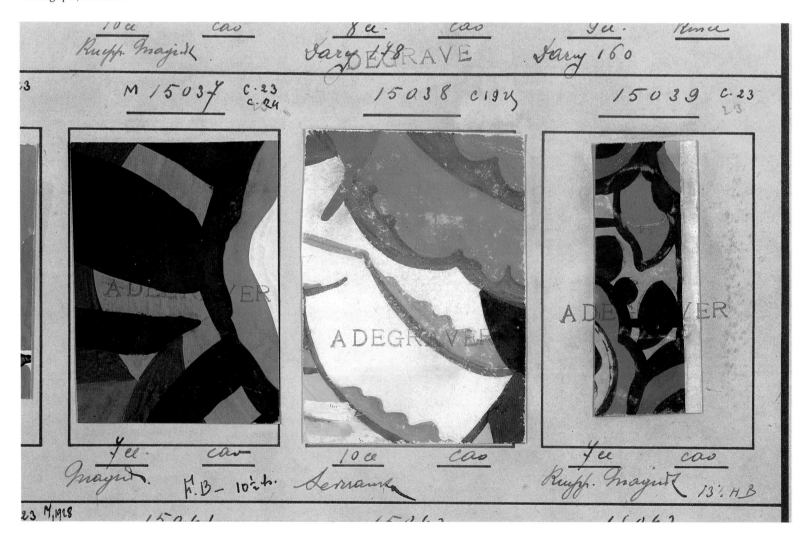

Plate 180

VICTOR SERVRANCKX (1897–1965)

"Ships," 1922 (reissued 1970).

Wallpaper, Peeters-Lacroix, Haren, Belgium. Servranckx
espoused the ideas of order and harmony and extolled the
beauty of machine-produced simplicity along with Le
Corbusier and Amédée Ozenfant. His "machine" paintings
were admired by fellow Purists, and his wallpaper shows a
streamlined, Futurist-inspired style. Private collection,
Kortenberg, Belgium.

some of his obsessive patterns—sleigh bells, clouds in a blue sky, wooden planks, the torso of a nude woman—make an interior background.[7] The trauma of Magritte's youth was the loss of his mother by suicide, and some recurring patterns, especially the nude torsos and the sleigh bells, may refer to this event.[8]

The culminating examples of Magritte's wallpaper images are in his huge oval mural *The Enchanted Domain* (1962), a *panorama surréaliste* 236 feet in length for the Casino Communal on the Belgian coast at Knokke-le-Zoute. For it the artist wove together a composite of many of the recurring motifs in his paintings; the eighth panel, for instance, contains the familiar perforated "wallpaper," as well as the healer-therapeutic birdcage, the lion couchant, and the Scheherazade face of pearls (plate 182). A prose poem cele-

brating the mural, written by Magritte's friend the poet Paul Colinet, offers this description of the panel: "In the warm darkness of their home, a pair of turtle doves watch over the health of a wayward healer. The pearls of a face bedeck his right hand. A garland of roses appeases its lion. A perforated wallpaper collects bits of sky."[9]

The most arresting surreal wallpaper motif used by Magritte in his paintings, and the one that has most caught the imagination of the world, is his interior wall pattern of blue sky and soft white clouds. This pattern appears in an adjacent panel of the casino mural where a painted door opens from the interior of sunlit blue sky to reveal a starry sky outside. Similarly, in *Personal Values* (1951–52), one of Magritte's best-known paintings, a giant comb dominates a small bed and casts a shadow against the wall of a room

Plate 181
René Magritte (1898–1967)
La Golconde, 1953.
Oil on canvas, 31½ x 39½ in. (80 x 100.3 cm).
Courtesy of the Menil Collection, Houston.

Plate 182
RENÉ MAGRITTE (1898–1967)
Lion and Vagrant, 1937.
Oil on canvas, 36¼ x 25⅝ in. (92 x 65 cm). This image is
also in the mural at the Casino Communal, Knokke-le-Zoute,
Belgium, 1962. Collection of Mr. and Mrs. J.B. Urvater.

completely papered in blue sky, except for a wooden cornice below the painted ceiling. In reference to this painting Magritte commented in a letter to Alexandre Iolas: "From the point of view of immediate usefulness, what would correspond to the idea that, for example, the sky covers the walls of a room . . . ?"[10] Blue sky wallpaper, no doubt inspired by Magritte, was in recent years available commercially.

Do these wallpaper images in Magritte's paintings have a meaning? Admittedly, meaning for Magritte was always something to transcend. If someone suggested an interpretation of a painting, he would quote Stéphane Mallarmé and say: "You are more fortunate than I am."[11] He wished the viewers of his paintings truly to enter an enchanted domain, a mysterious realm that would negate ordinary thought and stimulate a new kind of thinking, freed of symbolism.

Gablik reports that Magritte "particularly liked to refuse the name of artist saying he was a man of *thought*."[12] In 1922 he was moved to tears by De Chirico's *The Song of Love,* and remarked admiringly on the ascendancy of poetry over painting.[13] Mary Mathews Gedo sees Magritte's obsession with "poetic" painting as his wish for "poetic mysteries" rather than symbols, "mysteries that he evidently intended his public to contemplate but not to penetrate."[14] To promote the mystery in his enchanted domain it is not surprising that he sometimes chose to jolt the onlooker with astonishing images as wallpaper motifs, or with the shock of an inside-outside reversal. With such surprising images, he hoped "the limited evidence of the common-sense world [could] be transcended."[15]

Another Belgian artist, Jean-Michel Folon, created his

own plumper, more vulnerable small-man motif, and for his one wallpaper repeated this image in *irisé,* or a kind of rainbow coloring, handsomely produced by Zuber in 1969 in two color combinations (plate 183). Folon's *Foultitude* poster of 1969 is very similar to the wallpaper. Folon wrote that the theme was *le grand nombre,* perhaps representing the world's unimportant but numerous human beings, in this case all men. About his art Folon has said: "Imagination is stronger than we are. To design is to walk the streets and look at life. I do not understand my designs."

Many wallpaper images created by later twentieth-century artists seem at once superficial and deeply revealing; as such they have a mysterious force. Salvador Dalí's one wallpaper, published by the German firm of Rasch Brothers in 1960, has been called variously "Cervantes," "L'Age d'or," and "Don Quixote" (plate 184). Quixotic it is, a detailed pattern of a Spanish landscape with windmills and churches, dry hills and a stream; amid them are some leaf-clad dancing figures and dark trees. The colors are not noteworthy; there is no Don Quixote in sight. This art wallpaper presents a challenging puzzle: Why did Dalí create it?

Dalí was always fiercely nationalistic. Velázquez and Gaudí were his idols; they were masters and they were Spanish. Cervantes was in his soul. In 1956 he was commissioned by Joseph Foret to illustrate a magnificent French edition of *Don Quixote,* with both color plates and original lithographs.[16] Among the color plates is a large, two-page illustration of much of the wallpaper scene, with some changes. In this illustration, Dalí's real interest is in the knight-errant, or "fantastic cavalier," as the artist dubbed Quixote, in the foreground. The knight is ceremoniously holding up an acorn. The caption for this illustration quotes the Don, who as a stranger has been extended warm hospitality by a group of goatherds—hospitality that included a meal of kid stew and dried acorns amid much kindness. "O happy age," Quixote intones, "which our first parents called the age of gold!"[17] Of course the romantic knight is unable to realize that he has just experienced such an age in the present: great kindness and human unselfishness, copious food from the earth, the words *mine* and *thine* unknown. As shepherdesses are brought into the conversation by the goatherds, Quixote recalls shepherdesses of the past and finishes with a rhapsodic embroidery: "their lovely hair sometimes loose and flowing, clad in no other vestment but what was necessary to cover decently what modesty would always have concealed . . . yet bedecked with more becoming leaves and flowers."[18] It is the perfect description of the female figures in the wallpaper. For this repeated pattern, the artist chose to omit the knight but evoke the golden world, emphasizing the dancing figures and the landscape of Don Quixote's windmills. Thus Dalí's evocative wallpaper is Quixote's dream-scene of the past.

About the film *L'Age d'or* (also one of the titles of the wallpaper) Dalí's collaborator Luis Buñuel once remarked: "Dalí and I used every gag that occurred to us and we relentlessly threw out everything that might have meaning."[19] The illustrations in the *Don Quixote* edition are spattered with spots of ink from lithographic stones that had been bombarded with pellets, giving a surrealistic appearance to the plates. The wallpaper, however, is only lightly touched in this way, and the splotches have become tree foliage. Perhaps Dalí was presenting an image he found satisfying in a straightforward manner and enjoying the likely reaction of surprise to such an act from him. In any case the wallpaper is pleasing and old-fashioned as well as inordinately interesting, partly because of the rich literary and philosophical allusions, and partly because the viewer keeps seeking the surreal in it.

Plate 183   *Opposite*
Jean-Michel Folon (b. 1934)
"Foultitude," 1969.
Wallpaper, Zuber et Cie., Rixheim, France. Courtesy of Zuber et Cie. and the Musée des Arts Décoratifs, Paris.

Plate 184
Salvador Dalí (1904–1989)
"Cervantes" ("Don Quixote," "L'Age d'or"), c. 1960.
Wallpaper, Gebruder Rasch and Co. Courtesy of Gebruder Rasch and Co., Bramsche, Germany.

Plate 185

ALEXANDER CALDER (1898–1976)

"Calder #1," 1949.

Wall textile, Laverne Originals, New York. Courtesy of the
Whitney Museum of American Art, New York.

It is not surprising that Alexander Calder designed wallpapers with the same exuberance and delight he took in creating anything. In fact, he *asked* for his first commission of wallpaper, from Erwin Laverne, when he installed a mobile in the Laverne studio in 1949. Laverne published wallpapers and Calder is reported to have said: "I'd like to try my hand at doing some wallpapers, too."[20]

"Calder #1" was his first wallpaper for Laverne; it was also produced as a textile (plate 185). The Spanish painter Joan Miró was a lifelong friend of Calder's and "Calder #1," with its childlike motifs repeated in primary colors, is strongly Miró-inspired. It is perhaps more successful in its textile version, in which the folds soften the blocky repeat. "Splotchy" (plate 177), Calder's second design for Laverne, is masterful. Handsomely printed in red, green, and black on heavy white paper, the design is very large and is ingeniously reversed and turned on end for the full pattern. It was also produced as a textile but is more dramatic and exciting seen quite flat as a wallpaper. The title is an amusing, if accurate, Calder touch (plate 186).

Both wallpapers display the two major influences on Calder's art: his love of the circus and the inspiration he derived from the movement, splendor, and awesome power of the universe. He once said: "I felt there was no better model for me to choose than the Universe. . . . Spheres of different sizes, densities, colors and currents of air, viscosities and odors—of the greatest variety and disparity."[21] What a combination these two influences were: "Calder #1" might be a child's view of the cosmos; "Splotchy" might be a sophisticated banner for a mystery play.

From childhood, Calder demonstrated great inventiveness. For his sister he designed a small cannon to shoot off one-inch firecrackers; for his college friends he solved the problem of holes in sock heels by placing black India ink on the skin underneath. In his early days in Paris he worked on a toy bird that could laboriously pull a toy worm out of the ground. Later he performed his famous Circus to an admiring art world; his friend Fernand Léger would operate the victrola while Calder played all the parts, even sweeping up after his small homemade menagerie. His friend and critic James Johnson Sweeney once observed: "The solemnity of the conventional restricts him."[22] Because he was able to approach art uniquely and fearlessly, he was able to devise unique art, most importantly his famous mobiles. Calder was able to work in wallpaper, wire, tin from coffee cans, or whatever he chose without feeling the need to please critics. He declared: "I have developed an attitude of indifference to the reception of my work, which allows me to go about my business."[23] When Frank Lloyd Wright directed that the mobile for the Guggenheim Museum be made of gold, Calder replied that it might be made of gold, but that it would be painted black.[24] The same free spirit enabled Calder to create his "Splotchy" wallpaper.

Plate 186
ALEXANDER CALDER (1898–1976)
"Splotchy," 1949.
Wallpaper; *in situ,* home of Mrs. Dorothy Rautford, Glencoe, Illinois. Courtesy of the Whitney Museum of American Art, New York.

The designs of Saul Steinberg's wallpapers celebrate the same comic and sad imaginary world of the Steinberg drawings and cartoons. Steinberg also made cartoons of "wallpaper" events. Among these is the drawing of the empty room: the unseen mirror, the pictures, and the man in the chair have all been against the wall so long that the wallpaper around their shapes has faded. Another poignant cartoon shows a Steinberg woman making her own wallpaper pattern by patiently tracing around her hand on the wall.[25]

Early in his career Steinberg made the decision to be an artist whose work was reproducible; thus his wallpapers for Piazza Prints and Greeff Fabrics (c. 1950), although rarely mentioned in biographical notes about him, fit into his oeuvre as democratically and satisfyingly as do his cartoons and drawings. Steinberg's wallpaper is art that enhances everyday life as if it were theater. Although Morris might have found Steinberg's designs lacking in repose, they are clearly art expressive of the twentieth century, which itself has been seriously bereft of repose.

As he designed at least seven wallpapers, and probably more, Steinberg must have had an interest in this work. He has always enjoyed the flatness of his art; an example is his sculpture of a flat lady painted languishing on the upholstery of a real chair, her painted hand resting on a real table. He has equally enjoyed his own world of the inkwell in which he could draw himself drawing himself as well as a fantastic universe full of decorative, inky flourishes with underlying truths. The flatness and decorative charm of this imaginary world inhabit the wallpapers, and many of the motifs of the cartoons are there too.

Consider the drawing of "Birds," or "Aviary" (plate 187), a wallpaper design of the early 1950s produced by Piazza

Plate 187 *Opposite*
SAUL STEINBERG (b. 1914)
"Birds" ("Aviary"), c. 1950.
Drawing for wallpaper, pen and ink, 29 x 23 in.
(73.6 x 58.5 cm). Courtesy of Cooper-Hewitt,
National Museum of Design, Smithsonian Institution;
Gift of Harvey Smith/Art Resource, New York.

Plate 188
SAUL STEINBERG (b. 1914)
"Wedding," 1950.
Wallpaper, screen printed by hand, Piazza Prints,
New York. Courtesy of Cooper-Hewitt, National
Museum of Design, Smithsonian Institution; Gift
of Harvey Smith/Art Resource, New York.

Prints. The onlooker has to admit these are thoughtful, enigmatic birds. Are they a comment about bird life or about human life? Perhaps both. The free yet complex imagination in this drawing is straight from the Steinberg world we know best in the cartoons. How would such a wallpaper work on the wall? Its filigree patterns provide both a thoughtful and a cheerful wall design, as well as an unobtrusive background. This wallpaper has horizontal friezes but

because of the intricacy and delicacy of the design even the most obvious band of repeat—the very small birds—is not oppressive. In fact, this band is like a comic dado.

"Flowers" is a bolder multiple-block design that was produced as both wallpaper and fabric by Piazza Prints. "Wedding" (plate 188) is a witty, happy, high-spirited image that would repeat in a block or half-drop pattern on the wall.

Plate 189
SAUL STEINBERG (b. 1914)
"Views in Paris," 1946.
Wallpaper, screen printed by hand, Piazza Prints, New York.
By courtesy of the Board of Trustees of the Victoria and Albert
Museum, London.

Plate 190   *Opposite*
SAUL STEINBERG (b. 1914)
"Trains," c. 1950.
Wallpaper, screen printed by hand, Piazza Prints, New York.
By courtesy of the Board of Trustees of the Victoria and Albert
Museum, London.

Other Steinberg wallpaper patterns were derived from his travels and his past. An insatiable traveler until he saw only "tourists and waiters" on his trips, Steinberg "loved to arrive in a new place and face the new situations like one newly born who sees life for the first time, when it still has the air of fiction."[26] It lasts one day, he says. One of his wallpaper— as well as cartoon—subjects is the railway station. "Trains" (plate 190) is a greeting to an enchanting older world, perhaps Romania, where Steinberg was born in 1914, or Paris. In it the curlicues and Art Nouveau flourishes of the second-

class railway carriages drawn by the decorated steam engine share melodrama with the great glass roof of the station itself. This wallpaper, with an alternate block design, is one of Steinberg's best, a black-on-white drawing with clear, beautiful colors, finely printed by Piazza Prints.

Steinberg appears to have been most devoted to the architecture of Paris. At midcentury he designed two wallpapers of Paris buildings that demonstrate the enticing hold that city once must have had on his imagination. "Views in Paris" (1946; plate 189) portrays those extensive and no

Plate 191
SAUL STEINBERG (b. 1914)
"Horses," c. 1950.
Wallpaper, screen printed by hand, Piazza Prints, New York.
By courtesy of the Board of Trustees of the Victoria and Albert
Museum, London.

Plate 192 *Opposite*
SAUL STEINBERG (b. 1914)
"Paris Opera," c. 1950.
Wallpaper, Greeff Fabrics, New York. Courtesy of Cooper-
Hewitt, National Museum of Design, Smithsonian Institution;
Gift of Mrs. Howard Adams/Art Resource, New York.

doubt endlessly bureaucratic Paris buildings, which Steinberg was able to extend indefinitely and wittily on the wall in black and white. The other, "Paris Opera" (plate 192), produced by Greeff as both fabric and wallpaper, is lovingly bedecked with angels bearing harps, lavishly explored in pastels and gold.

Steinberg once complained that he couldn't draw horses, but they were the subject (and title) of his most interesting wallpaper (plate 191). As in "Trains," the background is white and the drawing black with vivid multicolor passages. As in "Birds," Steinberg uses a horizontal pattern, in this case four friezes, one above the other in different scales. The horses are pure Steinberg, some awkward, some jaunty. They perform variously: pulling chariots, galloping to foxhunts, carrying polo players, dogs, little girls, coachmen, French generals. The people are on the move, costumed as for some marvelous and crazy stage setting.

The absurd and comic predicaments of human beings are essential to the drama in Steinberg's art, including his wallpapers. Harold Rosenberg has portrayed Steinberg himself as a masquerader, wearing the masks and uniforms of "Mr. Anybody (and his wife) in their countless poses, self-

disguises and self-creations."[27] Steinberg once appeared for an interview photograph in a large grocery-bag mask, an appropriate symbol for the Steinbergian theater of everyday life. Although they were once widely available, Steinberg's wallpapers can no longer be had by Mr. or Mrs. Anybody. As with so many things intended originally for ordinary people, Steinberg's wallpaper art, all produced around 1950, is now only for the collector.

G raham Sutherland, the British artist most famous for his work at Coventry Cathedral, designed two spirited wallpapers shortly after World War II. One was a conventional diaper pattern, using an unconventional corn-dolly motif; the other, more playful design was a treatment of the letters *OXO* from the English bedtime health drink (plate 194). This jolly yellow-and-white wallpaper was produced in a series designed for the small home in 1950 (plate 193).

In 1972 the firm of Marburger in Kassel, then West Germany, asked a group of artists to design wallpapers for them. The response was enlightening, since each artist made this invitation an opportunity for an artistic statement in a personal idiom, at the same time carefully considering the wallpaper format and, to an extent, exploiting it. Jean Tinguely, the French constructionist and painter, opted for an all-over design of his familiar flotsam and jetsam, with no one focus and with every effort to avoid a pattern. Appropriately he titled his design "Vive la Liberté" (plate 195), spoofing the ordered repetition of conventional wallpaper.

Plate 195   *Opposite*
JEAN TINGUELY (1925–1991)
"Vive la Liberté," 1972.
Wallpaper, Marburger Tapetenfabrik. Marburger Tapetenfabrik, Kirchain, Germany.

Plate 194   *Below*
OXO advertisement, 1928. The *OXO* letters were the source for Sutherland's "Abstract" wallpaper. Courtesy of Santoro Graphics, Ltd., London.

Plate 193
GRAHAM SUTHERLAND (1903–1980)
"Abstract," 1950.
Wallpaper, block printed, John Perry for Cole and Son, London. For folio, issued by the Council of Industrial Design, *Wallpaper for the Small Home,* 1950. By courtesy of the Board of Trustees of the Victoria and Albert Museum, London.

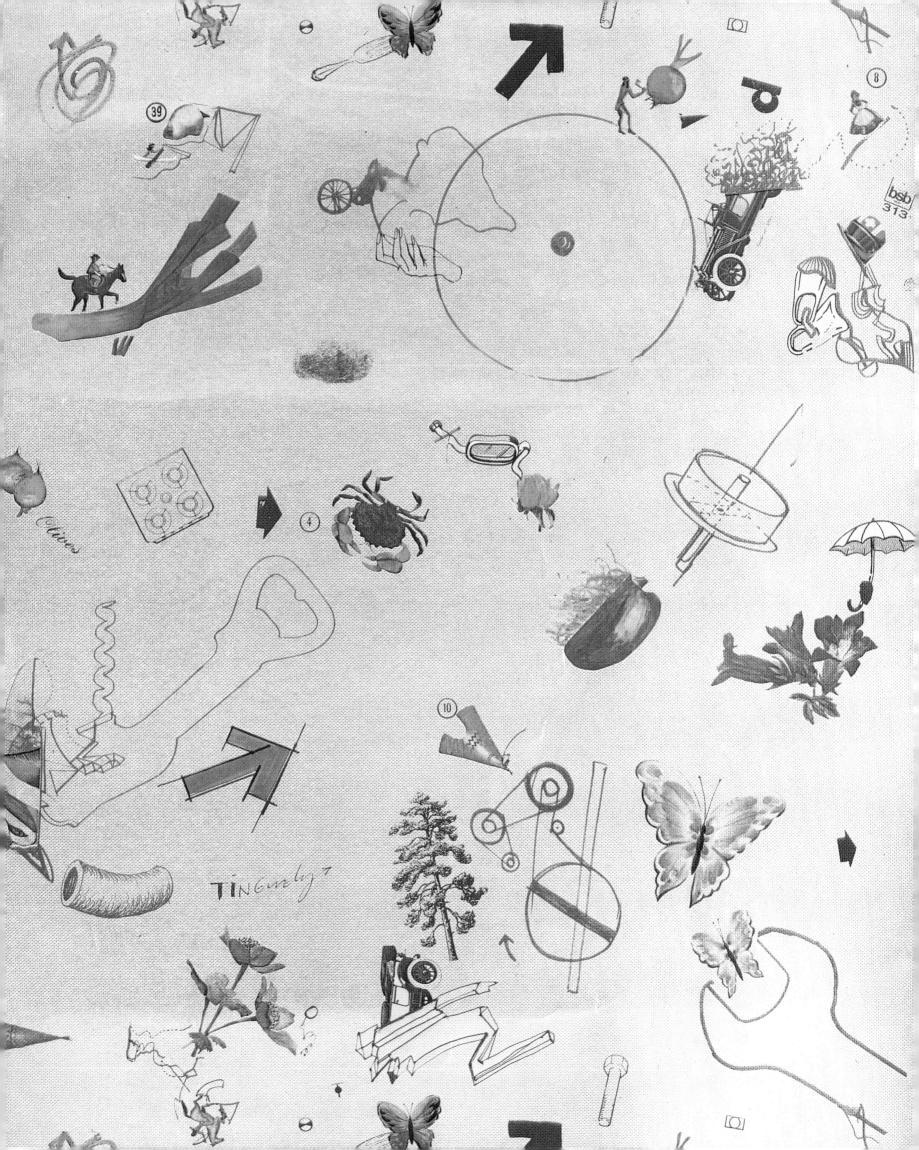

Plate 196
ALLEN JONES (b. 1937)
"Right-Hand Lady," 1972.
Wallpaper, Marburger Tapetenfabrik. Marburger
Tapetenfabrik, Kirchain, Germany.

Plate 197
WERNER BERGES (b. 1941)
"Beauty," 1972.
Wallpaper, Marburger Tapetenfabrik. Marburger
Tapetenfabrik, Kirchain, Germany.

Three other artists exploited the repetitiveness of wallpaper design to add emphasis to their already exaggerated images of women's sexual appeal. Allen Jones, the British Pop artist, designed a pattern titled "Right-Hand Lady" (plate 196) featuring his typical aggressive brunette, a nearly nude woman with boots and hoop, staring directly at the onlooker. Werner Berges, a Berliner, designed a wallpaper in brilliant, almost violent colors featuring a negative photographic image of a woman's face against stripes (plate 197). Paul Wunderlich, one of the best known of German artists, designed a pattern of a trompe l'oeil drapery covering a woman's breasts, entitling it "Faltenwurf" ("Shadow-folds"). All of these designs, meant to appear on the wall repetitively, could fairly be called spoofs of wallpaper traditions.

ndy Warhol is the artist who more than once stage-managed a triumphant wallpaper spoof. His decision to place his portraits over his own "Cow" wallpaper in a major retrospective in 1970 has been seen by one observer as sabotaging that show.[28] But did it? Warhol often used his own wallpapers as backgrounds for his paintings and sometimes exhibited his paintings massed almost as wallpaper. Indeed, some of the repeated motifs in the paintings (Coke bottles, dollar bills, soup cans) *look* like the repeated motifs of a wallpaper. For an early, on-the-edge show at the Castelli Gallery in 1966, Warhol exhibited only the "Cow" wallpaper (plate 198) and his silver Mylar pillow-cloud sculptures. In "Cow" the familiar Borden logo of Elsie was enlarged to a giant pattern in fuchsia on a citron background. For the retrospective four years later, the same wallpaper was printed in pinks and blues; Warhol's paintings, including many portraits of celebrities, were placed over it in a typical Warhol double statement. Warhol said he thought the paintings would be less *visible* against the wallpaper background.[29] There is a legend that Warhol once explained that the "Cow" wallpaper was designed for Leo Castelli's barn in Connecticut, though Leo Castelli disclaims ever having had a barn, in or out of Connecticut.[30]

Warhol once admitted that he made up his past as he went along. "I'd prefer to remain a mystery; I never like to give my background and, anyway, I make it all different all the time I'm asked. It's not just that it's part of my image not to tell everything, it's just that I forget what I said the day before and I have to make it all up over again. I don't think I have an image anyway, favorable or unfavorable."[31] On another occasion he said: "If you want to know all about Andy Warhol, just look at the surface of my paintings and films and me, and there I am. There's nothing behind it."[32] He was clearly reluctant to reveal himself in the retrospective. Charles Stuckey relates that Warhol's first proposal for the show was to present three hundred of his Flower paintings and his second was for the show to consist simply of "Cow" wallpaper hung backward.[33] In an earlier exhibit at the Galerie Ileana Sonnabend in Paris in 1965, Warhol had placed the Flower paintings over "Cow," and in a memorable gesture at the Moderna Museet in Stockholm in 1968, he had managed to have real steers grazing in front of the museum, which had been swathed on the outside with—

Plate 198
Andy Warhol hanging "Cow" wallpaper at the Castelli Gallery, New York, 1966.

Plate 199
ANDY WARHOL (1928–1987)
"Mao," 1974.
Wallpaper installation at Margo Leavin Gallery, Los Angeles,
1975. Courtesy of Castelli Gallery, New York.

what else?—the ubiquitous "Cow" wallpaper. In 1975, in Frascati, Italy, the wallpaper covered doorways as well as walls, on which were hung the Ladies and Gentlemen series of drag-queen portraits. Viewers burst through the wallpaper to enter.

Warhol's second wallpaper rhymed with "Cow" and was titled "Mao." It appeared, along with the Hammer and Sickle paintings and paintings of Chairman Mao, about the time of Nixon's rapprochement with China and thus was very timely, or very audacious; its biggest exhibition was in Paris at the Musée Galliera in 1974. An exceedingly simple

wallpaper, it was composed of purple ovals of Mao's face repeated in diaper pattern (plate 199). On it Warhol placed all of his portraits of Mao, silkscreened in different colors, but all of the same pose. In 1978 he designed yet another wallpaper, a self-portrait pattern with pink and purple swatches (plate 200), which he used for a show at the Kunsthaus in Zurich. This last wallpaper appears to have been exhibited only once.

In addition to using these three deadpan but potent wallpapers, Warhol often treated his paintings as wallpaper. At the Heiner Friedrich Gallery in New York in 1979 he hung his series of Shadow paintings at floor level and edge to edge. In 1964 he hung his Flower paintings like wallpaper at the Galerie Sonnabend in Paris. And for a retrospective at the Whitney in 1979, he placed his portraits in pairs (as a "decoration") against brown, lacquered walls.

Both his paintings and his wallpapers indicate that Warhol was absorbed with the idea of a repetitive image. He declared that he himself wanted to be a machine. He fixed his record player to repeat the same pop song for any visitors from the art world.[34] Considering the idea of a society stamped out in machine pattern, he once concluded that Communism was forcing people to say the same thing, but that in America people were choosing to do so on their own.[35] He liked to say that he wanted everybody alike, in the sense that then everyone could be an artist. So why not stamped-out machine-patterned art? "Should he devise a vending machine that, for 50 cents, would dispense a plastic sculpture that was made before the buyer's eyes?"[36]

The question of wallpaper in Warhol's work thus becomes an essentially moral but ambiguous one. Like many artists, he wanted to produce art that could be owned by many people. When Leo Castelli was asked how much "Cow" wallpaper was made, he replied: "So much that we just gave it away."[37] Warhol once declared: "I think somebody should be able to do all my paintings for me. I haven't been able to make every image clear and simple and the same as the first one. I think it would be so great if more people took up silk screens so that no one would know whether my picture was mine or somebody else's."[38] Throwaway wallpaper fitted this image of the artist perfectly.

It seems that Warhol was telling us a great deal about ourselves by denying in his deadpan way what he actually believed about life—and death—in America. He once said as much in the early days before he perfected his detached posture: "I adore America. . . . My image is a statement of the symbols of the harsh, impersonal products and brash materialistic objects on which America is built today. It is a projection of everything that can be bought and sold, the practical but impermanent symbols that sustain us."[39] A repeated image in his paintings could show something of this, especially a well-chosen one like the American Indian, the electric chair, a car crash, or a tragic and vulnerable glamour icon like Marilyn Monroe. Place these repeated motifs from the paintings against another expressive repeat in a wallpaper and a powerful statement is produced. The repetition of wallpaper—in the case of the "Cow" wallpaper the studied banality, in the case of the "Mao" wallpaper the genuine daring—helped Warhol insure that people could not ignore his images.

Plate 200
ANDY WARHOL (1928–1987)
Self-portrait wallpaper, 1978.
Collage of offset, film, colored paper, 41½ x 31¾ in. (105.5 x 81 cm). Private collection; courtesy of Thomas Ammann, Zurich.

ART AND WALLPAPER

ritic Harold Rosenberg once described Action Painting as the work of "a tube of paint squeezed by the Absolute.... The painter need keep himself on hand solely to collect the benefits of an endless series of strokes of luck.... The result is an apocalyptic wallpaper."[1] Another critic, Marina Vaizey, has aptly called the dominance of photography in our society "that never-ending visual wallpaper that surrounds us."[2] Clement Greenberg once predicted that viewers would look at a Jackson Pollock and say "Nothing but wallpaper."[3] Such analogies with the idea of wallpaper are examples of the many ways in which—beyond the actual wallpapers designed by artists—wallpaper and art have intersected. Most literally, of course, reproductions of paintings have been printed on wallpaper, to be pasted on the wall. In many twentieth-century collages and constructions, actual pieces of ordinary wallpaper have been prominent. Painted-in wallpaper patterns have adorned the backgrounds of literally thousands of important paintings, contributing to a variety of artistic effects; inked-in wallpaper patterns have also given comic point to numerous cartoons. Intersections between wallpaper and art seem ubiquitous.

In the eighteenth century (see chapter 1) John Baptist Jackson badly reproduced Titian, Veronese, and Tintoretto, each on a small individual wallpaper panel. Horace Walpole then patronizingly used these works around 1750 in the "little parlor" of his neo-Gothic villa of Strawberry Hill. Later, between 1780 and 1789, some extraordinary paintings were reproduced as wallpaper in France. Perhaps it was because Madame de Pompadour was so influential—already a patron of French and English wallpapers—that we have examples of *demi-lunes* (half-moons) of the series Four Seasons and Four Amours by her chosen artist François Boucher, in wallpaper. These surmounted panels of wallpaper by noted painters of the day. Jean-Honoré Fragonard is thought to have created several of the paintings reproduced in wallpaper that were crowned with Boucher's work; *Pygmalion and His Statue* (plate 203) and *Eurydice Frightened by the Serpent* were attributed to him in a 1938 wallpaper exhibition.[4] These and other remarkable wallpapers (plate 204) were produced by Arthur and Grenard in sepia and grisaille about the time of the French Revolution: both men were

Plate 201   *Preceding pages*
PABLO PICASSO (1881–1973)
Femmes à leur toilette, 1938.
Collage of wallpaper, 117⅝ x 176⅜ in. (299 x 488 cm).
Musée Picasso, Paris.

Plate 202   *Opposite*
VINCENT VAN GOGH (1853–1890)
Portrait of Joseph Roulin, 1888–89.
Oil on canvas, 25⅜ x 20⅝ in. (64.4 x 52.2 cm). Collection, The Museum of Modern Art, New York; Gift of Mr. and Mrs. William A. M. Burden, Mr. and Mrs. Paul Rosenberg, Nelson A. Rockefeller, Mr. and Mrs. Armand Bartos, Sidney and Harriet Janis, and Mr. and Mrs. Werner E. Josten (by exchange).

guillotined during the Terror and few of the works were printed. Their wallpapers are considered masterpieces of wood-block printing.

The nineteenth century was addicted to such wallpaper panels of master artists and preferred to reproduce instructive, moralistic painters. These reproductions would ordinarily replace paintings and be pasted on the wall. Some, such as Thomas Couture's "Les Prodigues" ("The Prodigals"; plate 205), a large wallpaper panel from the Vices series, could in a sense be considered scenic wallpaper panels. The painting from which Couture adapted this wallpaper was titled *Supper after the Masked Ball,* a symbolic depiction of the artist (Pierrot in the painting) amid the debauchery of the Second Empire.

Plate 203
JEAN-HONORÉ FRAGONARD[?] (1732–1836)
"Pygmalion and His Statue," c. 1785.
Wallpaper panel, grisaille, 34⅜ x 26⅜ in. (87 x 67 cm), from a series by Arthur and Grenard, Paris. The lunette is from the series Four Seasons and Four Amours by François Boucher (1703–1770), grisaille, Arthur and Grenard, Paris, c. 1785. Musée des Arts Décoratifs, Paris.

Plate 204   *Opposite, top*
ANONYMOUS
"Venus Rising from the Waters," c. 1785.
Overdoor wallpaper, Arthur and Grenard, Paris.
Museum of Art, Rhode Island School of Design, Providence, Rhode Island; Mary B. Jackson Fund.

Plate 205   *Opposite, bottom*
THOMAS COUTURE (1815–1879)
"Les Prodigues," 1862.
Wallpaper panel, 73½ x 102 in. (186.6 x 259.1 cm), from The Vices and the Virtues, Jules Desfosse, Paris. After Couture's *Supper after the Masked Ball,* 1855. By courtesy of the Board of Trustees of the Victoria and Albert Museum, London.

In the mid-twentieth century something comparable resulted when the New York wallpaper firm of Katzenbach and Warren approached Alexander Calder, Henri Matisse, Roberto Matta, and Joan Miró and commissioned each of them to create a "Mural Scroll," a design to be silk-screened on canvas in a small edition of two hundred copies. Each of the four artists produced a fine design typical of his oeuvre (plates 206; 207; 208) and contributed enthusiastic comments about the Mural Scrolls to an advertising booklet.

Calder's "A Piece of My Workshop" is a panel of mobile motifs, six feet high by ten feet wide. Calder wrote: "Of course I wish I had invented this medium of Mural Scrolls myself. But as I didn't—the Orientals having been doing this for many years—I am still very enthusiastic about smearing up somebody's wall." Matisse rejoiced in "the possibility of reproducing without hindrance the great qualities of mural art" and of "bringing to all" the results of this effort. Matta poeticized: "One should wear a Mural-Scroll like a woman

Plate 206
HENRI MATISSE (1869–1954)
"Arbre en Fleur," 1948.
Mural Scroll wallpaper, silkscreen on canvas, 5 x 6 ft. (152.4 x 182.9 cm), Katzenbach and Warren, New York. Plates 206, 207, and 208 courtesy of Cooper-Hewitt, National Museum of Design, Smithsonian Institution; Gift of Katzenbach and Warren, Inc./Art Resource, New York.

Plate 207   *Top*
Roberto Matta (b. 1911)
"Sun-Dice," 1948.
Mural Scroll wallpaper, silkscreen on canvas, 9 x 6 ft. (274.3 x 182.9 cm), Katzenbach and Warren, New York.

Plate 208   *Bottom*
Joan Miró (1893–1983)
"El Sol," 1948.
Mural Scroll wallpaper, silkscreen on canvas, 4 x 6 ft. (121.9 x 182.9 cm), Katzenbach and Warren, New York.

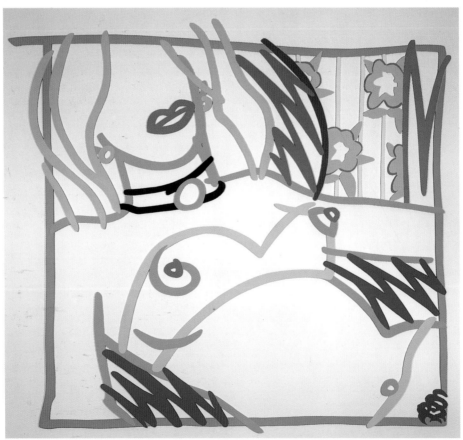

wears a dress. It is to hang oneself, in full color, upon the wall, as a sunny day." Miró responded with wishes to address "oneself in a more direct way to men in the collaboration . . . of the painter, the artisan and the technician." Calder concluded his statement in his most earthy, direct manner: "I would neither wear it, as Matta, nor collaborate it, as Miró, but just spit on the back of it, and stick it up where it can best give pleasure, or diminish gloom."[5]

Actual wallpapers, usually the most traditional and innocuous patterns, have been incorporated in artists' collages and constructions. Picasso's very large collage *Femmes à leur toilette* (1938; plate 201) is made wholly of quite ordinary wallpapers. It is a scene of women, one of whom is looking in a mirror held by another whose face is turned away. The mirror reflects a face composed of a particularly aggressive pattern of wallpaper, and the effect of the whole is of a considerable misogyny. Picasso once commented: "The artist is a receptacle for emotions . . . whether they spring from heaven, from earth, from a scrap of paper, from a passing face, or from a spider's web."[6] For him, a scrap of wallpaper could lead to a work of art. An everyday wallpaper is also used, but for a totally different effect, in Red Grooms's construction *Maine Room* (1964; plate 209). The wallpaper message here, of down-home togetherness with its varying satisfactions, is delivered instantly to the viewer. On the other hand, Max Ernst's use of wallpaper in collage gives an intentionally deceptive air of everyday life to his startling Dada images. In his 1920 *Little Tear Gland That Says Tic Tac* (plate 211), the brown wallpaper border strips used verti-

cally serve as a "tear gland machine." Ernst must have chosen these strips carefully for his feigned realism because the strips have a machinelike metallic look as well as "knobs" (in paper). Real metal has recently represented wallpaper in art constructions: the "wallpaper" in Tom Wesselmann's metal-strip paintings, or "steel drawings" (one in 1985 titled *Bedroom Nude with Black Choker and Wallpaper*), is there for garish effect, both mocking and celebrating pop culture and gaudy blondes, and composed of brightly colored, flat metal strips and metal flowers (plate 210).

Plate 211
MAX ERNST (1891–1976)
The Little Tear Gland That Says Tic Tac, 1920.
Gouache on wallpaper, 14⅜ x 10 in. (36.2 x 25.4 cm).
The Museum of Modern Art, New York; Purchase.

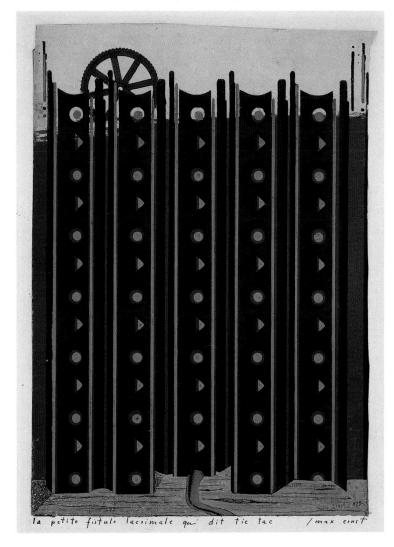

Plate 209   *Opposite, top*
RED GROOMS (b. 1937)
Maine Room, 1964.
Watercolor on cardboard and wood in Plexiglas box,
12 x 23 x 23 in. (30.5 x 58.4 x 58.4 cm). Courtesy of
Kimiko and John Powers, New York.

Plate 210   *Opposite, bottom*
TOM WESSELMANN (b. 1931)
Bedroom Nude with Black Choker and Wallpaper, 1985.
Enamel on cutout aluminum, 81 x 89 in. (205.7 x 226 cm).
Courtesy Sidney Janis Gallery.

To cartoonists, the flat and repetitive images of wallpaper are a source of the human comedy. There is the cartoon of the wife who decorates everything in the room—including her husband—to match the wallpaper.[7] Or the swain who plucks one of the patterned paper bouquets off the wall to extend to his beloved. Or the artist carefully studying the flower for the hundredth time that he is about to paint as a repeat for the wallpaper. Max Beerbohm's most memorable wallpaper cartoon presents small, repeated images of a prickly-haired Henrik Ibsen in the wallpaper pattern, mirroring the great dramatist himself in the foreground (plate 213). Ibsen's disciple, the drama critic William Archer, is abjectly kneeling before him. Thus Beerbohm conveys in one cartoon Ibsen's self-adulation and Archer's excessive prostration in his reviews of Ibsen's plays. William Steig's inimitable cartoon of a surpassingly flat wallpaper family is inspired (plate

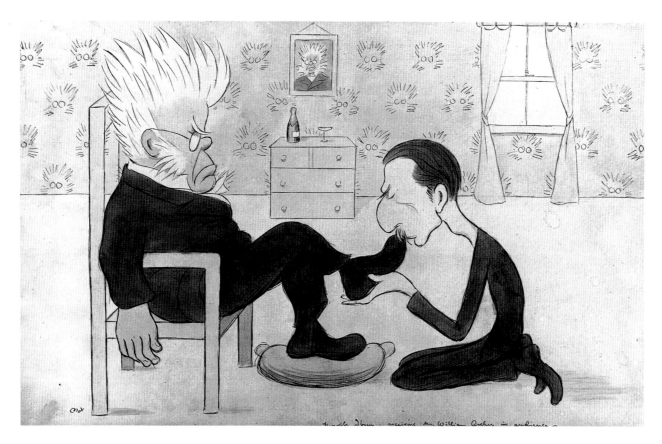

Plate 212 *Top*
WILLIAM STEIG (b. 1907)
"Wallpaper," 1986.
Cartoon. Courtesy of *The New Yorker*/copyright 1986
The New Yorker Magazine.

Plate 213
MAX BEERBOHM (1872–1956)
"Henrik Ibsen, Receiving Mr. William Archer in Audience," 1904.
Cartoon. The Hugh Lane Municipal Gallery of Modern Art, Dublin.

Plate 214

The Samuel Sargent Family, c. 1800.

Oil on canvas, 38⅜ x 50⅜ in. (97.4 x 128 cm).

National Gallery of Art, Washington, D.C.; Gift

of Edgar William and Bernice Chrysler Garbisch.

212). Is this decorative black and white group from the Wiener Werkstätte?

A most interesting and very common intersection between wallpaper and fine art is to be found in the many paintings that include the artist's idea of wallpaper painted into their backgrounds. In part, of course, such depictions of wallpaper simply reflect the reality the artist sees; yet fre-

quently other values are also evident. Artists know that the simple patterns of wallpaper express an aura of everyday life and humanity that communicates instantly while adding richness of color and texture to a painting. A regularly spaced wallpaper pattern, usually floral, repeated to the limit of the artist's patience, is a favorite device. *The Samuel Sargent Family,* an anonymous folk painting (c.1800; plate

214), has a simple stenciled pattern above the wainscot that lends an inviting touch to this charming group. A wrinkle appears just under the window where a strip of the paper without the design may have been used. This pattern is presented quite regularly, but very often artists are unwilling to present a wallpaper pattern in perfect formal rows, and will take liberties, as does James Tissot in *Portrait of Mlle. L. L.* (1864; plate 215). The wallpaper in this scene is indeed hand-painted, its carefree placement of floral sprigs far from formal but adding needed lightness to the background and harmonizing perfectly with the costume of Mademoiselle L. L. For a different mood, in John Everett Millais's *Black Brunswicker* (1860; plate 216) the poignancy of the soldier's farewell (most men of this regiment did not return from the Battle of Waterloo) is enhanced by the domestic realism of the wallpaper peeling away from the wall. In his infinitely painstaking style, Millais was careful to portray this sad damask wallpaper quite faithfully.

Plate 215
JAMES TISSOT (1836–1902)
Portrait of Mlle. L. L., 1864.
Oil on canvas, 48¾ x 39¼ in. (124 x 99.5 cm).
Musée d'Orsay, Paris.

Plate 216

JOHN EVERETT MILLAIS (1829–1896)

The Black Brunswicker, 1860.

Oil on canvas, 41 x 27 in. (104.1 x 68.6 cm). Courtesy of the
Lady Lever Art Gallery, Port Sunlight, England.

Plate 217

Roger Parry (1905–1977)

Banalité, 1930.

Gravure print. Spencer Collection, The New York Public
Library, Astor, Lenox and Tilden Foundations.

In some works of art, wallpaper backgrounds may take on a dominant role, as in Roger Parry's gravure print *Banalité* (1930; plate 217). The sepia wallpaper with dark floral diaper design is as significant as the upside-down portrait, the rope, and the rolled-up carpet in conveying an environment of utter despair. One of van Gogh's impassioned patterned backgrounds has, in art critic John Russell's words, "the astonishing wallpaper with which van Gogh shuts out the rest of the world." Russell calls the wallpaper flowers behind the figure in the painting *Portrait of Joseph Roulin* (plate 202) "giddy blooms" that echo the cosmic stars in the artist's *Starry Night*.[8] In Harold Gilman's painting *The Shopping List* (1912; plate 218) the hackneyed but respectable wallpaper is as important a piece of social commentary as the working-class woman beside it. As a member of the Camden Town group of artists who painted the social milieu of north London early in the twentieth century, Gilman used stereotyped wallpaper patterns to help portray drab, dutiful lives. Cecil Beaton once dismissed such wallpapers as papers whose taste was "spoilt by respectability."[9]

Plate 218
Harold Gilman (1876–1919)
The Shopping List, 1912.
Oil on canvas, 61½ x 31 in. (156.2 x 78.7 cm).
The British Council, London.

Plate 219
EDOUARD VUILLARD (1868–1940)
Interior with Pink Wallpaper I, I, III, 1899.
Color lithographs, each 13⅜ x 10⅝ in. (34 x 27 cm).
From the series Landscapes and Interiors. Sterling
and Francine Clark Art Institute, Williamstown,
Massachusetts.

Plate 220   *Opposite*
Misia Natanson in her apartment at rue Saint-Florentin,
photograph by Edouard Vuillard, c. 1897.
The painting shown is Vuillard's *The Embroiderer;*
the wallpaper in the photograph often appeared in
Vuillard's paintings of Misia Natanson. Editions
Hazan, Paris.

Only a few years earlier and for different purposes, Edouard Vuillard was devotedly painting wallpapered interiors of French bourgeois everyday life, which he celebrated by means of his colors, textures, patterns, and gentle treatment of figures. His paintings are often dominated by the wallpapers, giving the works a patterned look of a single plane. As a Nabi, Vuillard was deeply interested in decorative art, even morally committed to it. Floral wallpapers cover his canvases; one of the most enchanting of his decorative and expressive works is a triptych in lithograph, *Interior with Pink Wallpaper I, II, III* from the series Landscapes and Interiors (1899; plate 219). These spatially complicated, floral-wallpapered interiors evoke the pat-terned charm achieved by Suzuki Harunobu in his series Eight Views of Indoor Life (1765). Harunobu's work may have been known to Vuillard: Gabriel Weisberg suggests similarities, pointing out in both artists' work the "warm interiors depicted with complicated perspective systems and the juxtaposition of contrasting patterns of wallpaper, furnishings and dress."[10] Even the titles of the two series are similar. Vuillard's flattened planes and multitude of patterns exaggerate Harunobu's.[11] And in none of his work does Vuillard so literally paint the wallpaper as when he depicts scenes in the home of Misia Natanson, whom he loved (plate 220). The yellow-flowered wallpaper of her salon is distinct and quite recognizable in painting after painting.

It requires a considerable mental leap to adjust to more fantastic derivations from wallpaper in later twentieth-century art. The British artist Howard Hodgkin's repeated "spots" in his painted interiors often recall wallpapered rooms. Yet in Hodgkin's paintings the recollection of places, moods, and faces is filtered repeatedly, with paint on top of paint, and finally the scenes he portrays are abstract and tantalizing. Hodgkin has said: "My pictures are finished when the subject comes back."[12] Two dinner-party paintings at the Tate Gallery, London, *Dinner at West Hill* and *Dinner at Smith Square* (plate 221), recall what may have been formidable evenings in wallpapered rooms. Although the wallpaperlike spots in Hodgkin's paintings are many times removed from Vuillard's patterned domesticity, more than one critic has seen a connection between the two artists.[13] Hodgkin himself has acknowledged that he is fascinated with domestic interiors and ornament, and that he has always been a "fanatical admirer of Vuillard."[14] In 1984, for a room commissioned by the Arts Council of Great Britain, Hodgkin created a fabric wall pattern in blues entitled "Water" (plate 222). Its design is reminiscent of the Japanese line swirls in Maurice Denis's wallpapers. This room, including its large, Hodgkin-designed wall panel of a decorative tree with Hodgkin spots, recalled Vuillard and Chinese wallpapers as well.

Plate 222
HOWARD HODGKIN (b. 1932)
The Hodgkin Room; from *Four Rooms,* exhibition, London,
1984. South Bank Centre/Arts Council of Great Britain,
London.

Plate 221   *Opposite*
HOWARD HODGKIN (b. 1932)
Dinner at Smith Square, 1975–79.
Oil on wood panel, 37¼ x 49¼ in. (94.6 x 125 cm).
The Tate Gallery, London/Art Resource, New York.

Plate 223
VENTURI, SCOTT BROWN AND ASSOCIATES
Best Products Co., Oxford Valley, Pennsylvania, 1979.
The design of the tiled exterior is from a favorite
wallpaper pattern. Courtesy of Venturi, Scott Brown
and Associates, Inc., Philadelphia.

Plate 224
JAMES ENSOR (1860–1949)
Attributes of the Studio, 1889.
Oil on canvas, 32⅝ x 44½ in. (83 x 113 cm). Bayerische
Staatsgemäldesammlungen, Munich, Germany.

Plate 225   *Opposite*
CLAES OLDENBURG (b. 1929)
Light Switches, 1966.
Watercolor and crayon, 9½ x 7 in. (24.1 x 17.8 cm).
Courtesy Maurice Payne, London.

The sculptor Claes Oldenburg thought that the eerie paintings of James Ensor summoned up wallpaper images and memories. The flat, patterned backgrounds of faces give many of Ensor's paintings a jolting power. After seeing them, Oldenburg in fact wrote "Ensor" and "wallpaper" on his own watercolor of London light switches and blurry wallpaper (1966; plate 225). Ensor's *Attributes of the Studio* (1889; plate 224) has in the background what seems to be a wallpaper of faces, often masked, with leering expressions. *Banquet of the Starved* (1925) is haunted with "wallpaper" of skeletal death

figures; *Masks* (1896) conjures fantastic, bodiless spirits on the wall. All these images are derived from masks; Ensor lived for a time in Ostend with his aunt, who sold the traditional masks worn in Belgium for fêtes throughout the year. The artist must have seen the masks hung in rows on the back wall of her shop year after year. Indeed, in some works the masked images in the background wallpapers are a reprise of Ensor's great painting *The Entry of Christ into Brussels in 1889* (1888), in which the multitude covering most of the canvas is composed of masked figures.

Architects, too, have joined painters in celebrating wallpaper fantasies and the metaphor of wallpaper. Philip Johnson's Glass House of 1949 was prophetic of René Magritte's spellbinding, surreal painting *Personal Values*—a bedroom papered below the painted cornice with blue sky and soft white clouds. Like Magritte, Johnson celebrated the resonances of wallpaper: "[The house] turns the landscape into wallpaper, rather expensive wallpaper to be sure, with the sun and the stars and the moon," he once commented.[15] "The wallpaper needed pushing out," he remarked on another occasion, adding that the trees were "suffocating"

the house.[16] Robert Venturi's use of a favorite wallpaper pattern placed in giant-size tile on the exterior of a vast merchandising showroom in Pennsylvania is a similar metaphor in postmodern form (plate 223). Venturi has been a persuasive spokesman for the banal but meaningful art images of our time. "Convention can be good and ordinary can be good—everything doesn't have to be high art," he has stated.[17] A case in point is the Italian design group Memphis, which has exaggerated Art Deco colors and forms with humor and verve, giving their wallpapers the look of "fantastic sweets wrappers." Memphis artist Nathalie du

Plate 226
ROBERT S. ZAKANITCH (b. 1935)
Blue Monk, 1978.
Acrylic on canvas, 78 x 66 in. (198.1 x 167.6 cm).
Robert Miller Gallery, New York.

Plate 227

Henri Matisse at work on *The Parakeet and the Mermaid,* 1952.
Paris Match.

Pasquier has designed chintzes that on a wall could look aboriginal as well, a decoration that, as she says, "lays bare the soul of things."[18]

Wallpaper has inspired a surprising number of contemporary artists who use repeat patterns for whole paintings. Kathy Halbreich writes of the late-twentieth-century "proliferation of repeats, reprocessing, reproduction and repression."[19] The parallel with wallpaper has been expressed most obviously in the group of Pattern Painters that emerged in the United States in the 1970s. Many of them were drawn to wallpaper images. Robert Zakanitch has painted wallpaper flowers in patterned panels with borders (plate 226). Robert Kushner has been inspired by the rich decorative patterns he saw in Iran and by patterns in wallpaper books, and has deliberately sought to unify the decorative and fine arts. Kushner is notable for changing

each of his multiple views of an image slightly, to considerable effect. Cynthia Carlson has been described as having a "wallpaper gestalt."[20] She has done whole-room installations of patterns in acrylic paint, thickly squeezed from the tube and looking remarkably like three-dimensional wallpaper. Her installations attempt to reflect the setting: at the Massachusetts Institute of Technology in urban Cambridge, Massachusetts, she created a bedraggled but lively weed pattern; at Oberlin College in rural Ohio a garden plant pattern; and in the Victorian architecture of the Pennsylvania Academy of the Fine Arts, Philadelphia, a gilded grid of red and blue rosettes. More recently, Robert Gober's stark wallpaper pattern of a white man sleeping soundly near a black man who has been lynched ("Hanging Man, Sleeping Man," 1989) has an impact that one image alone, however fearful, could not give. The quiet presentation of such an image repeated calmly in wallpaper is terrifying.[21]

Most of the Pattern Painters have paid homage to Henri Matisse, who himself late in life created cut-paper wall murals that demonstrate the perfect fusion of the fine and decorative arts. In his early career (1906–11), Matisse was sternly accused by one critic of exhibiting a painting that to his eyes resembled wallpaper: "Where are we? Who is this? No expression, no attention, no life! A wallpaper image, imprecise, floating."[22] Matisse was devoted to the decorative in art, and even described his work as "decorative" without flinching, adding that he sought an art "of purity and serenity, devoid of troubling or depressing subject matter . . . a soothing, calming influence on the mind, something like a good armchair which provides relaxation from physical fatigue."[23] This is a statement that sounds very much like one of Morris's statements on repose: "We must provide ourselves with lesser art . . . with which to surround our common workaday or restful times, and for those times, I think, it will be enough for us to clothe our daily and domestic walls with ornament."[24]

In these beliefs Morris and Matisse were kindred spirits. Each spoke of nature stylized, and of decorative art that reminds the viewer of much more than the thing itself. But Matisse managed to do what Morris said could not be done, to "bring a whole countryside, or a whole field, into your room."[25] In the last years of his life, when he was bedridden and could no longer walk or swim, Matisse cultivated gardens and seas and skies with giant cutout paper murals pasted on the white walls of his bedroom at the Hôtel Régina in Nice. "I often have to keep to my bed because of my health, so I created a little garden around me where I could walk," he once said (plate 227).[26] In Paris in 1946, for two maquettes for linen wall hangings he had placed his paper versions of *Oceania the Sea* and *Oceania the Sky* on his walls above the wainscot, and even a small strip above the door, so that the ensemble was like Matisse wallpaper. These paper trials were remembered images of his trip in 1930 to Tahiti, a paradise of water and sky. There, as he later described it, he could swim under the water and then surface to be almost blinded to the wonders of the scene by the brilliant light.[27] Some of that glorious light is present in Matisse's great later wall decorations where, as he said, he used "the wall instead of a trellis," and created patterns with

slight and fascinating variations from his shears and gouached paper.

These overwhelming walls of the early 1950s are saturated with both light and color. There may not be one exact repeat in the many-fingered paper leaf forms of the magnificent *Parakeet and the Mermaid* (1952; plate 228) but, because the forms are very similar, the effect is of repeat in a bountiful and beloved tropical world, as the eye follows the familiar contours with wonder and "repose." "No leaf of a fig tree is identical to any other, each has a form of its own, but each

cries out: Fig tree!" Matisse stated in his pochoir masterpiece, *Jazz*.[28] He believed totally that decoration could be expressive—could express no less than the spirit of man.

Existing in Matisse's great decorations are the flatness, the pattern, the meaning, the concern with every inch of the mat, even the mystery and poetry that have distinguished some of the best decorative art, and that in the hands of a great artist can become fine art. These murals achieve a kind of transcendence; what we experience in Matisse's last paper murals may be a true "apocalyptic wallpaper."

ARTISTS' WALLPAPERS FOR CHILDREN

(1860–1980)

Plate 229 *Preceding pages*
HORST ECKERT (Janosch) (b. 1931)
"Zirkus," c. 1980.
Nursery wallpaper. Copyright 1988 by Janosch, all rights reserved.

Plate 230 *Opposite*
WALTER CRANE (1845–1915)
"Miss Mouse at Home" ("Ye Frog He Would A-Wooing Go"), 1877.
Nursery wallpaper design, Jeffrey and Co. By kind permission of Roger Warner and the Board of Trustees of the Victoria and Albert Museum, London.

n 1874 Samuel and Olivia Clemens built a splendid new house in Hartford, Connecticut; a few years later, having more money after the success of *Tom Sawyer,* they decorated the nursery with a wallpaper by the English artist Walter Crane. The Clemenses were well-traveled; they shopped for their home on their travels and could have chosen this wallpaper on a European trip, but Crane's wallpapers were also newly available in America. A sophisticated and elaborate tile design in subdued colors of browns, greens, and dull reds, it was titled by the artist "Miss Mouse at Home" and is commonly called "Ye Frog He Would A-Wooing Go." Crane's original design for this wallpaper was painted in pale colors: blues, greens, and yellows, befitting the aesthetic age and its stipulation of light colors for the young (plate 230). (Crane also designed "aesthetic" clothes for young people.) However, in these darker shades and in this setting it was a handsome paper and must have pleased the Clemens children and their parents, because it was not changed while they lived in the house. In fact, the Crane wallpaper can still be seen in the nursery in a fine reproduction copied from a fragment found behind the fireplace mantel. In November 1879 Olivia Clemens wrote to her mother: "The nursery is perfect. . . . When I remember the sense of being taken care of . . . I feel I must give the same sense to the children—What an intense love of home I always had as a young lady!"[1] The Clemens children often entertained their parents in the nursery suite, and in 1881 the whole family was, as Clemens put it, "living like a gang of tramps" on the second floor with the children, while the first floor was being decorated by Louis Comfort Tiffany with elegant stenciled and leather wallpapers.[2]

No doubt the Clemens children as well as thousands of others in the United States knew Walter Crane's children's books *The Baby's Opera* and *The Baby's Bouquet* from which his first nursery wallpapers were derived. Crane himself related with some amusement that he became a wallpaper designer in self-defense, because an "enterprising but somewhat unscrupulous manufacturer" in America pirated the pictures from his storybooks very successfully.[3] Crane's own first wallpaper designs, "Queen of Hearts" (1875; plate 231)

and "Hey Diddle Diddle" or "Humpty Dumpty" (1876; plate 232), were book illustrations translated into wallpaper, but always achieved with new and imaginative drawings. The Clemens family's nursery design appeared in 1877 and was derived from songs in *The Baby's Opera*. A later nursery pattern, "Fairy Garden" (1886), was an equally ingenious use of book illustration translated masterfully for wallpaper, using the flower fairies of Crane's children's book *Flora's Feast* in an intertwined and glowing Art Nouveau design.

In all, Crane produced seven machine-printed wallpapers for the nursery, each with a child-centered motif, each meticulously drawn, nonthreatening, intricate. There wasn't a crane in the lot (Crane liked to sign his work with the drawing of a crane standing on one foot), but there were duck gargoyles on a picturesque gingerbread house in "The House That Jack Built," a briar-rose forest where "Sleeping Beauty" reclined (1879; plate 233), and peacocks and topiary trees as well as cockleshells for the garden of "Mistress Mary" (1903). Crane created a special design of nursery rhyme figures for the nursery at Castle Howard, Yorkshire. The Howards, the earl and countess of Carlisle, were friends of many artists, among them William Morris, Edward Burne-Jones, and Crane. Each of their homes was decorated with Morris wallpapers, in some cases the same Morris paper. They apparently liked the Crane wallpaper of nursery rhymes and used it in a second castle, Naworth, in Cumberland.[4]

Crane's rivals in the nursery were Kate Greenaway and Randolph Caldecott. The much-admired Greenaway nursery wallpaper of 1893 somewhat resembled the Howards' Crane wallpaper, as both are composed of nursery figures

Plate 231 *Opposite*
WALTER CRANE (1845–1915)
"Queen of Hearts" ("Baby's Opera"), 1875.
Wallpaper, machine printed, Jeffrey and Co.
By courtesy of the Board of Trustees of the
Victoria and Albert Museum, London.

Plate 232
WALTER CRANE (1845–1915)
"Hey Diddle Diddle" ("Nursery Rhymes,"
"Humpty Dumpty"), 1876.
Wallpaper, machine printed, Jeffrey and Co. Courtesy of
Cooper-Hewitt, National Museum of Design, Smithsonian
Institution; Gift of the Essex Institute/Art Resource, New York.

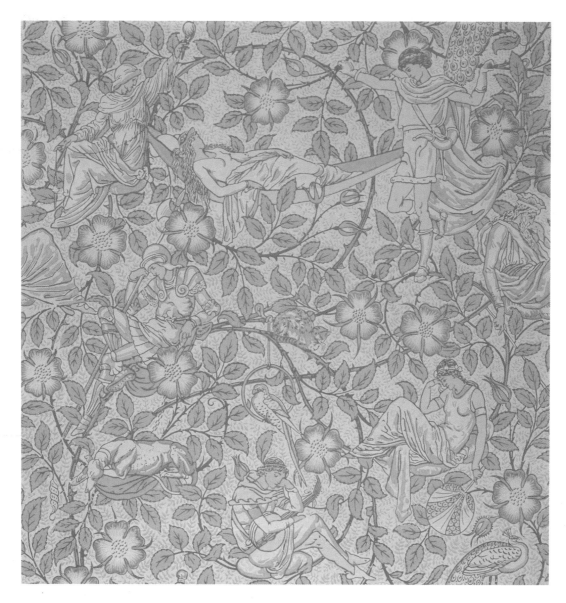

Plate 233
WALTER CRANE (1845–1915)
"Sleeping Beauty," 1879.
Wallpaper, machine printed, Jeffrey and Co. By courtesy of the
Board of Trustees of the Victoria and Albert Museum, London.

encircled with foliage or flowers. Because she needed the money, Greenaway allowed her *Almanac* drawings to be issued by David Walker and Co. in both filling and frieze, known as "The Months" and "The Seasons" (plate 234). She was pleased with the high quality of the wallpaper, which today seems remarkable for its pervading quality of gentleness, perhaps because of the soft colors of the costumes, its aura of childhood goodness and delight (some might say docility), and the affection pictured between child and adult.

The book illustrations of Randolph Caldecott were also made into a nursery wallpaper, similar in design to Greenaway's with spaced vignettes of figures but no dividing foliage (plate 235). The sportive illustrations were taken directly from the Caldecott *Picture Books,* their merry scenes of English country life accompanied by traditional nursery rhymes. The wallpaper was produced in circa 1900 by Allan Cockshut and Co. and was much loved.

Neither Greenaway nor Caldecott themselves coped with

Plate 234
KATE GREENAWAY (1846–1901)
"The Months," 1893.
Wallpaper, machine printed, David Walker and Co. The frieze
of this wallpaper is entitled "The Seasons." The Whitworth
Art Gallery, University of Manchester, England.

the problems of designing wallpaper; instead, they simply allowed their book illustrations to be purchased for that use. Like Walter Crane, however, two other children's book artists themselves attacked this rather demanding art form. Beatrix Potter's letters to her publisher Norman Warne in 1904–5 describe her chagrin when an acquaintance approached her with Potter's own drawings redrawn and made into a wallpaper frieze, which the acquaintance proposed to market. "The idea of rooms with badly drawn rabbits is appalling,"[5] Potter grumbled good-naturedly in her letter, and set about making a wallpaper herself—taking, as she put it humorously, "possession of the field."[6] However, in a subsequent letter she admitted: "The wallpapers proved a heavy job," especially the "piecing together." Nevertheless, "they are less frightful than might have been expected, and Mr. McGregor is magnificent on the frieze." She further explained: "We have done them flat, like stencil colors." By then she was beginning to feel that this might not be her field after all: "I feel as if I should like to persevere and get *one* printed though I certainly don't intend to go into that line of business."[7] Sandersons eventually offered ten pounds (which she thought was too little) for her Benjamin Bunny

Plate 235   *Opposite*
RANDOLPH CALDECOTT (1846–1886)
Wallpaper, adapted by J. Cheetham Cockshut, machine printed, Allan, Cockshut and Co., c. 1900. From his *Nursery Books.* By courtesy of the Board of Trustees of the Victoria and Albert Museum, London.

Plate 236
EDMUND DULAC (1882–1953)
Nursery wallpaper drawing; for the Central Institute of Art and Design, London, 1945. Collection of Colin White.

wallpaper, rejecting Peter Rabbit. She wrote her publisher: "If they were taking the Benjamin Bunny only and if that would preclude my offering Peter elsewhere, I think that would be a pity. Peter would be the one that would catch the public. The original Peter went all around the town before he found a publisher, but I should not like you to take all that trouble for the wallpapers."[8] She wrote more hopefully a bit later, "I wonder whether Liberty would care for that paper?"[9] Sadly, there is no record of Potter's selling her wallpaper designs of Benjamin Bunny and Peter Rabbit to a wallpaper firm, and her wallpaper drawings have not been identified among her papers. However, her book illustrations have been used in various wallpapers and friezes and are today perhaps the most famous and best-loved childhood images in the world.

Edmund Dulac, known for his splendid children's book illustrations, also tackled wallpaper. In 1923 he decorated the nursery of the Queen's Dollhouse at Windsor Castle with fairytale scenes on the miniature wallpapers. When he set about making a nursery wallpaper twenty years later, he proceeded with exacting study and care.[10] The result is stylized and flat, admirable traits in a wallpaper, but static. The nursery-rhyme children are dressed in circa 1945 clothes and the enclosing meandering flowers are streamlined (plate 236). This pattern was designed for an exhibition of wallpapers sponsored by the Central Institute of Art and Design, London, just after World War II. Wallpaper manufacturers had struggled through years of a paper shortage and were encouraging its use again. Many artists contributed to this show, among them Graham Sutherland (see plate 194) and children's book illustrator Mabel Lucie Attwell.

Attwell's most memorable children's wallpaper, however,

Plate 237
WILL OWEN (1869–1957)
"Bo Peep" and "Simple Simon," 1910.
Friezes, machine printed, Lightbown, Aspinall and Co.
By courtesy of the Board of Trustees of the Victoria and Albert Museum, London.

Plate 238
WILLIAM MORRIS (1834–1896)
"Brother Rabbit," 1881.
Chintz. William Morris Gallery, Walthamstow, London.

was designed in 1910 before she became famous for her cherubic illustrations of children in the Victorian novel *Water Babies* by Charles Kingsley. The wallpaper was a classic Mother Goose frieze with appealingly picturesque characters. By 1910 the wallpaper frieze had become a nursery staple. From the turn of the century illustrators John Hassall, Cecil Aldin, and somewhat later Will Owen designed simple, flat, stylized friezes in primary colors (plate 237); these were immensely popular for children's rooms, "as much a part of Edwardian households as potted ferns and antimacassars."[11] Nursery friezes had as their subjects Noah's Ark and its parade of animals, processions of people, as in the tale of "The Gingerbread Man," successions of dolls, toys, or the sweep of a seashore with its wide expanse of human activity. The fashion continued into the twenties, when Ernest Shepard's book illustrations of characters from *Winnie the Pooh* decorated a frieze (1929), which used the long space at the top of a wall effectively by depicting amid the vast sweeps of the North Pole the small figures from the Pooh books. Rocket men, jet planes, and racing cars, subjects for today's nursery wallpapers, seem light years rather than decades removed from these charming if archaic images.

Hassall's masterful wallpaper panels "Morning," "Noon,"

Plate 239
WILLIAM MORRIS (1834–1896)
"Trellis," designed 1862, produced 1864.
Wallpaper, block printed, Jeffrey and Co. Courtesy of Arthur
Sanderson and Sons, Ltd., Middlesex, England.

Plate 240   *Opposite*
WILLIAM MORRIS (1834–1896)
"Willow Boughs," c. 1887.
Wallpaper; *in situ,* the nursery at Stanway House, Stanway,
England. By kind permission of Stanway House.

and "Night," depicting these times of day in a child's life, were used in the nurseries of both the Dutch and Spanish royal families.[12] Art for children had become a serious matter: Crane remarked that the earlier, cheap children's "toy" books published before his own "were good for trade if bad for babies,"[13] and his own high-quality draftsmanship set a new standard for inexpensive books and wallpapers for the

young. The needs of children were not a preoccupation of society before the last half of the nineteenth century, and nursery wallpapers were virtually unknown. When such wallpapers were produced, it is not surprising that so many of them were done by illustrators of books for children. Not only was their work already familiar, but it was typically full of the fine details that children love to examine. Illustrators did not, however, have a monopoly on the field. From William Morris through the artists of the first half of the twentieth century, many of those already surveyed in this book designed wallpapers for children, or had their work used in children's rooms.

Morris himself, although devoted to his daughters (both born in the early 1860s), designed no wallpapers specifically for children. He did create a chintz, "Brother Rabbit" (1882; plate 238), when the family was reading the *Uncle Remus* stories by Joel Chandler Harris.[14] (Crane had recently designed his early children's wallpapers.) When Morris's daughter May remembered her childhood room in London, the wallpaper she recalled vividly was "Trellis" (plate 239), designed by Morris about 1862 when the family was still at Red House with its rose trellises in the garden. It is a pattern of wild roses on a solid and square-shaped trellis interspersed with birds and insects. Tradition credits Philip Webb, the architect of Red House, with the birds in this wallpaper, but May Morris disputed this, saying her father was perfectly capable of drawing birds. She later recalled: "In my Father's 'Trellis' there was a certain one of the birds who gave anxiety to a child in her cot high-up in the Queen Square house because he was thought to be wicked and very alive, but there were such interesting things going on behind that rose-trellis that one had not time to worry very much about him."[15] When she designed and embroidered bed hangings for Morris's great bed at Kelmscott Manor, she included a rose trellis for remembrance.

Many of Morris's wallpapers have been used in children's rooms. That perennial favorite, "Daisy" (see plate 36), must have often been found very appropriate, as would another favorite Morris pattern, "Willow Boughs." May Morris's room at Kelmscott Manor was decorated with this wallpaper, because of "the pleasant river scenes they recall."[16] The beautiful Cotswold house called Stanway has its nursery in the historic Morris "Willow" room (plate 240). At Standen, the Morris-decorated house in East Grinstead, Sussex, one

Plate 241
C.F.A. Voysey (1857–1941)
"Four and Twenty Blackbirds," c. 1925.
Design for nursery chintz. British Architectural
Library, Royal Institute of British Architects, London.

Plate 242   *Opposite*
Maurice Denis (1870–1943)
"Les Poussins," 1893.
Wallpaper design, gouache. Private collection,
Paris.

of the daughter's bedrooms is hung with Morris's charming "Powdered" wallpaper, with its delicate, many-colored flowers strewn on a miniaturized background of "Willow." It is unlikely that any of these wallpapers would offer an image "wicked and alive" to a child.

Like Morris, C.F.A. Voysey, the nineteenth-century architect and designer of many wallpapers, did not design children's wallpapers; Voysey did create several remarkable nursery chintzes. These were very animated in Voysey's droll way and, for the most part, child-centered. They include "Four and Twenty Blackbirds" (plate 241), "I Love Little Pussy," "Alice in Wonderland," and "Three Men of Gotham." Voysey's original sketch for "The House That Jack Built" was designed around a gigantic rat, removed in the final version. For his children's schoolroom in his home near London in 1898, Voysey used his own adult pattern "The Squire's Garden," a rather severe design of trellises, topiary trees, and peacocks.

In the 1890s Maurice Denis designed two wallpapers that may have been meant for children. The pattern of "Les Poussins" ("The Chicks") uses nursery colors of pink and yellow, and is composed of three small chicks facing each other against a tiny flower repeat (plate 242). The other pattern, "Les Fillettes" (see plate 88), is a design of small girls with joined hands, a motif that Denis repeated in 1912 in the oil painting *Au Paradis* (see plate 87).

Plate 243 *Opposite*
FRANZ VON ZÜLOW (1883–1963)
Cartoons for a wallpaper frieze, c. 1908; for the nursery, Palais
Stoclet, Brussels. Courtesy Franz-Joachim von Zülow.

Plate 244
JOSEPH MARIA OLBRICH (1867–1908)
Drawing for a nursery at Villa Friedmann, 1898. Staatliche
Museen Preussischer Kulturbesitz, Berlin.

The American Will Bradley composed a children's wallpaper for the 1896 "women's issue" of *Bradley: His Book,* his own magazine. He called this wallpaper "The Babies' Garden" and drew the linear design of cherubs' faces in green on white, their hair like foliage tying the pattern together.

At the turn of the century, Joseph Maria Olbrich designed a Secession nursery (1898; plate 244) for the Villa Friedmann outside Vienna, anticipating later Wiener Werkstätte interiors with hints of rectangular forms and plain surfaces. The concession to the sinuous lines of Art Nouveau in the nursery drawing is restrained. The Crane nursery wallpapers would have been too effusive here; indeed it would be hard to imagine the wallpapers of any of the nineteenth-century children's book illustrators in this room. Nevertheless the

room can be recognized as a child's room: the furniture is undersized, and the bold new look of the decoration of trees and meadows is done in a lively nursery style. As with so much of Austrian decorative art early in the century, this nursery has elements of Art Deco design.

The wallpapers designed by Wiener Werkstätte artists for children in the first decade of the twentieth century are dramatic and exciting, the motifs peasant-inspired. When Franz von Zülow's engaging, fragmented figures in a frieze for the Palais Stoclet nursery (plate 243) were rejected by the client, another member of the Werkstätte, Ludwig Heinrich Jungnickel, contributed the final designs in 1908, which were produced in a wallpaper. Entitled "Hochwald," this memorable design in deep colors is, magically, both lively and dignified. Used in a frieze, its drama would not have been overpowering, but today we might think the intensity of its figures frightening for very young children (plate 245).

The art of Paul Poiret's Maison Martine in Paris (see chapter 6) was frequently childlike but often urbane, as in one lively and fresh wallpaper of multicolored, decorated squares on a white background, for a simple white nursery enlivened with touches of bright blue. The wallpaper (c. 1925) in this case was restrained and even geometric.

There were other notable artists' wallpapers for nurseries in the Art Deco period. In the 1920s Jean-Emile Laboureur designed a bestiary wallpaper with rounded shapes for the animals and glowing color. In 1913 Vanessa Bell designed animal motifs for the display nursery of the Omega Workshop (plate 246), using large jagged shapes of painted and cut paper on walls and ceiling—the ceiling because, as she observed, that's the part of the room the baby looks at most.[17] P. G. Konody, writing about Bell's nursery in the *Observer,* commented waggishly: "It is—well, a landscape, expressed with some freedom. A blue, uneasy ribbon of colour is a range of mountains; a paler blue blob is a pond, and, unmistakably, on the stretch of yellow that may be sand, is the black silhouette of a huge mammoth elephant. . . .

Above on the roof a terrific sky is in progress, and what one takes to be a sunset is stuck on to the cornice. The whole room is gaudy with an effect like a piano-organ."[18] Bell's conception predates Matisse's paper cutouts; the dark, expressionistic, jagged shapes in this design, however, could seem threatening.

Architect Pierre Chareau designed a nursery with airplane wallpaper for the fourteenth Salon des Artistes Décorateurs in 1923 (plate 247). This wallpaper is quite surprising since it is an entire small aviation scene repeated block by block on the wall. The airplane, which must have been extremely interesting and topical for 1923 viewers, would likely have been more important than the art. Otherwise this nursery was sophisticated, with a puppet-show theater and a toy box and furniture all in wicker. Chareau's wallpapers were often designed by the painter Jean Lurçat, whose Dada wallpaper "Les Mazeraies" was shown in a young girl's bedroom in 1924 (see plates 155; 156). Another Lurçat wallpaper bears, among the leaves, birds, and musical staffs in the design, a message that must have delighted children: "Celui qui aime écrit sur les murs" ("One who loves writes on the walls"; see plate 154).

Emile-Jacques Ruhlmann's famous nursery, which

Plate 245

Ludwig Heinrich Jungnickel (1881–1965)

"Hochwald," 1908–9

Wallpaper; for the nursery, Palais Stoclet, Brussels.

Graphische Sammlung Albertina, Vienna.

Plate 246 *Top*
VANESSA BELL (1879–1961)
Nursery for the Omega Workshops, 1913.
Witt Library, Courtauld Institute of Art, London.

Plate 247 *Bottom*
PIERRE CHAREAU (1883–1950)
Nursery for the fourteenth Salon des Artistes Décorateurs,
Paris, 1923. Bibliothèque Forney, Paris.

Plate 248
EMILE-JACQUES RUHLMANN (1879–1933)
Nursery. From *Harmonies of Ruhlmann,*
edited by Jean Badovici (Paris, 1924).
Bibliothèque Forney, Paris.

Plate 249   *Opposite*
EMILE-JACQUES RUHLMANN (1879–1933),
Nursery wallpaper, c. 1920.
Musée des Arts Décoratifs, Paris.

appeared in Jean Badovici's pochoir volume *Harmonies of Ruhlmann* in 1924, is classic Art Deco (plate 248). Not for Ruhlmann a noisy or overlarge design. All is calm in this nursery; the wallpaper appears to be simply dotted. Ruhlmann did design one nursery wallpaper that was produced, of two child figures in a black line drawing enlivened with pale blue accents on a beige background (plate 249). The lines of the drawing, as often with Ruhlmann, are wavering and expressive, the colors serene and even elegant.

In the 1930s John Piper designed a children's frieze for the Curwen Press, a double scene of sea and shore that was too large for the press and was done elsewhere.[19] Titled "Nursery Frieze," it was lithographed in reds, blues, and black.

As artists and architects of the last half-century have frequently rejected both ornament and wallpaper, few major fine artists have created nursery wallpaper designs. However, some very familiar popular figures for children have often been printed on wallpaper. Among these important icons, almost totem beings, are Mickey Mouse, Snoopy, the Muppets, Paddington Bear, and many other worldwide

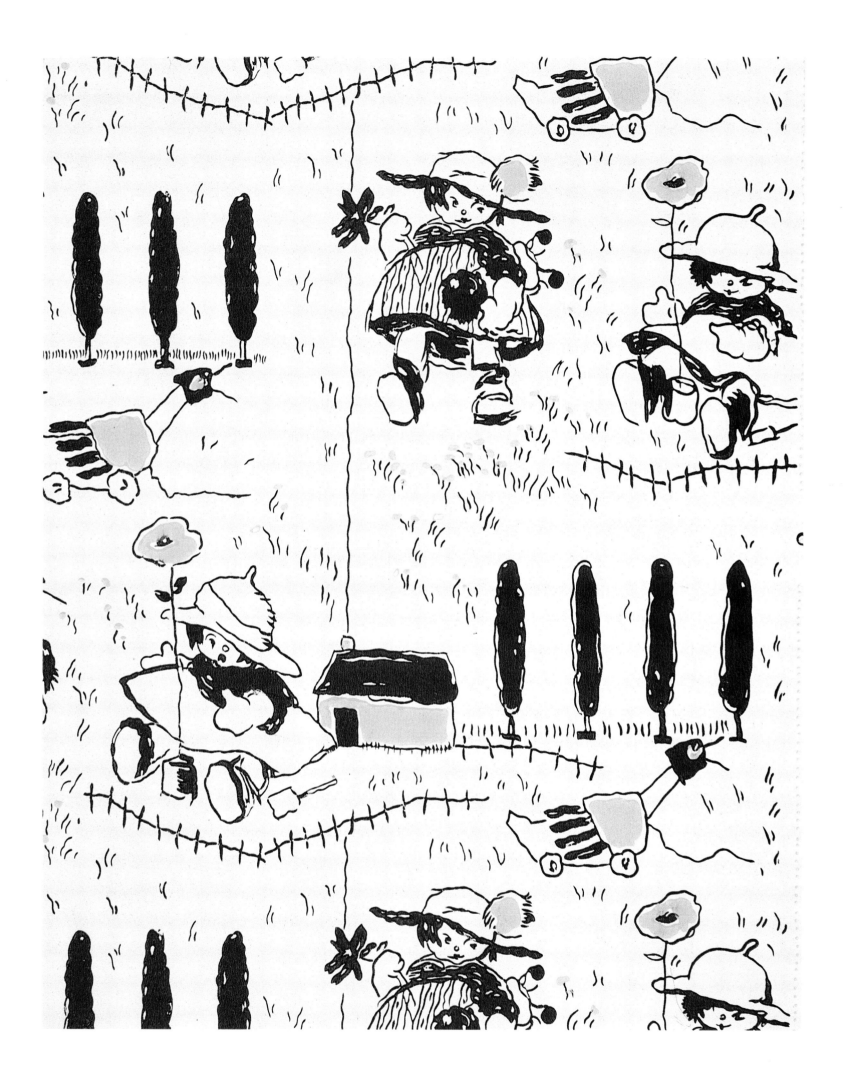

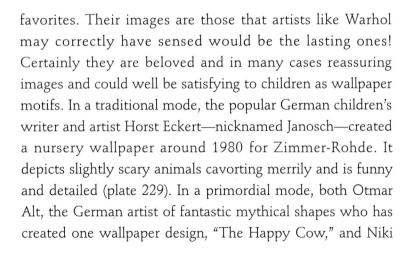

Plate 250
NIKI DE SAINT PHALLE (b. 1930)
"Nana," 1972.
Wallpaper. Marburger Tapetenfabrik, Kirchain, Germany.

Plate 251
OTMAR ALT (b. 1940)
"The Happy Cow," 1972.
Wallpaper, Marburger Tapetenfabrik. Marburger
Tapetenfabrik, Kirchain, Germany.

favorites. Their images are those that artists like Warhol may correctly have sensed would be the lasting ones! Certainly they are beloved and in many cases reassuring images and could well be satisfying to children as wallpaper motifs. In a traditional mode, the popular German children's writer and artist Horst Eckert—nicknamed Janosch—created a nursery wallpaper around 1980 for Zimmer-Rohde. It depicts slightly scary animals cavorting merrily and is funny and detailed (plate 229). In a primordial mode, both Otmar Alt, the German artist of fantastic mythical shapes who has created one wallpaper design, "The Happy Cow," and Niki

de Saint Phalle, the French painter and sculptor who has designed children's playgrounds and one wallpaper, "Nana," have somewhat the same massive forms and simple primary colors in both wallpapers and paintings (1972; plates 250; 251). Their wallpapers, made for the Marburger firm, may not have been intended for children, but more than one observer has watched very young children absorb this kind of image in a fascinated way. For the youngest children, these two late-twentieth-century artists' wallpapers may be curiously right.

APPENDIX B: ARTISTS' WALLPAPERS
A Guide to Manufacturers and Shops

The following is a sampling of manufacturers and shops where wallpaper designs by major artists may be obtained. In most cases, the sublistings are of wallpapers rather than fabrics. They are handprints unless noted. Handprints are likely to stay in the line of a manufacturer for years. They are, however, much more expensive than machine prints, which are more ephemeral. Nevertheless, machine prints of artists' wallpapers do become available from time to time. Because the complete list of each manufacturer or shop changes from year to year, one should always inquire about the current list and ask for major artists' designs that may be included. In some cases such patterns may be obtained only through decorators.

ArtCodif Boutique
Musée des Arts Décoratifs
Palais du Louvre
107 rue de Rivoli
Paris 75001, France

Prelle et Cie.: Réveillon designs, circa 1790, in toile.

Artcurial
9 avenue Matignon
Paris 75008, France

Sonia Delaunay: "Ulysses" and "Jazz," circa 1930, wall linens.

Laura Ashley
New York and London

From the Bloomsbury series:
Vanessa Bell: "The Waves," circa 1940, machine-printed wallpaper.
Vanessa Bell and Duncan Grant: "Charleston Grapes" and "Charleston Border," 1932, in linen union; from the Omega decoration of the Lefevre Gallery, London.
Duncan Grant: "West Wind," 1931, in linen union.
Owen Jones: "Dandelion," "Albert," "Mr. Jones," and "Palmetto," machine printed; "Swinburne" and "Byron," wallpaper borders.

Joh. Backhausen & Sohne GmbH
Karntner Strasse 33
A-1010 Vienna, Austria
Josef Hoffmann: "Kunstschau," "Paradies," "Harlekin," "Zick-Zack," and many other original textile designs.

Alexander Beauchamp
One Church Street
Douglas, Isle of Man, U.K.

Archibald Knox: "Magnolia," "Tea Rose," "Rosy Buds," and "Corn," all circa 1900; extradordinary Celtic Art Nouveau.
Many seventeenth-century wallpapers.

Celia Birtwell
71 Westbourne Park Road
London W2 5QH, England

David Hockney: "Green Punchinellos," circa 1980, cotton fabric; can be used on walls.

Boussac of France, Inc.
D.&D. Building, 979 Third Avenue
New York, New York 10022

Raoul Dufy: "Les Ecailles," "L'Exotique," and "La Chasse," all circa 1928, wall toiles.

Bradbury and Bradbury
P.O. Box 155
Benicia, California 94510

Walter Crane: "Deer and Rabbit Frieze," circa 1890.
William Morris: "Marigold," "Bird and Anemone," "Willow," all circa 1875.

Brunschwig et Fils
D.&D. Building, 979 Third Avenue
New York, New York 10022

Raoul Dufy: "La Peche," circa 1928, wall toile.

The Royal Pavilion, Brighton, Collection:
"Royal Dolphin," "Pavilion Fret," "Royal Glade."

Coles of Mortimer Street
18 Mortimer Street
London W1, England

Coles's remarkable handprints are from the famous John Perry firm in London.

The Bardfield Collection: the wallpapers of Edward Bawden and fellow artist John Aldridge, available in handprint.
Edward Bawden: "Stone Ivy," circa 1938–50, Art Deco faux stone design; "Flute," early 1950s, used in the Royal Box, Royal Festival Hall, London; "Swan and Grass," circa 1938, with freshness of the earlier Curwen Press wallpapers by Bawden.

John Aldridge: "Lace" and "Moss"; although designed circa 1938, have a postmodern look.

From Coles's Victoria and Albert Museum series:
"Chinese Trellis" and "Regency Bamboo," both circa 1820; bamboo patterns from the Brighton Pavilion.
"Shepherd and Sheep," circa 1850; Print Room design from Doddington Hall.
A.W.N. Pugin: "Scarisbrick," "Lough Cutra," "Tudor Rose and Fleur-de-Lis," "Crace Diaper," and "Golden Lily," all circa 1850; designed for Scarisbrick and Lough Cutra castles, and for the Houses of Parliament.
Cecil Beaton: "Love Birds" and "Great Poppy," circa 1965; wallpapers from *My Fair Lady*, variations of C.F.A. Voysey designs.
"Owen Jones," mid-1800s; small foliate design.
"Besford Court," circa 1570; Elizabethan design.
Graham Sutherland: "Abstract OXO," circa 1950; a playful "design for the small home."

Crown Publishers
Belgrave Mills
Belgrave Mills Road
Darwen, Lancashire BB3 2RR, England

Beatrix Potter: "Nursery Tales," machine-printed wallpaper.

A. L. Diament and Co.
P.O. Box 230
309 Commerce Drive
Exton, Pennsylvania 19341

Many French scenic wallpapers, in reproduction by silk screen, reprinted from original blocks, or original papers.
Handpainted Chinese papers.

Dragons of Walton Street, Ltd.
23 Walton Street
London SW3, England

Beatrix Potter: "Nursery Frieze."

Eco Tapeter AB
S-570
23 Anneberg, Sweden

Carl Larsson: "Nursery Frieze," circa 1910; machine printed; can best be used with plain white wallpaper. This ribbon bow design is in a Larsson painting.

MARIANO FORTUNY, INC.
509 Madison Avenue
New York, New York 10022

Many elegant, inimitable cotton wallcoverings from this artist, including "Orsini," "Fragonard," "Boucher," and "Murillo."

IDEAL DECOR USA, INC.
69 Bloomingdale Road
Hicksville, New York 11801

A blue sky, white cloud wallpaper reminiscent of Magritte.
A Mucha champagne poster as a wallpaper panel.

KATZENBACH AND WARREN
950 Third Avenue
New York, New York 10022

"Mandarin and Pine Tree," circa 1700; early folk design.
"Charles II," circa 1690; early block print.

MAISON MAUNY
25 bis rue Franklin
Paris 75016, France

George Barbier: "Parrots and Peonies," "Oranges."
Jean-Emile Laboureur: "Raspberries, Thorns and Bees," "Strawberries and Snails," "Bouquet de Mariée," "Carnation," "Le Marin," "Bestiary."
Marie Laurencin: "Apollinaire," "Les Singes."
Charles Martin: "Angel in Cage."
All are brilliant Art Deco designs, circa 1930.

MARBURGER TAPETENFABRIK GMBH
D-3575 Kirchain 1, Germany

From the remarkable X-Art Walls collection of contemporary artists' designs, 1972:
Otmar Alt: "Happy Cow."
Getulio Alviani: "Testura Graphica."
Werner Berges: "Beauty."
Allen Jones: "Right Hand Lady."
Peter Philips: "Kenya."
Niki de Saint Phalle: "Nana."
Jean Tinguely: "Vive la Liberté."
Paul Wunderlich: "Faltenwurf."

JOHN OLIVER, LTD.
33 Pembridge Road
London W11 3HG, England

C.F.A. Voysey: "Fool's Parsley," circa 1900, titled here "Lovebirds."

PIERRE DEUX
870 Madison Avenue
New York, New York 10021

Jean-Baptiste Huet: "Fragonard" and "Lafayette," circa 1790.
Jean-Baptiste Greuze: "Le Couronnement de la Rosière," circa 1725.
These are classic toiles de Jouy, traditionally used on walls.

GEBRUDER RASCH TAPETENFABRIK
Postfach 120
4550 Bramsche, Germany

Walter Gropius: three wallpaper designs, circa 1928.
Many Bauhaus designs, circa 1930, are available.

ARTHUR SANDERSON AND SONS, LTD.
52 Berners Street
London W1P 3AD, England

William Morris: Sanderson's handprints superbly many William Morris patterns, including "Daisy," "Trellis," "Fruit," "Larkspur," "Bachelor's Button," "Chrysanthemum," "Willow Boughs," and "Sunflower." Many machine prints of Morris designs are also available.
C.F.A. Voysey: "Rowan," "The Allerton," "Ilmore," "Lerena," "Fool's Parsley," and "Tulip and Bird," all circa 1890–1900.
Walter Crane: "The Orange Tree," 1907.

SCALAMANDRÉ
950 Third Avenue
New York, New York 10022

William Morris: "Pimpernel," "Wallflower," "Myrtle," "Morris Iris," "Borage," and "Morris Ceiling," all circa 1875–90; "Brother Rabbit," circa 1882, is available as a chintz for wall hanging in the Morris style, as is "Daffodil," circa 1891.

F. SCHUMACHER & CO.
939 Third Avenue
New York, New York 10022

Frank Lloyd Wright: "Design 102," circa 1950; "Imperial Peacock," "Stained Glass Mosaic," "Coonley Playhouse," "Ennis Block," "Geometric," circa 1930, designs adapted for wallpaper, machine printed.

TEKKO AND SALUBRA
18 Newman Street
London W1P 4AB, England

Distinctive wallpapers in the styles of Chippendale, Sheraton, and Adams.
"Styles Nobles," circa 1760, machine printed.

THE TWIGS
5700 Third Avenue
San Francisco, California 94124

"Monuments of Paris," circa 1815; a faithful reproduction of the original.

WARNER'S AND SONS, LTD.
7 Noel Street
London W1, England

Howard Hodgkin: "Water," circa 1984, wall fabric; has not been in production recently.

WATERHOUSE WALLHANGINGS
38 Wareham Street
Boston, Massachusetts 02118

"Lady Pepperell House," circa 1750, Print Room design.

WATTS AND CO.
7 Tufton Street
London SW1, England
(United States address: Christopher Hyland, D.&D. Building, Suite 1708, 979 Third Avenue, New York, New York 10022)

A.W.N. Pugin: "Shrewsbury," "Rose and Coronet," "Trellis," "Pineapple," "Tudor Rose and Fleur-de-Lis."
G. F. Bodley: chinoiserie "Bird," Morris-influenced "Bamboo Jasmine," Art Nouveau "Sunflower," all circa 1870.
Anonymous: "The Pear," circa 1735; large-scale flock design formerly in the Queen's Drawing Room, Hampton Court.

KURT WEBER GMBH
Gutenbergstrasse 2
2803 Weyhe, Germany

Albrecht Dürer: "The Satyr Family," circa 1500; this very early wallpaper is beautifully printed as a large poster.

ZIMMER-ROHDE GMBH, CoKG
Zimmersmuhlenweg 14-18
Postfach 1245
6370 Oberursel, Germany

German artist Horst Eckert, or "Janosch": "Zirkus," circa 1980, machine printed, nursery design.

ZOFFANY, LTD.
27a Motcomb Street
London SW1, England

Red flock 18th-century small diaper pattern from Temple Newsam.
"Reveillon," circa 1790.
"Chintz," circa 1868, chinoiserie wall hanging from Temple Newsam.
"Owen Jones."
"Dufour," circa 1804, grisaille.

Preface, *pages 8–11*

1. "I remember the wallpaper in my bedroom in Paris when I was five—those giraffes!" George Plimpton, May 1987, U.S. Public Television.
2. Marcel Proust, *Le Côté de Guermantes* (1921), in *Remembrance of Things Past;* quoted in E.A. Entwisle, *Literary History of Wallpaper* (London: B.T. Batsford, 1960), 8.
3. *Building News,* 20 February 1885, 279.
4. Fyodor Dostoyevsky, *Crime and Punishment;* quoted in Françoise Teynac, Pierre Nolot, and Jean-Denis Vivien, *Wallpaper: A History* (New York: Rizzoli, 1982), 198.
5. Guy de Maupassant, *Bel Ami, The Wolf and Other Stories* (New York: Thompson-Barlow, 1923), 35.
6. John Updike, *Just Looking* (New York: Alfred A. Knopf, 1989), 115.
7. John Peter, "How to Wrap an Opera in Musical Wallpaper," *London Sunday Times,* 23 April 1989, Arts section.
8. Henry Miller, *Tropic of Cancer* (New York: Grove Press, 1961), 165.
9. "Le papier peint à l'état embryonnaire est encore plus fait que cette marine-là!" Louis Leroy, "L'Exposition des impressionistes," *Le Charivari,* 25 April 1874; quoted in Steven Z. Levine, *Monet and His Critics* (New York: Garland, 1976), 16.
10. Charlotte Perkins Gilman, *The Yellow Wallpaper* (Old Westbury, N.Y.: Feminist Press, 1973), 13.

12. Quoted in Robert Goldwater, *Paul Gauguin* (New York: Harry N. Abrams, 1957), 44.
13. See Denise Domergue, *Artists Design Furniture* (New York: Harry N. Abrams, 1984).
14. E.H. Gombrich, *The Sense of Order* (Ithaca, N.Y.: Cornell University Press, 1979), 208.
15. William Morris, "Some Hints on Pattern-Designing," *Collected Works,* 22:191.
16. Ibid., 179.

ONE From Dürer to Rowlandson, *pages 13–29*

1. Horst Appuhn and Christian von Heusinger, *Riesenholzschnitte und Papiertapeten der Renaissance* (Unterschneidheim, Germany: Verlag Dr. Alfons Uhl, 1976).
2. See Lynn Frier Kaufman, *The Noble Savage:*

Satyrs and Satyr Families in Renaissance Art (Ann Arbor, Mich.: UMI Research Press, 1984).
3. See Christian von Heusinger, "Ein neuentidecktes Exemplar der Dürertapete auf schwarzen Grund," *Jahrbuch der Berliner Museen* 25 (1983): 143–59.
4. Christian von Heusinger, interview with author, London, 6 October 1988.
5. Janey S. Byrne, *Renaissance Ornament Prints and Drawings* (New York: Metropolitan Museum of Art, 1981), 26.
6. Ibid., 26–27.
7. Von Heusinger, "Ein neuentidecktes Exemplar," 150.
8. The pomegranate portraits are dated 1519 and were painted after the emperor's death. One is in Vienna at the Kunsthistorisches Museum, the other in Nuremberg at the Germanisches National-almuseum.
9. Christian von Heusinger, "Ornamente und Tapeten von Dürer, Beham, Altdorfer und Jörg Seld," in Appuhn and von Heusinger, *Reisenholzschnitte,* 22–23.
10. Erwin Panofsky, *The Life and Art of Albrecht Dürer* (Princeton, N.J.: Princeton University Press, 1955), 179. Seven hundred copies of the *Triumphal Arch* have been identified as being produced. See Larry Silver, "Prints for a Prince: Maximilian, Nuremberg, and the Woodcut," in *New Perspectives on the Art of Renaissance Nuremberg,* ed. Jeffrey Chipps Smith (Austin, Tex.: Huntington Art Gallery, University of Texas, 1985), 13 n. 27.
11. William Martin Conway, *Literary Remains of Albrecht Dürer . . . with Transcripts from the British Museum Manuscripts* (Cambridge: Cambridge University Press, 1889), 89–91.
12. The Altdorfer section of the frieze showing laurel crowns can be seen in Jacqueline Guillaud and Maurice Guillaud, *Altdorfer and Fantastic Realism in German Art* (Paris: Guillaud Editions; Rizzoli, 1985), plates 175–86.
13. Lewis W. Spitz, *The Protestant Reformation, 1517–1559* (New York: Harper and Row, 1985), 149. See also Heinrich Wölfflin, *The Art of Albrecht Dürer,* trans. Alastair Grieve and Heide Grieve (London: Phaidon Press, 1971), 31; Walter L. Strauss, *The German Single-Leaf Woodcut, 1550–1600* (New York: Abaris Books, 1975) 1:149.
14. From Dürer's *Third Book on Human Proportions* (1528); quoted in Conway, *Literary Remains of Albrecht Dürer,* 243.

15. See John Fowler and John Cornforth, *English Decoration in the Eighteenth Century* (Princeton, N.J.: Pyne Press, 1974), 136–39.
16. Jacques Savary des Bruslons, *Dictionnaire universel du commerce* (Geneva, 1723); quoted in Francoise Teynac, Pierre Nolot, and Jean-Denis Vivien, *Wallpaper: A History* (New York: Rizzoli, 1982), 22.
17. Jean-Michel Papillon, *Traité historique et pratique de la gravure en bois* (Paris, 1766).
18. Thomas Sheraton, *The Cabinet-Maker and Upholsterer's Drawing-Book,* 3d ed. (London: T. Bensley, 1802), plate 4.
19. Horace Walpole, *Strawberry Hill Accounts,* ed. Paget Toynbee (Oxford: Clarendon Press, 1927), 60–61.
20. See *Sayer and Bennett's Catalogue of Prints for 1775* (London: Holland Press, 1970), 110.
21. Jackson, J.B., *An Essay on the Invention of Engraving and Printing in Chiaro Oscuro as practised by Albert Durer, Hugo di Carpia, and the Application of it to the making of Paper Hangings of Taste, Duration and Elegance. By Mr. Jackson of Battersea* (London, 1754); quoted in Charles C. Oman and Jean Hamilton, *Wallpapers* (London: Sotheby Publications and the Victoria and Albert Museum, 1982), 24.
22. Quoted in A.V. Sugden and J.L. Edmondson, *A History of English Wallpaper* (New York: Charles Scribner's Sons, 1926), 49–50.
23. Susan Lambert, ed., *Pattern and Design* (London: Victoria and Albert Museum, 1983), 64–66.
24. Joseph Grego, *Rowlandson the Caricaturist* (London: Chatto and Windus, 1880), 1:94.
25. Ibid.
26. Ronald Paulson, *Rowlandson: A New Interpretation* (London: Studio Vista, 1972), 15.
27. See A. Paul Oppe, *Thomas Rowlandson, His Drawings and Watercolours* (London: The Studio, 1923), 7.
28. Rowlandson's inscription on a drawing in the Widener collection, Harvard University, reads: "It holds good through the whole scale of the creation / That the great and the little have need of one another." See John Riely, *Rowlandson Drawings from the Paul Mellon Collection* (New Haven: Yale Center for British Art, 1977), xxii.
29. Paulson, *Rowlandson,* 65.

TWO Before William Morris, *pages 31–49*

1. Françoise Teynac, Pierre Nolot, and Jean-Denis Vivien, *Wallpaper: A History* (New York: Rizzoli,

1982), 112–13, 117. See also Nancy McClelland, *Historic Wall-papers* (Philadelphia: J.B. Lippincott, 1924), for a translation of Dufour's booklet.

2. Quoted in E.A. Entwisle, *French Scenic Wallpapers* (Leigh-on-Sea, England: Frank Lewis, 1972), 48.

3. George Leland Hunter, *Decorative Textiles* (Philadelphia: J.B. Lippincott, 1918), 362.

4. See Entwisle, *French Scenic Wallpapers,* 48. Balzac believed that the banquet scene was from the "Telemachus" wallpapers; however, this particular section was from the scenic series "Antenor." See Teynac, Nolot, and Vivien, *Wallpaper,* 167.

5. John James Audubon to his wife, 22 September 1834, in *Letters of John James Audubon, 1826–1840,* ed. Howard Corning (Boston: Club of Odd Volumes, 1930), 46. See also Christopher Gilbert, "Lady Hertford, John James Audubon and the Chinese Drawing Room at Temple Newsam," *Leeds Art Calendar* 61 (1968): 14–17; Anthony Wells-Cole, *Historic Paper Hangings from Temple Newsam* (Leeds, England: City Art Galleries, 1983), 15.

6. From the Crace Ledgers, Royal Pavilion Archives, Brighton, England. See John Morley, *The Making of the Royal Pavilion, Brighton* (Boston: David R. Godine, 1984), 88.

7. Robert Blake, ed., *The English World* (London: Thames and Hudson, 1982), 188.

8. Benjamin Ferrey, *Recollections of A.N. Welby Pugin and His Father, Augustus Pugin* (London: Edward Stanford, 1861), 187.

9. A.W.N. Pugin to J.G. Crace, 10 October 1851 (with sketch in margin); Crace MSS PUG 8/55, British Architectural Library of the Royal Institute of British Architects, London. See Alexandra Wedgwood, *A.W.N. Pugin and the Pugin Family* (London: Victoria and Albert Museum, 1985), 280.

10. Quoted in M. Trappes-Lomax, *Pugin, a Medieval Victorian* (London: Sheed and Ward, 1932), 28.

11. Trappes-Lomax, *Pugin,* 50, 280.

12. A.W.N. Pugin, *True Principles of Pointed or Christian Architecture* (1841; reprint, New York: St. Martin's Press, 1973), 1.

13. Ibid., 29.

14. Quoted in J. Mordaunt Crook, *William Burges and the High Victorian Dream* (Chicago: University of Chicago Press, 1981), 22.

15. Crook, *William Burges,* 22.

16. Brenda Greysmith, *Wallpaper* (New York: Macmillan, 1976), 140.

17. Crook, *William Burges,* 294 and 406, n. 3.

18. *Building News,* 11 October 1872, 291.

19. Owen Jones, *The Grammar of Ornament* (London: Bernard Quaritch, 1868), 5.

20. Jones, *Grammar* (1868), 2. See also Patrick Conner, *The Inspiration of Egypt* (Brighton, England: Brighton Museums, 1983), 98.

21. *Builder,* 9 May 1874, 385.

22. Owen Jones and Joseph Bonomi, *Description of the Egyptian Court* (1854), 13; quoted in Conner,

Inspiration of Egypt, 93.

23. Jones, *Grammar* (1868), 24–25.

24. Jones, *Grammar* (1868), 5.

25. Owen Jones, "Color in the Decorative Arts," in *On the Manufacture of Glass,* ed. George Shaw (1852), 286.

26. Jones, *Grammar* (1868), 7.

27. "No one can forget the harmony . . . of the three primary colors . . . distributed and balanced over that sea of glass and light without a tawdry effect." See *Building News,* 24 April 1874, 440.

THREE William Morris and His Followers,
pages 51–85

1. William Morris, "The Lesser Arts of Life," in *Collected Works of William Morris,* ed. May Morris (New York: Russell and Russell, 1966), 22:260.

2. W.R. Lethaby, *Philip Webb and His Work* (Oxford: Oxford University Press, 1935), 94.

3. Robin Spencer, *The Aesthetic Movement* (London: Studio Vista; New York: E.P. Dutton, 1972), 7.

4. See Peter Floud, "The Wallpaper Designs of William Morris," *Penrose Annual* 54 (1960): 44.

5. Joanna Banham, *A Decorative Art* (Manchester, England: Whitworth Art Gallery, 1985), 51.

6. William Morris to Thomas Wardle, 1 August 1876, in *Collected Letters of William Morris,* ed. Norman Kelvin (Princeton, N.J.: Princeton University Press, 1984), 1:311. See also "Sixty Letters from William Morris to Thomas Wardle on Dyeing and Printing, 1875–77," typescript in National Art Library, Victoria and Albert Museum, London.

7. Morris, "Some Hints on Pattern Designing," in *Collected Works,* 22:199.

8. William Morris, "Making the Best of It," in *Collected Works,* 22:109.

9. William Morris, "Textiles," in *Arts and Crafts Essays* (New York: Charles Scribner's Sons, 1893; facsimile edition, New York: Garland, 1977), 37.

10. Sambourne cartoons can be seen in Elizabeth Aslin, *The Aesthetic Movement* (New York: Frederick A. Praeger, 1969), plates 68, 114.

11. See Charles Mitchell, "William Morris at St. James Palace," *Architectural Review* 101 (January 1947): 37–39; reprinted by the William Morris Society, 18 June 1960.

12. E.A. Entwisle, *A Literary History of Wallpaper* (London: B.T. Batsford, 1960), 132.

13. William Morris, "Some Hints on Pattern-Designing," *Collected Works,* 22:177–78.

14. Morris, "Making the Best of It," *Collected Works,* 22:109.

15. Morris, "Some Hints on Pattern-Designing," *Collected Works,* 22:186.

16. Georgiana Burne-Jones, *Memorials of Burne-Jones* (London: Macmillan and Co., 1904), 2:196.

17. William Waters and Martin Harrison, *Burne-*

Jones (New York: Putnam, 1973), 136. Waters and Harrison give the year for this collaboration as circa 1880. Georgiana Burne-Jones describes for the year 1889 the advent of the Merry Mermaid, a tavern room addition to their house at Rottingdean, but does not mention a wallpaper. See Burne-Jones, *Memorials of Burne-Jones,* 2:196–97.

18. *Letters of Dante Gabriel Rossetti to William Allingham,* ed. G.B. Hill (London: T. Fisher Unwin, 1897), 251. An example of the "crown" effect can be seen in "Tropical," a wallpaper of 1895 by English architect M. H. Baillie Scott. See James D. Kornwolf, *M. H. Baillie Scott and the Arts and Crafts Movement* (Baltimore and London: Johns Hopkins Press, 1972), 129–30.

19. Rossetti's Blake Notebook, now at the British Museum, is also known as the Rossetti manuscript. See Whitworth Art Gallery, *British Sources of Art Nouveau* (Manchester, England: Whitworth Art Gallery, 1969), 8.

20. *Building News* 36 (1879): 198.

21. See Rodney K. Engen, *Walter Crane as a Book Illustrator* (New York: St. Martin's Press, 1975), 13.

22. Walter Crane, *William Morris to Whistler* (London: G. Bell and Sons, 1911), 232.

23. George Leland Hunter, *Decorative Textiles* (Philadelphia: J.B. Lippincott, 1918), 375.

24. Metford Warner, "History of Paperhangings" (1896), lecture to Art Workers' Guild, British Architectural Library of the Royal Institute of British Architects, London.

25. *Magazine of Art* 2 (1904): 211.

26. Nikolaus Pevsner, *Pioneers of Modern Design* (Harmondsworth, England: Penguin, 1964), 148.

27. "An Interview with Mr. Charles F. Annesley Voysey, Architect and Designer," *Studio* 1 (September 1893): 233.

28. *British Architect* 73 (4 March 1910): 160; quoted in Duncan Simpson, *C.F.A. Voysey, an Architect of Individuality* (New York: Watson-Guptill, 1981), 17.

29. C.F.A. Voysey, "Ideas in Things," in *The Arts Connected with Building* (London: B.T. Batsford, 1909), 115, 130; quoted in Simpson, *C.F.A. Voysey,* 119, 127.

30. Voysey, "Ideas in Things," 120; quoted in Simpson, *C.F.A. Voysey,* 120.

31. C.F.A. Voysey, "Aims and Conditions of the Modern Decorator" (lecture), *Journal of Decorative Arts* 15 (April 1895): 88.

32. Margaret Richardson, "Wallpapers by C.F.A. Voysey, 1857–1941," *Journal of the Royal Institute of British Architects* 72 (1965): 403.

33. Simpson, *C.F.A. Voysey,* 146.

34. Manifesto of the first issue of the *Hobby Horse,* 1884.

35. James A. McNeill Whistler, *The Gentle Art of Making Enemies* (London: Heinemann, 1892; reprint, New York: Dover Publications, 1967), 143.

36. Hilary Taylor, *James McNeill Whistler* (London:

Studio Vista, 1978), 90.

37. The original leather wallpaper can still be seen under Whistler's paint in the Peacock Room, Freer Gallery, Washington, D.C.

38. John Ruskin, "Burne-Jones," *Fors Clavigera* (2 July 1877). See Robert L. Herbert, *Art Criticism of John Ruskin* (New York: Doubleday, 1964), 407.

39. Whistler (quoting Tom Taylor, art critic of *Punch*), *Gentle Art of Making Enemies,* 18.

40. Max Beerbohm, "1880" (essay); quoted in J. Mordaunt Crook, *William Burges and the High Victorian Dream* (Chicago: University of Chicago Press, 1981), 90, 360 n. 71.

41. Elizabeth Aslin, *E.W. Godwin, Furniture and Interior Decoration* (London: John Murray, 1986), 16.

42. Brenda Greysmith, *Wallpaper* (New York: Macmillan, 1976), 141.

43. Whistler, *Gentle Art of Making Enemies,* 136.

FOUR The Art Nouveau Style, *pages 87–113*

1. Robert Schmutzler, *Art Nouveau* (New York: Harry N. Abrams, 1962), 7.

2. Nikolaus Pevsner, *Pioneers of Modern Design* (Harmondsworth, England: Penguin, 1964), 90.

3. Hector Guimard, *Le Castel Béranger* (Paris: Rouam, 1898).

4. See Peter Selz, "Introduction," in *Art Nouveau,* ed. Peter Selz and Mildred Constantine (New York: Museum of Modern Art, 1959), 10–11.

5. Owen Jones, *The Grammar of Ornament,* proposition 36 (London: Day and Son, 1856).

6. Eugène-Emmanuel Viollet-le-Duc, *Histoire d'une maison* (Paris: J. Hetzel, 1873), 228–29.

7. Eugène-Emmanuel Viollet-le-Duc, *Discourses on Architecture,* vol. 2 (Boston: James R. Osgood & Co., 1875).

8. Stuart Durant, *Ornament* (Woodstock, N.Y.: Overlook Press, 1986), 28.

9. Quoted in Elizabeth Aslin, *The Aesthetic Movement* (New York: Frederick A. Praeger, 1969), 177.

10. Henry van de Velde, "Artistic Wallpapers," *L'Art moderne* 13 (1893): 193–95; van de Velde, "Essex and Co.'s Westminster Wallpapers," *L'Art moderne* 14 (1894): 254–55.

11. S. Tschudi Madsen, *Art Nouveau* (New York: McGraw-Hill, 1970), 54.

12. See Susan Canning, *A History and Critical Review of the Salons of Les XX, 1884–93,* Ph.D. Diss., Pennsylvania State University (Ann Arbor, Mich.: University Microfilms, 1980), 174–75.

13. Francoise Dierkens, conservator of the Musée Horta, Brussels, to author, 20 July 1988. All data on Horta wallpapers (except for information on the Solvay House) is from the Musée Horta.

14. L. Wittamer–De Camps, Solvay House, Brussels, to author, 29 July 1988.

15. The office of the Tassel House is now wallpa-

pered with Voysey's "Tokyo." This famous pattern was adapted when the photographer and stage designer Cecil Beaton was designing wallpapers for *My Fair Lady.* Beaton called his own version "Great Poppy." Another, of lovebirds, was inspired by Voysey's bird designs. I am indebted to Dennis Hall, of John Perry Co., London, for the information on Beaton's wallpapers.

16. Robert Koch, "Introduction," in Samuel Bing, *Artistic America: Tiffany Glass and Art Nouveau* (Cambridge, Mass.: MIT Press, 1970), 4–5.

17. Samuel Bing, *Artistic Japan* (May 1888), 6; quoted in Robert Koch, *Louis C. Tiffany, Rebel in Glass* (New York: Crown, 1964), 73.

18. Samuel Bing, "L'Art Nouveau," *Craftsman* 5 (5 October 1903): 1. Reprint in Bing, *Artistic America,* 227–50.

19. Jan Verkade, *Le Tourment de Dieu* (Paris: Librairie de l'Art Catholique, 1923), 94; quoted in Selz, "Painting and Sculpture, Prints and Drawings," in *Art Nouveau,* ed. Selz and Constantine, 55.

20. Victor Arwas, *Berthon and Grasset* (New York: Rizzoli, 1978), 20.

21. Maurice Denis, *Theories, 1890–1910* (Paris: Bibliothèque de l'Occident, 1913); cited in E.H. Gombrich, *The Sense of Order: A Study in the Psychology of Decorative Art* (Ithaca, N.Y.: Cornell University Press, 1979), 58.

22. Quoted in Walter Koschatzky, "Introduction," in Horst-Herbert Kossatz, *Ornamental Posters of the Vienna Secession* (New York: St. Martin's Press, 1974), 10.

23. Maurice Denis, "Notes picturales du voyage de noces," in *Journal* (Paris: La Colombe, 1957), 1:102: "Pour le papier peint.—des méandres et reflets d'eau, vert et blanc, comme dans la mer près du canot. Dessins de glace (voy. de Gide). Ronces sur un ruisseau. Le blé (ton sur ton)—des feuilles sombres sur un fond blanc et bleu.—Des bourgeons de marronnier rose et creme et gris vert. . . . Pour un plafond . . . harpistes, belles attitudes."

24. Denis, *Theories,* 162; cited in Patricia Eckert Boyer, "The Nabis, Parisian Humorous Illustrators, and the Chat Noir," in *The Nabis and the Parisian Avant-Garde,* ed. Patricia Eckert Boyer (New Brunswick, N.J., and London: Rutgers University Press, 1988), 1.

25. See Elizabeth Prelinger, "The Art of the Nabis: From Symbolism to Modernism," in Boyer, *The Nabis,* 82.

26. Dominique Maurice-Denis, two interviews with author, October and December 1987.

27. Arwas, *Berthon and Grasset,* 11.

28. Eugène Grasset, "Introduction," in M.P. Verneuil, *L'Animal dans la décoration* (Paris: Librairie Centrale des Beaux-Arts, 1897); quoted in Arwas, *Berthon and Grasset,* 62.

29. Jiří Mucha, *Alphonse Maria Mucha* (New York: Rizzoli, 1989), 142, 156–61.

30. Peter Wittlich, *Art Nouveau Drawings* (London: Octopus, 1974), 19.

31. William Allmann, White House archivist, interview with author, Washington, D.C., 6 July 1987.

32. See Clarence Cook, *What Shall We Do with Our Walls?* (New York: Warren Fuller & Co., 1880).

33. Wilson H. Faude, "Associated Artists and the American Renaissance in the Decorative Arts," *Winterthur Portfolio* 10 (1975): 124.

34. Catherine Lynn, *Wallpaper in America* (New York: W.W. Norton, 1980), 402–3, 426.

35. Isabelle Anscombe, *A Woman's Touch* (New York: Viking, 1984), 39.

36. "Selected Statements by Louis C. Tiffany," in Robert Koch, *Louis C. Tiffany's Art Glass* (New York: Crown, 1977), 38.

37. Will Bradley, *Bradley: His Book* 1, no. 3 (1896).

38. Henry James in 1889 wrote in *Century* magazine, "If the centuries are ever arranged at some bar of justice to answer in regard to what they have given of good or bad, to humanity, our interesting age might perhaps do worse than put forth the plea, 'Dear me! I have given it a fresh interest in black and white.'" Quoted in Roberta Wong, *Will H. Bradley: American Artist and Craftsman* (New York: Metropolitan Museum of Art, 1972), 1.

39. "Mr. Roosevelt's Address," *Harvard Crimson* 26, no. 41 (10 November 1894): 1; quoted in Diane Chalmers Johnson, *American Art Nouveau* (New York: Harry N. Abrams, 1979), 213.

40. Bradley's series of interiors appeared in *Ladies' Home Journal* from November 1901 to August 1902. See Robert Judson Clark, ed., *The Arts and Crafts Movement in America* (Princeton, N.J.: Princeton University Press, 1972), 32; Johnson, *American Art Nouveau,* 303. Bradley's drawings for these interiors are at the Metropolitan Museum of Art, New York.

41. Quoted in Ernst Wolfgang Mick, *Wallpaper Design in the Deutsches Tapeten Museum* (Tokyo: Gakken, 1981), 242.

42. Ibid., 245.

43. Quoted in Martin Filler, "Grand Finale: Vienna 1900," *House and Garden* 158 (July 1986): 158.

44. Mick, *Wallpaper Design,* 244.

45. Maurice Denis, *Theories 1890–1910* (Paris: Rouart et Watelin, 1920), 149; quoted in Alan M. Fern, "Graphic Design," in *Art Nouveau,* ed. Selz and Constantine, 45.

46. Quoted in Madsen, *Art Nouveau,* 54.

47. Ibid.

FIVE Movements toward Restraint, *pages 115–41*

1. Quoted in Alison Filippo, *Charles Rennie Mackintosh as a Designer of Chairs* (Woodbury, N.Y.: Barron's, 1977), 13.

2. Hermann Muthesius, *The English House* (New York: Rizzoli, 1979), 52.

3. See Daniele Baroni and Antonio d'Auria, *Kolo Moser: Graphic Artist and Designer* (New York: Rizzoli, 1986), 138.

4. Thomas Howarth, *Charles Rennie Mackintosh and the Modern Movement* (Boston: Routledge and Kegan Paul, 1977), 201.

5. Mackintosh to Hoffmann and Wärndorfer, 17 March 1903, in Eduard F. Sekler, *Josef Hoffmann* (Princeton, N.J.: Princeton University Press, 1985), 66.

6. Wendy Kaplan, *The Art That Is Life* (Boston: Museum of Fine Arts, 1987), 91.

7. Emily Bardack Kies, "The Secession," in *Vienna 1900* (newsletter), ed. Gertje Utley, Emily Bardack Kies, and Kirk Varnedoe (New York: Museum of Modern Art, 1986), 3.

8. Kirk Varnedoe, *Vienna 1900* (New York: Museum of Modern Art, 1986), 83.

9. Quoted in Edward Lucie-Smith, *Furniture: A Concise History* (New York and Toronto: Oxford University Press, 1979), 161.

10. Josef Hoffmann, "Architectural Matters from the Island of Capri, *Der Architekt* 3 (1897): 13; quoted in Sekler, *Josef Hoffmann,* 479.

11. Josef Hoffmann to S. Tschudi Madsen, September 1954; quoted in Madsen, *Art Nouveau* (New York: McGraw-Hill, 1967), 30.

12. Quoted in Sekler, *Josef Hoffmann,* 8.

13. Ibid., 63.

14. Sekler, *Josef Hoffmann,* 132.

15. Elsie de Wolfe, *The House in Good Taste* (New York: The Century Co., 1913), 66.

16. Adolf Loos, "Ornament and Crime" (1908); see Ludwig Munz and Gustav Kunstler, *Adolf Loos, Pioneer of Modern Architecture,* trans. Harold Meek (New York: Frederick A. Praeger, 1966), 226–31.

17. Ibid., 231.

18. In *Neue Wiener Tagblatt* (26 April 1900); reprinted as "The Poor Little Rich Man," in *Adolf Loos: Spoken into the Void: Collected Essays, 1897–1900,* ed. Joan Ockman, trans. Jane O. Newman and John H. Smith (Cambridge, Mass.: MIT Press, 1982), 127.

19. The wallpaper appeared in *Deutsche Kunst und Dekoration* 19 (1906–7): 469.

20. Quoted in Jane Kallir, *Viennese Design and the Wiener Werkstätte* (New York: Galerie St. Etienne; George Braziller, 1986), 112 n. 25.

21. This was the Ausstellung der Österreichischen Tapeten, Linkrusta und Linoleum Industrie, 20 May–July 1913.

22. See Max Eisler, *Dagobert Peche* (Vienna: Gerlach und Weidling, 1925); cited in Kallir, *Viennese Design and the Wiener Werkstätte,* 107.

23. See Waltraud Neuwirth, *Wiener Werkstätte, Avantgarde, Art Deco, Industrial Design* (Vienna: Selbstverlag Dr. Waltraud Neuwirth, 1984).

24. Werner J. Schweiger, *Wiener Werkstätte: Design in Vienna, 1903–1932* (New York: Abbeville Press, 1984), 187.

25. Peter Behrens, "Zur Aesthetik des Fabrikhaus," *Gerwerbefleiss* 108, nos. 7/9 (July/September 1929); quoted in Alan Windsor, *Peter Behrens* (New York: Watson-Guptill, 1981), 82.

26. Windsor, *Peter Behrens,* 126 n. 24.

27. See Gillian Naylor, *The Arts and Crafts Movement* (Cambridge, Mass.: MIT Press, 1971), 183, 187.

28. Quoted in Nancy J. Troy, *The De Stijl Environment* (Cambridge, Mass.: MIT Press, 1983), 161–62. Calder recalled that "the mobiles started when I went to see Mondrian. I was impressed by several colored rectangles he had on the wall. Shortly after that I made some mobiles; Mondrian claimed his paintings were faster than my mobiles." In Katherine Kuh, *The Artist's Voice* (New York: Harper and Row, 1960), 41.

29. Troy, *De Stijl Environment,* 138.

30. Ibid.

31. Piet Mondrian, *Plastic Art and Pure Plastic Art and Other Essays* (New York: Wittenborn-Schultz, 1945), 14; quoted in Hans L.C. Jaffé, *De Stijl, 1917–1931: The Dutch Contribution to Modern Art* (Cambridge, Mass. and London: Harvard University Press, 1986), 180.

32. Piet Mondrian, "No Axiom but the Plastic," *De Stijl* 6, nos. 6/7:83–85; quoted in Hans L.C. Jaffé, *De Stijl* (New York: Harry N. Abrams, 1970), 189.

33. Quoted in Troy, *De Stijl Environment,* 164.

34. Ibid.

35. Walter Gropius, "Program of the Staatliche Bauhaus in Weimar, April 1919," in Hans M. Wingler, *The Bauhaus* (Cambridge, Mass.: MIT Press, 1969), 31.

36. Walter Gropius, "Concept and Development of the State Bauhaus" (1924); quoted in Frank Whitford, *Bauhaus* (London: Thames and Hudson, 1984), 23.

37. Whitford, *Bauhaus,* 187.

38. Wingler, *Bauhaus,* 518.

39. Le Corbusier, *Decorative Art of Today,* trans. James I. Dunnett (Cambridge, Mass.: MIT Press, 1987), 200; Le Corbusier, *Mon Oeuvre,* trans. James Palmer (London: Architectural Press, 1960), 24.

40. Mary Patricia Sekler, *Early Drawings of Le Corbusier, 1902–1908* (New York: Garland, 1977), 104–5.

41. See photograph C17/5, DR, Fondation Le Corbusier, Paris.

42. Drawing 30080, Fondation Le Corbusier, Paris.

43. Le Corbusier, *Mon Oeuvre,* 24.

44. Charles-Edouard Jeanneret and Amédée Ozenfant, *Après le cubisme* (Turin, Italy: Bottega d'Erasmo, 1975), 59.

45. Le Corbusier, *Towards a New Architecture,* trans. Frederick Etchells (New York: Frederick A. Praeger, 1960), 107.

46. Le Corbusier, *Decorative Art of Today,* 42.

47. Le Corbusier, *Towards a New Architecture,* 115.

48. Le Corbusier, *Decorative Art of Today,* 188.

49. Salvador Dalí, *Dalí on Modern Art,* trans. Haakon M. Chevalier (New York: Dial Press, 1957), 29.

50. Le Corbusier, *Decorative Art of Today,* 46.

51. Ibid., 67.

52. Ibid., 81.

53. Ibid., 114.

54. Quoted in "Second Salubra Collection by Le Corbusier" (Grenzach-Wyhlen, Germany: Forbo-Salubra GmbH, 1959).

55. Ibid.

56. Ibid.

57. Frank Lloyd Wright, "The Art and Craft of the Machine," in *Frank Lloyd Wright: Writings and Buildings,* ed. Edgar Kauffmann and Ben Raeburn (New York: Horizon Press, 1960), 55–73.

58. Ibid., 56.

59. Ibid., 71.

60. See Vincent Scully, *Frank Lloyd Wright* (New York: George Braziller, 1960), 114 n. 29.

61. Frank Lloyd Wright, *Genius and the Mobocracy* (New York: Horizon Press, 1971), 71.

62. Frank Lloyd Wright, "The Sovereignty of the Individual," in *Ausgeführte Bauten und Entwürfe* (Berlin: Wasmuth, 1910). Reprinted in *Frank Lloyd Wright,* ed. Kauffmann and Raeburn, 102.

63. Ibid.

SIX The Art Deco Years, *pages 143–73*

1. Paul Poiret, *My First Fifty Years,* trans. Stephen Hayden Guest (London: Victor Gallancz, 1931), 160.

2. Quoted in Palmer White, *Poiret* (London: Studio Vista, 1973), 132.

3. Poiret, *My First Fifty Years,* 159.

4. René Simon Lévy, "The Fabrics of Raoul Dufy: Genesis and Context," in Hayward Gallery, *Raoul Dufy, 1877–1953* (London: Arts Council of Great Britain, 1983), 99.

5. Sarah Wilson, "Raoul Dufy: Tradition, Innovation, Decoration, 1900–1925," in Hayward Gallery, *Dufy,* 74.

6. White, *Poiret,* 119.

7. White, *Poiret,* 119.

8. Poiret, *My First Fifty Years,* 158. Poiret in the same passage mentions Martine's leaping tigers, another Dufy motif.

9. Quoted in Giulia Veronesi, *Style and Design, 1909–1929* (New York: George Braziller, 1968), 116 n. 9.

10. Dora Perez-Tibi, *Dufy* (New York: Harry N. Abrams, 1989), 86.

11. Lévy, "The Fabrics of Raoul Dufy," in Hayward Gallery, *Dufy,* 106.

12. Georges Remon, "L'Habitation d'aujourd'hui,"

L'Art vivant 1 (1 January 1925), 11–13.

13. Wilson, "Raoul Dufy," in Hayward Gallery, *Dufy,* 86.

14. André Dunoyer de Segonzac, "Testimonial," in Alliance Française, *Jean-Emile Laboureur, 1877–1943* (New York: Alliance Française, 1977), 11.

15. Robert Allen, "Introduction," in Alliance Française, *Jean-Emile Laboureur,* 5–9.

16. Martin Battersby, *The Decorative Thirties* (New York: Walker and Co., 1971), 95–96.

17. See Frances Steegmuller, *Apollinaire: Poet Among the Painters* (New York: Farrar Straus and Co., 1963), 175.

18. The poem of the Dove is in *Le Bestiaire, ou cortège d'Orphée,* a description in quatrains of each animal in the procession following Orpheus. See Guillaume Apollinaire, *Oeuvres poétiques* (Paris: Librairie Gallimard, 1959), 28: "Colombe, l'amour et l'esprit/Qui engendrates Jesus-Christ,/Comme vous j'aime une Marie./Qu'avec elle je me marie." J.-E. Laboureur's wallpaper "Bouquet de Mariée" may also be a tribute to Marie Laurencin.

19. Quoted in Florence Camard, *Ruhlmann: Master of Art Deco,* trans. David Macey (New York: Harry N. Abrams; London: Thames and Hudson, 1984), 32.

20. Ibid., 14.

21. Sonia Delaunay, *Nous irons jusqu'au soleil* (Paris: Editions Robert Laffont, 1978), 77: "Nous voici ruinés bel et bien, mais l'espérance du peuple russe nous fait pleurer de joie." See also Arthur A. Cohen, *Sonia Delaunay* (New York: Harry N. Abrams, 1975), 76.

22. Cohen, *Sonia Delaunay,* 77.

23. Quoted in Sherry A. Buckberrough, "An Art of Unexpected Contrasts," in Albright-Knox Art Gallery, *Sonia Delaunay, a Retrospective* (Buffalo: Albright-Knox Art Gallery, 1980), 108.

24. Ibid., 111.

25. Quoted in Marie-Noël de Gary, *Edouard Bénédictus: Rythme et couleur de l'art deco* (Paris: Musée des Arts Décoratifs; Flammarion, 1986), 20.

26. Jean Lurçat, *Designing Tapestry* (New York: Macmillan, 1951), 8.

27. Roger Fry to George Bernard Shaw, 11 December 1912, Manuscripts Department, British Library, London.

28. Vanessa Bell to Roger Fry, 6 February 1913, 93, Tate Gallery Omega Archive; quoted in Judith Collins, *The Omega Workshops* (Chicago: University of Chicago Press, 1984), 47.

29. Winifred Gill to Duncan Grant, 4 July 1966, from collection of Richard Shone; quoted in *The Omega Workshops 1913–1919,* ed. Fiona MacCarthy (London: Crafts Council of Great Britain, 1984), 17.

30. Vanessa Bell to Clive Bell, 2 April 1913, 95, Tate Gallery Omega Archive; quoted in Collins, *Omega Workshops,* 44.

31. See Virginia Woolf, *Roger Fry: A Biography* (London: Hogarth Press, 1940), 191.

32. See Collins, *Omega Workshops,* 45 n. 51.

33. Collins, *Omega Workshops,* 32.

34. Entry dated 7 April 1918, in *The Diary of Virginia Woolf,* ed. Anne Olivier Bell (London: Hogarth Press, 1977), 1:134.

35. Roger Fry, "The Artist as Decorator," *Colour* (April 1917), 92–93; quoted in Richard Cork, *Art Beyond the Gallery* (New Haven, Conn.: Yale University Press, 1985), 170.

36. Cork, *Art Beyond the Gallery,* 173–74.

37. Frances Spalding, *Roger Fry* (Berkeley and Los Angeles: University of California Press, 1980), 223.

38. Quoted in Andrew Causey, *Paul Nash* (Oxford: Clarendon Press, 1980), 49, note d.

39. Ibid.

40. Collins, *Omega Workshops,* 84.

41. Roger Fry to Arnold Bennett, 2 June 1919, collection of University College Library, London University; quoted in Collins, *Omega Workshops,* 172.

42. Woolf, *Roger Fry,* 216.

43. Charles C. Oman and Jean Hamilton, *Wallpapers* (London: Sotheby Publications and the Victoria and Albert Museum, 1982), 451–52.

44. Douglas Percy Bliss, *Edward Bawden* (London: Godalming, 1979), 165.

45. Quoted in E.A. Entwisle, *A Literary History of Wallpaper* (London: B.T. Batsford, 1960), 179.

46. Quoted in Battersby, *Decorative Thirties,* 166.

47. Ibid.

SEVEN The Wallpapers of Charles Burchfield, *pages 175–83*

1. Charles E. Burchfield, journal, 20 January 1916, in Burchfield Papers, Charles E. Burchfield Center, Buffalo.

2. *Exhibition of Wallpaper, Historical and Contemporary* (Buffalo: Buffalo Fine Arts Academy and Albright Art Gallery, 1937–38), entries 173–78. Pamphlet.

3. Charles E. Burchfield Center, *Wallpapers by Charles E. Burchfield* (Buffalo: Charles E. Burchfield Center, 1973).

4. Quoted in Edna M. Lindemann, "Introduction," in Charles E. Burchfield Center, *Wallpapers,* 3.

5. Burchfield, journal, spring 1923; quoted in Charles E. Burchfield Center, *Wallpapers,* 11.

6. Ibid., 13.

7. "'The Birches,' the first design I made for the Birge Co. and just about my favorite." Quoted in Charles E. Burchfield Center, *Wallpapers,* 13.

8. Burchfield, journal, November 1925; quoted in Charles E. Burchfield Center, *Wallpapers,* 11.

9. Charles Burchfield, manuscript for John I.H. Baur; quoted in Baur, "Introduction," in *Charles E. Burchfield: The Early Years at Kennedy Galleries 1915–1929* (New York: Kennedy Galleries, 1977), unpaginated.

EIGHT From Surrealism to Spoof, *pages 185–207*

1. Georges Roque, *Ceci n'est pas un Magritte* (Paris: Flammarion, 1983), 154–55.

2. The manifesto, "L'Art pur," was destined for *Ça Ira* but was not published. Fonds Servranckx, Archives de l'Art Moderne, Brussels.

3. Quoted in Suzi Gablik, *Magritte* (Greenwich, Conn.: New York Graphic Society, 1970), 16.

4. Gablik, *Magritte,* 66.

5. Ibid., 23.

6. Suzi Gablik, "A Conversation with René Magritte," *Studio International* 173 (March 1967): 128.

7. Richard Calvocoressi, *Magritte* (Oxford: Phaidon Press, 1979), 10.

8. Mary Mathews Gedo, "Meditations on Madness: The Art of René Magritte," in Dawn Ades et al., *In the Mind's Eye: Dada and Surrealism* (Chicago: Chicago Museum of Contemporary Art; New York: Abbeville Press, 1985), 83 n. 24.

9. From Paul Colinet, "Le Domaine enchanté," in Patrick Waldberg, *René Magritte,* trans. Austryn Wainhouse (Brussels: André de Rache, 1965), 276.

10. René Magritte to Alexandre Iolas, 24 October 1952, in Harry Torczyner, *Magritte: Ideas and Images,* trans. Richard Miller (New York: Harry N. Abrams, 1977), 233.

11. Gablik, *Magritte,* 10.

12. Ibid., 9.

13. This event is described in Magritte's "Esquisse autobiographique," which is now in the Palais des Beaux-Arts, Brussels. See Gablik, *Magritte,* 25; see also Casino Communal of Knokke-le-Zoute, *L'Oeuvre de René Magritte* (Brussels: Editions de la Connaissance, 1962), in which the "Esquisse autobiographique" appears.

14. Gedo, "Meditations on Madness"; in Ades et al., *In the Mind's Eye,* 167.

15. Gablik, *Magritte,* 126.

16. See Miguel de Cervantes, *Don Quichotte de la Manche* (Paris: Joseph Foret, 1957), 28–29. A later Italian "magazine" edition is *Don Quixote della Mancia* (Milan: Aldo Palazzi Editore, 1965), 40–41. For a description of Dalí's bombardment technique for the *Don Quixote* illustrations, see Robert Descharnes, *World of Salvador Dalí* (New York: Viking, 1968), 75; see also Dalí's own description in *Diary of a Genius* (London: Hutchinson, 1964), 165–68.

17. Miguel de Cervantes, *Don Quixote de la Mancha,* trans. Peter Motteux (New York: Harper and Bros., 1915), 136.

18. Ibid., 138.

19. Quoted in Uwe M. Schneede, *Surrealism* (New

York: Harry N. Abrams, 1974), 40.

20. Quoted in Jean Lipman, *Calder's Universe* (New York: Whitney Museum of American Art and Viking, 1976), 334.

21. Ibid., 18.

22. Ibid., 39.

23. Ibid., 33.

24. Ibid., 35.

25. Saul Steinberg, *The Art of Living* (New York: Harper, 1945), 6.

26. Harold Rosenberg, *Saul Steinberg* (New York: Alfred A. Knopf; Whitney Museum of American Art, 1978), 239.

27. Rosenberg, *Saul Steinberg,* 11.

28. John Coplans, "Andy Warhol, 1928–87," *Art in America* 75 (May 1987): 141.

29. Charles F. Stuckey, "Andy Warhol's Painted Faces," *Art in America* 68 (May 1980): 103.

30. Leo Castelli, interview with author, New York, 6 May 1987.

31. Quoted in Harold Rosenberg, *Art on the Edge* (New York: Macmillan, 1975), 105.

32. Quoted in Andy Warhol et al., eds., *Andy Warhol* (Stockholm: Moderna Museet, 1968), unpaginated.

33. Stuckey, "Andy Warhol's Painted Faces," 103.

34. David Bourdon, "Andy Warhol, 1928–87," *Art in America* 75 (May 1987): 139.

35. G.R. Swenson, "What Is Pop Art?" *Art News* 62 (November 1963): 26.

36. Bourdon, "Andy Warhol, 1928–87," 140.

37. Leo Castelli, interview with author, New York, 6 May 1987.

38. Quoted in Swenson, "What Is Pop Art?" 26.

39. Quoted in Lawrence Alloway, *American Pop Art* (New York: Macmillan, 1974), 109 n. 4.

NINE Art and Wallpaper, *pages 209–33*

1. Harold Rosenberg, *The Tradition of the New* (London: Thames and Hudson, 1962), 34.

2. Marina Vaizey on BBC Radio, "The Critics," March 1989.

3. Clement Greenberg, quoted in W.J.T. Mitchell, "Ut Pictura Theoria," *Critical Inquiry* 15 (Winter 1989): 366.

4. See Henri Clouzot and Charles Follot, *Histoire du papier peint en France* (Paris: Editions d'Art Charles Moreau, 1935), 110–11; see also *Exhibition of Wallpaper, Historical and Contemporary* (Buffalo: The Buffalo Fine Arts Academy and Albright Art Gallery, 1937–38), entry 54. Pamphlet.

5. Statements by the artists are in *Calder, Matisse, Matta, Miro: Mural Scrolls* (New York: Katzenbach

and Warren, 1949), unpaginated.

6. Quoted in Anni Albers, *On Designing* (New Haven: Pellango Press, 1959), 3.

7. See Gahan Wilson cartoon, *New Yorker,* 27 April 1987, 57.

8. John Russell, "Alpha and Omega of Late Van Gogh," *New York Times,* 13 August 1989, Arts and Leisure section, 1.

9. Cecil Beaton, *Vogue,* May 1945; quoted in E.A. Entwisle, *Literary History of Wallpaper* (London: B.T. Batsford, 1960), 175.

10. See Gabriel P. Weisberg, ed., *Japonisme: Japanese Influence on French Art, 1854–1910* (Cleveland: Cleveland Museum of Art, 1975), 107. In same volume see also Philip Dennis Cate, "French Prints 1883–1910," 64.

11. See Mario Praz, *An Illustrated History of Interior Decoration* (New York: Thames and Hudson, 1982), 380.

12. David Sylvester, "Howard Hodgkin Interviewed," in Nicholas Serota, ed., *Howard Hodgkin: Forty Paintings, 1973–84* (New York: George Braziller; London: Trefoil Books and Whitechapel Art Gallery, 1984), 97.

13. Michael Compton, *Howard Hodgkin's Indian Leaves* (London: Tate Gallery, 1982), 6; see also Sylvester, "Howard Hodgkin Interviewed," in Serota, ed., *Howard Hodgkin,* 100.

14. Sylvester, "Howard Hodgkin Interviewed," in Serota, ed., *Howard Hodgkin,* 100.

15. Philip Johnson, in PBS interview with Rosamond Bernier, 30 June 1986.

16. Joseph Giovannini, "Johnson and His Glass House: Reflections," *New York Times,* 16 July 1987, Home section.

17. Robert Venturi, interview with Peter Eisenman, *Skyline* (July 1982), 14; quoted in *High Styles: Twentieth-Century American Design* (New York: Whitney Museum of American Art and Summit, 1985), 197.

18. Quoted in Barbara Radice, *Memphis* (New York: Rizzoli, 1983), 88.

19. Kathy Halbreich, *Culture and Commentary: An Eighties Perspective* (Washington, D.C.: Hirshhorn Museum, 1990), 21.

20. Patricia Stewart, "High Decoration in Low Relief," *Art in America* 68 (February 1980): 100.

21. Halbreich, *Culture and Commentary,* 80–83.

22. André Fontainas, "Le Salon d'Automne," *L'Art moderne* (October 1910): 329–30; quoted in Jack D. Flam, *Matisse, the Man and His Art, 1869–1918* (Ithaca, N.Y.: Cornell University Press, 1986), 291.

23. Henri Matisse, "Notes of a Painter, 1908," in Jack D. Flam, *Matisse on Art* (London: Phaidon Press, 1973), 38.

24. William Morris, "Some Hints on Pattern-Designing," in *Collected Works of William Morris,* ed. May Morris (New York: Russell and Russell, 1966), 22:177.

25. Ibid., 181.

26. Jean Guichard-Meili, *Matisse Paper Cutouts,* trans. David Macey (New York: Thames and Hudson, 1984), 36.

27. Henri Matisse, "Interview with Verdet, 1952," in Flam, *Matisse on Art,* 145.

28. Henri Matisse, *Jazz* (Paris: Editions Verve, 1947); see Flam, *Matisse on Art,* 112.

APPENDIX A Artists' Wallpapers for Children, *pages 235–56*

1. Olivia Clemens to her mother, Olivia Langdon, November 1879, Mark Twain/Clemens Papers, Stowe-Day Library and Foundation, Hartford, Conn.

2. *Mark Twain's Notebooks and Journals,* ed. Frederick Anderson, Lin Salamo, and Bernard L. Stein (Berkeley: University of California Press, 1975), 2:399 n. 148.

3. Walter Crane, *Catalogue of a Collection of Designs* (Chicago: Art Institute, 1892), 12.

4. Castle Howard Archives, J23/105/15 and J23/105/28, Castle Howard, York, England, by kind permission of the Howard family.

5. Judy Taylor, *Beatrix Potter's Letters* (New York: Frederick Warne; Viking, 1989), 105.

6. Ibid., 109.

7. Ibid., 112.

8. Ibid., 113.

9. Ibid., 114.

10. Colin White, *Edmund Dulac* (New York: Charles Scribner's Sons, 1976), 184.

11. Roy Heron, *Cecil Aldin* (Exeter, England: Webb and Bower, 1981), 54.

12. See Colin White, *World of the Nursery* (London: Herbert Press, 1984), 70.

13. Crane, *Catalogue,* 4.

14. May Morris, *William Morris: Artist, Writer, Socialist* (New York: Russell and Russell, 1966), 1:44.

15. Ibid., 35–36.

16. May Morris, *Decorative Needlework* (London: Hughes & Co., 1893), 117.

17. Frances Spalding, *Vanessa Bell* (New Haven: Ticknor & Fields, 1983), 123.

18. P.G. Konody, *Observer,* 14 December 1913; quoted in Judith Collins, *The Omega Workshops* (Chicago: University of Chicago Press, 1984), 67.

19. Tate Gallery, *Artists at Curwen* (London: Tate Gallery, 1977), 86.

BIBLIOGRAPHY

This bibliography has as its subject the elusive interface between the fine and decorative arts, particularly as they relate to wallpaper. For the reader who is interested primarily in wallpaper history the extensive bibliography by E.A. Entwisle in Oman and Hamilton, cited below, is excellent. Lynn, also cited below, lists wallpaper collections in Europe and the United States.

Ackerman, Phyllis. *Wallpaper, Its History, Design and Use.* New York: Frederick A. Stokes, 1923.

Albers, Anni. *On Designing.* New Haven: Pellango Press, 1959.

Anscombe, Isabelle. *A Woman's Touch.* New York: Viking, 1984.

Appuhn, Horst, and Christian von Heusinger. *Riesenholzschnitte und Papiertapeten der Renaissance.* Unterschneidheim, Germany: Verlag Dr. Alfons Uhl, 1976.

Arnason, H.H. *A History of Modern Art.* New York: Harry N. Abrams, 1969.

Arts Council of Great Britain. *Four Rooms.* London: Arts Council of Great Britain, 1984.

Arwas, Victor. *Berthon and Grasset.* New York: Rizzoli, 1978.

———. *The Liberty Style.* New York: Rizzoli, 1979.

———. *Art Deco.* New York: Harry N. Abrams, 1985.

Aslin, Elizabeth. *The Aesthetic Movement.* New York: Frederick A. Praeger, 1969.

———. *E.W. Godwin, Furniture and Interior Decoration.* London: John Murray, 1986.

Badovici, Jean. *Harmonies: Interieurs de Ruhlmann.* Paris: A. Morance, 1924.

Banham, Joanna. *A Decorative Art: 19th-Century Wallpapers in the Whitworth Art Gallery.* Manchester, England: Whitworth Art Gallery, 1985.

Baroni, Daniele, and Antonio D'Auria. *Kolo Moser: Graphic Artist and Designer.* Translated by Jon Van de Grift and Hanna Hannah. New York: Rizzoli, 1984.

Battersby, Martin. *The Decorative Twenties.* New York: Walker and Co., 1969.

———. *The Decorative Thirties.* New York: Walker and Co., 1971.

Baur, John I.H. *The Inlander: Life and Work of Charles Burchfield 1893–1967.* Newark, N.J.: University of Delaware Press; New York and London: Cornwall Books, 1982.

Baynes, Ken. *Art in Society.* Woodstock, N.Y.:

Overlook Press, 1975.

Benedictus, Edouard. *Variations.* Paris: Librairie Centrale des Beaux-Arts, [1924].

———. *Nouvelles variations.* Paris: Editions Albert Levy, [1928].

———. *Relais.* Paris: Editions Vincent, Freal et Cie, [1930].

Bernus-Taylor, Marthe, et al. *Etoffes merveilleuses du Musée Historique des Tissus de Lyon.* Tokyo: Gakken, 1976.

Bibliothèque Forney. *Dessins originaux de la collection Isidore Leroy,* vols. 1, 2. Tokyo: Gakken, 1985.

Billcliffe, Roger. *Charles Rennie Mackintosh: The Complete Furniture, Furniture Drawings, and Interior Designs.* New York: Taplinger, 1979.

———. *Mackintosh Textile Designs.* London: The Fine Art Society, 1982.

Bing, Samuel. *Artistic America: Tiffany Glass and Art Nouveau.* Cambridge, Mass.: MIT Press, 1970.

Bliss, Douglas Percy. *Edward Bawden.* London: Godalming, 1979.

Bock, Judith. *The Wallpapers of Charles Voysey.* Ann Arbor, Mich.: University Microfilms, 1966.

Bouillon, Jean-Paul. *Art Deco 1900–1940.* New York: Rizzoli, 1989.

Bowlt, John E., ed. *Russian Art of the Avant-Garde: Theory and Criticism 1902–1934.* New York: Viking, 1976.

Boyer, Patricia Eckert, ed. *The Nabis and the Parisian Avant-Garde.* New Brunswick, N.J., and London: Rutgers University Press, 1988.

Brandon-Jones, John. *C.F.A. Voysey: Architect and Designer 1857–1941.* London: Lund-Humphries, 1978.

Burckhardt, Lucius, ed. *The Werkbund: History and Ideology 1907–1933.* Translated by Pearl Sanders. Woodbury, N.Y.: Barron's, 1980.

Byrne, Janet S. *Renaissance Ornament Prints and Drawings.* New York: Metropolitan Museum of Art, 1981.

Camard, Florence. *Ruhlmann: Master of Art Deco.* London: Thames and Hudson, 1984.

Casino Communal of Knokke-le-Zoute, ed. *L'Oeuvre de René Magritte.* Essays by Louis Scutenaire and others; *Esquisse autobiographique* by René Magritte; "Le Domaine enchanté" by Paul Colinet. Brussels: Editions de la Connaissance, 1962.

Chippendale, Thomas. *The Gentleman and Cabinet-Maker's Director.* London: 3d ed. 1762.

Clark, Fiona. *William Morris, Wallpapers and*

Chintzes. New York: St. Martin's Press, 1974.

Clark, Robert Judson, ed. *The Arts and Crafts Movement in America.* Princeton, N.J.: Princeton University Press, 1972.

Clouzot, Henri. *Le Style moderne dans la décoration intérieure.* Paris: C. Massin, [1921].

———. *La Décor moderne dans la tenture et le tissu.* Paris: C. Massin, 1929.

———. *Papiers peints et tentures modernes.* Paris: C. Massin, 1929.

———. *Tableaux-Tentures de Dufour & Leroy.* Paris: A. Calavas, Librairie des Arts Décoratifs, 1930.

———. *Le Papier peint en France du xvii au xix siècle.* Paris: G. van Oest, 1931.

Clouzot, Henri, and Charles Follot. *Histoire du papier peint en France.* Paris: Charles Moreau, 1935.

Collins, Judith. *The Omega Workshops.* Chicago: University of Chicago Press, 1984.

Compton, Michael. *Howard Hodgkin's Indian Leaves.* London: Tate Gallery, 1982.

Conner, Patrick. *The Inspiration of Egypt.* Brighton, England: Brighton Museums, 1983.

Conway, William Martin. *Literary Remains of Albrecht Dürer . . . with Transcripts from the British Museum Manuscripts.* Cambridge: Cambridge University Press, 1889.

Cook, Clarence. *What Shall We Do with Our Walls?* New York: Warren Fuller & Co., 1880.

Cooper, Jeremy. *Victorian and Edwardian Decor: From Gothic Revival to Art Nouveau.* New York: Abbeville Press, 1987.

Cooper-Hewitt Museum. *Wallpaper in the Collection of the Cooper-Hewitt Museum.* New York: Cooper-Hewitt Museum, 1981.

Cork, Richard. *Art Beyond the Gallery.* New Haven: Yale University Press, 1985.

Cowart, Jack, et al. *Henry Matisse Paper Cutouts.* Saint Louis: Saint Louis Art Museum, 1977.

Crane, Walter (subject). "A Designer of Paper Hangings." *The Studio* 4 (December 1894): 76–82.

Crane, Walter. *William Morris to Whistler.* London: G. Bell and Sons, 1911.

Crook, J. Mordaunt. *William Burges and the High Victorian Dream.* Chicago: University of Chicago Press, 1981.

Curry, David Park. "Whistler and Decoration." *Antiques* 126 (November 1984): 1186–99.

De Osma, Guillermo. *Mariano Fortuny, His Life and Work.* New York: Rizzoli, 1985.

Delaunay, Sonia. *Ses peintures, ses objets, ses tissus*

simultanes, ses modes. Paris: Librairie des Arts Décoratifs, [1925].

———. Compositions, couleurs, idées. Paris: Editions d'Art Charles Moreau, 1930.

———. Nous irons jusqu'au soleil. Paris: Editions Robert Laffont, 1978.

Denis, Maurice. Theories, 1890–1910. Paris: Bibliothèque de l'Occident, 1913.

Deschodt, Anne-Marie. Mariano Fortuny: Un Magicien de Venise. Tours, France: Editions du Regard, 1979.

Domergue, Denise. Artists Design Furniture. New York: Harry N. Abrams, 1984.

Duncan, Alastair. American Art Deco. New York: Harry N. Abrams, 1986.

———. Art Deco. New York: Thames and Hudson, 1988.

Durant, Stuart. Ornament. Woodstock, N.Y.: Overlook Press, 1986.

———. Decorative Designs of C.F.A. Voysey from the Drawings Collection of the British Architectural Library, Royal Institute of British Architects. Cambridge, England: Lutterworth Press, 1990.

Eisler, Max. Dagobert Peche. Vienna: Gerlach und Weidling, 1925.

Elderfield, John. The Cut-outs of Henri Matisse. New York: George Braziller, 1978.

Entwisle, E.A. A Literary History of Wallpaper. London: B.T. Batsford, 1960.

———. Wallpapers of the Victorian Era. Leigh-on-Sea, England: Frank Lewis, 1964.

———. The Book of Wallpaper. Bath, England: Kingsmead, 1970.

———. French Scenic Wallpapers. Leigh-on-Sea, England: Frank Lewis, 1972.

Evans, Joan. Pattern: A Study of Ornament in Western Europe from 1180 to 1900, 2 vols. Oxford, England: Clarendon Press, 1931. Reprint. New York: Hacker Art Books, 1975.

Faude, Wilson H. "Associated Artists and the American Renaissance in the Decorative Arts." Winterthur Portfolio 10 (1975): 101–30.

Feldman, Frayda, and Jorg Schellmann, eds. Andy Warhol Prints. New York: Abbeville Press, 1985.

Fenz, Werner. Koloman Moser: Graphik, Kunstgewerbe, Malerei. Salzburg, Austria: Residenz Verlag, 1984.

Ferrey, Benjamin. Recollections of A.N. Welby Pugin and His Father, Augustus Pugin. London: Edward Stanford, 1861.

Filippo, Alison. Charles Rennie Mackintosh as a Designer of Chairs. Woodbury, N.Y.: Barron's, 1977.

Flam, Jack D., ed. Matisse on Art. London: Phaidon Press, 1973.

———. Matisse, the Man and His Art 1869–1918. Ithaca, N.Y.: Cornell University Press, 1986.

Flick, Pauline. "Nursery Wallpapers in Victorian Times." Country Life 146 (December 1969): 1519–21.

Floud, Peter. "Wallpaper Designs of C.F.A. Voysey." Penrose Annual 52 (1958): 10–14.

———. "Dating Morris Patterns." Architectural Review 126 (July 1959): 14–20.

———. "The Wallpaper Designs of William Morris." Penrose Annual 54 (1960): 41–45.

Fowler, John, and John Cornforth. English Decoration in the Eighteenth Century. Princeton, N.J.: Pyne Press, 1974.

Gablik, Suzi. Magritte. Greenwich, Conn.: New York Graphic Society, 1970.

Gary, Marie-Noël de. Edouard Benedictus, Rythme et couleur de l'art deco. Paris: Musée des Arts Décoratifs; Flammarion, 1986.

Gilbert, Christopher. Life and Work of Thomas Chippendale. London: Studio Vista, 1978.

Gombrich, E.H. The Sense of Order; A Study in the Psychology of Decorative Art. Ithaca, N.Y.: Cornell University Press, 1979.

Grasset, Eugène. Introduction to M.P. Verneuil, L'Animal dans la décoration. Paris: Librairie Centrale des Beaux-Arts, 1897.

———. Les Plantes et ses applications ornamentaux. Paris: Librairie Centrale des Beaux-Arts, 1900.

Greenberg, Clement. Art and Culture: Critical Essays. Boston: Beacon Press, 1961.

Grego, Joseph. Rowlandson the Caricaturist, 2 vols. London: Chatto and Windus, 1880.

Greysmith, Brenda. Wallpaper. New York: Macmillan, 1976.

Guibert, Mireille. Papiers Peints 1800–1875. Paris: Société des Amis de la Bibliothèque Forney, 1980.

Guichard-Meili, Jean. Matisse Paper Cutouts. Translated by David Macey. New York: Thames and Hudson, 1984.

Guimard, Hector. Castel Béranger. Paris: Rouam, 1898.

Hamilton, Jean. An Introduction to Wallpaper. London: Her Majesty's Stationery Office, 1983.

Hammacher, A.M. Le Monde de Henry van de Velde. Translated by Claudine Lemaire. Paris: Librairie Hachette, 1967.

Hanks, David. Frank Lloyd Wright. Ann Arbor, Mich.: The National Center for the Study of Frank Lloyd Wright, 1988.

Hayward Gallery. Raoul Dufy. London: Arts Council of Great Britain, 1983.

Hochschule für Angewandte Kunst and Österreichisches Museum für Angewandte Kunst. Josef Hoffmann. Vienna: Österreichisches Museum für Angewandte Kunst and Hochschule für Angewandte Kunst, 1987.

Honour, Hugh. Chinoiserie. New York: E.P. Dutton, 1962.

Howarth, Thomas. Charles Rennie Mackintosh and the Modern Movement. London: Routledge and Kegan Paul, 1977.

Hunter, George Leland. Decorative Textiles. Philadelphia: J.B. Lippincott, 1918.

Impey, Oliver. Chinoiserie. New York: Charles Scribner's Sons, 1977.

Jacqué, Jacqueline, and Bernard Jacqué. Chefs-d'oeuvres du Musée de l'Impression sur Etoffes de Mulhouse, vol. 3. Edited by Takahiko Sano. Tokyo: Gakken, 1978.

Jenkinson, Hilary. "English Wallpapers of the Sixteenth and Seventeenth Centuries." Antiquaries Journal 5, no. 3 (1925): 237–53.

Jensen, Robert, and Patricia Conway. Ornamentalism. New York: Clarkson N. Potter, 1982.

Johnson, Diane Chalmers. American Art Nouveau. New York: Harry N. Abrams, 1979.

Jones, John Brandon. C.F.A. Voysey, Architect and Designer. London: Lund-Humphries, 1978.

Jones, Owen. The Grammar of Ornament. London: Day and Son, 1856. Reprint. New York: Van Nostrand Reinhold, 1972.

Justema, William. The Pleasures of Pattern. New York: Reinhold, 1968.

———. Pattern: A Historical Panorama. Boston: New York Graphic Society, 1976.

Kallir, Jane. Viennese Design and the Wiener Werkstätte. New York: Galerie St. Etienne; George Braziller, 1986.

Kaplan, Wendy. The Art That Is Life. Boston: Museum of Fine Arts, 1987.

Kardon, Janet. The Decorative Impulse. Philadelphia: Institute of Contemporary Art, 1979.

Katzenbach, Lois, and William Katzenbach. The Practical Book of American Wallpaper. Philadelphia: J.B. Lippincott, 1951.

Kery, Patricia. Art Deco Graphics. New York: Harry N. Abrams, 1986.

King, Donald, ed. British Textile Design in the Victoria and Albert Museum, 3 vols. Tokyo: Gakken, 1980.

Koch, Robert. Louis C. Tiffany: Rebel in Glass. New York: Crown, 1964.

———. Louis C. Tiffany's Art Glass. New York: Crown, 1977.

Komanecky, Michael, and Virginia Fabbri Butera. The Folding Image: Screens by Western Artists of the 19th and 20th Centuries. New Haven: Yale University Art Gallery, 1984.

Konody, P.G. The Art of Walter Crane. London: G. Bell, 1902.

Kossatz, Horst-Herbert. Ornamental Posters of the Vienna Secession. New York: St. Martin's Press, 1974.

Kuh, Katherine. The Artist's Voice. New York: Harper and Row, 1960.

Kunzle, David. The Early Comic Strip. Berkeley: University of California Press, 1973.

Lambert, Susan, ed. Pattern and Design: Designs for the Decorative Arts, 1480–1980. London: Victoria and Albert Museum, 1983.

Lambourne, Lionel. *Utopian Craftsmen*. Salt Lake City: Peregrine Smith, 1980.

Larner, Gerald, and Celia Larner. *The Glasgow Style*. New York: Taplinger, 1979.

Le Corbusier [Charles-Edouard Jeanneret]. *Mon Oeuvre*. Translated by James Palmer. London: Architectural Press, 1960.

———. *Towards a New Architecture*. Translated by Frederick Etchells. New York: Frederick A. Praeger, 1960.

———. *Decorative Art of Today*. Translated by James I. Dunnett. Cambridge, Mass.: MIT Press, 1987.

Lethaby, W.R. *Philip Webb and His Work*. Oxford: Oxford University Press, 1935.

Lipman, Jean. *Calder's Universe*. New York: Whitney Museum of American Art and Viking Press, 1976.

Lurçat, Jean. *Designing Tapestry*. New York: Macmillan, 1951.

Lynn, Catherine. *Wallpaper in America*. New York: W.W. Norton, 1980.

MacCarthy, Fiona. "Roger Fry and the Omega Idea." In MacCarthy, Fiona, ed. *The Omega Workshops, 1913–19*. London: Crafts Council of Great Britain, 1984.

McClelland, Nancy. *Historic Wall-papers from Their Inception to the Introduction of Machinery*. Philadelphia: J.B. Lippincott, 1924.

Madsen, S. Tschudi. *Art Nouveau*. New York: McGraw-Hill, 1970.

Marchesseau, Daniel. *The Intimate World of Alexander Calder*. New York: Harry N. Abrams, 1989.

Mick, Ernst Wolfgang. *Wallpaper Design in the Deutsches Tapeten Museum*. Tokyo: Gakken, 1981.

———. *The Deutsches Tapeten Museum*. Kassel, Germany: Hessische Brandversicherungsanstalt, 1983.

Mitchell, Charles. "William Morris at St. James's Palace." *Architectural Review* 101 (January 1947): 37–39. Reprint. London: William Morris Society, 1960.

Morley, John. *The Making of the Royal Pavilion, Brighton*. Boston: David R. Godine, 1984.

Morris, May. *William Morris: Artist, Writer, Socialist*, 2 vols. New York: Russell and Russell, 1966.

Morris, William. *Collected Letters of William Morris*, vol. 22. Edited by May Morris. New York: Russell and Russell, 1966.

———. "Textiles." In *Arts and Crafts Essays*. New York: Charles Scribner's Sons, 1893. Facsimile edition. New York: Garland, 1977.

———. *Collected Letters of William Morris*. Edited by Norman Kelvin. Princeton, N.J.: Princeton University Press, 1984.

Moussinac, Léon. *Etoffes imprimés et papiers peints*. Paris: Editions Albert Levy, 1924.

———. *Etoffes d'ameublement tissés et brochés*. Paris: Editions Albert Levy, 1925.

Mucha, Jiří. *Alphonse Maria Mucha*. New York: Rizzoli, 1989.

Munz, Ludwig, and Gustav Künstler. *Adolf Loos, Pioneer of Modern Architecture*. Translated by Harold Meek. New York: Frederick A. Praeger, 1966.

Musée des Arts Décoratifs. *Trois siècles de papiers peints*. Paris: Musée des Arts Décoratifs, 1967.

Muthesius, Hermann. *The English House*. Translated by Janet Seligman. London: Crosby Lockwood Staples, Granada; New York: Rizzoli, 1979. Originally published as *Das Englische Haus* (Berlin: Ernst Wasmuth, 1904).

Naylor, Gillian. *The Arts and Crafts Movement*. Cambridge, Mass.: MIT Press, 1971.

———. *The Bauhaus Reassessed: Sources and Design Theory*. New York: E.P. Dutton, 1985.

———. *William Morris by Himself*. London: Macdonald Orbis, 1988.

Nebehay, Christian M. *Ver Sacrum: 1898–1903*. Vienna: Edition Tusch, 1975.

Nerdinger, Winfried, ed. *Richard Riemerschmid: Vom Jugendstil zum Werkbund*. Munich: Prestel Verlag, 1983.

Neuwirth, Waltraud. *Wiener Werkstätte, Avantgarde, Art Deco, Industrial Design*. Vienna: Selbstverlag Dr. Waltraud Neuwirth, 1984.

Nouvel, Odile. *Papiers Peints Français 1800–1850*. Fribourg, Switzerland: Office du Livre, 1981.

Nouvel-Kammerer, Odile. *Papiers peints panoramiques*. Paris: Musée des Arts Décoratifs and Flammarion, 1990.

Nouvel-Kammerer, Odile, and Bernard Jacqué. *Le Papier peint: Décor d'illusion*. Schirmeck, France: J.P. Gyss, 1987.

Nylander, Richard C. *Wallpapers for Historic Buildings*. Washington, D.C.: The Preservation Press, 1983.

Nylander, Richard C., Elizabeth Redmond, and Penny J. Sander. *Wallpaper in New England*. Boston: Society for the Preservation of New England Antiquities, 1986.

Olligs, Heinrich. *Tapeten, Ihre Geschichte bis zur Gegenwart*, 3 vols. Braunschweig, Germany: Klinkhardt & Biermann, 1970.

Oman, Charles C. *Catalogue of Wallpapers in the Victoria and Albert Museum*. London: Board of Education, 1929.

Oman, Charles C., and Jean Hamilton. *Wallpapers: A History and Illustrated Catalogue of the Collection in the Victoria and Albert Museum*. London: Sotheby Publications and the Victoria and Albert Museum, 1982.

Oppé, A. Paul. *Thomas Rowlandson, His Drawings and Watercolours*. London: The Studio, 1923.

Panofsky, Erwin. *The Life and Art of Albrecht Dürer*, vols. 1, 2. Princeton, N.J.: Princeton University Press, 1955.

Papillon, Jean-Michel. *Traité historique et pratique de la gravure en bois*. Paris, 1766.

Parry, Linda. *William Morris Textiles*. London: Weidenfeld and Nicolson, 1983.

———. *Textiles of the Arts and Crafts Movement*. London: Thames and Hudson, 1988.

Paulson, Ronald. *Rowlandson: A New Interpretation*. London: Studio Vista, 1972.

Pennell, E.R., and J. Pennell. *The Life of James A. McNeill Whistler*. Philadelphia: J.B. Lippincott, 1908.

Percival, MacIver. "Wallpaper of the Sheraton Period." *Journal of Decorative Art,* September 1925, pp. 297–300.

Perez-Tibi, Dora. *Dufy*. New York: Harry N. Abrams, 1989.

Peterson, Harold. *Americans at Home*. New York: Charles Scribner's Sons, 1971.

Pevsner, Nikolaus. *Pioneers of Modern Design: From William Morris to Walter Gropius*. Harmondsworth, England: Penguin, 1964.

———. *Studies in Art, Architecture and Design,* 2 vols. New York: Walker, 1968.

Poiret, Paul. *My First Fifty Years*. Translated by Stephen Hayden Guest. London: Victor Gallancz, 1931.

Praz, Mario. *An Illustrated History of Interior Decoration*. New York: Thames and Hudson, 1982.

Pugin, A.W.N. *True Principles of Pointed or Christian Architecture,* 1841. Reprint. New York: St. Martin's Press, 1973.

Radice, Barbara. *Memphis*. New York: Rizzoli, 1983.

Ratcliff, Carter. *Warhol*. New York: Abbeville Press, 1983.

Rheims, Maurice. *The Flowering of Art Nouveau*. New York: Harry N. Abrams, 1966.

Richardson, Margaret. "Wallpapers by C.F.A. Voysey 1857–1941." *Journal of the Royal Institute of British Architects* 72 (1965): 399–403.

Riely, John. *Rowlandson Drawings from the Paul Mellon Collection*. New Haven: Yale Center for British Art, 1977.

Rix, Brenda D. *Our Old Friend Rolly*. Toronto: Art Gallery of Ontario, 1987.

Roque, Georges. *Ceci n'est pas un Magritte: Essai sur Magritte et la publicité*. Paris: Flammarion, 1983.

Rosenberg, Harold. *Artworks and Packages*. New York: Horizon Press, 1969.

———. *Saul Steinberg*. New York: Alfred A. Knopf and Whitney Museum of American Art, 1978.

Rosoman, Treve. "A Chippendale Wallpaper Discovered." *Country Life* (November 14, 1985): 1501.

Sanborn, Kate. *Old Time Wallpapers*. Greenwich, Conn.: The Literary Collector Press, 1905.

Savage, George. *French Decorative Art*. New York: Frederick A. Praeger, 1969.

Sayer and Bennett's Catalogue of Prints for 1775. London: Holland Press, 1970.

Schmutzler, Robert. *Art Nouveau.* New York: Harry N. Abrams, 1962.

Schoeser, Mary. *Fabrics and Wallpapers: Twentieth-Century Design.* New York: E.P. Dutton, 1986.

Schweiger, Werner J. *Wiener Werkstätte: Design in Vienna, 1903–1932.* New York: Abbeville Press, 1984.

Scully, Vincent. *Frank Lloyd Wright.* New York: George Braziller, 1960.

Seale, William. *The Tasteful Interlude: American Interiors through the Camera's Eye 1860–1917.* New York: Frederick A. Praeger, 1975.

Séguy, E.A. *Les Fleurs et leurs applications décoratives.* Paris: A. Calavas, 1902.

———. *Floréal.* Paris: A. Calavas, [1914].

———. *Samarkande.* Paris: C. Massin, 1920.

———. *Papillons.* Paris: Talmer, 1927.

———. *Suggestions pour étoffes et tapis.* Paris: C. Massin, [1927].

———. *Prismes.* Paris: Editions d'Art Charles Moreau, [1930].

Sekler, Eduard F. *Josef Hoffmann.* Princeton, N.J.: Princeton University Press, 1985.

Sekler, Mary Patricia. *Early Drawings of Le Corbusier, 1902–1908.* New York: Garland, 1977.

Selz, Peter, and Mildred Constantine, eds. *Art Nouveau.* New York: Museum of Modern Art, 1959.

Serota, Nicholas, ed. *Howard Hodgkin: Forty Paintings 1973–1984.* New York: George Braziller, 1984.

Sheraton, Thomas. *The Cabinet-Maker and Upholsterer's Drawing-Book.* 3d ed. London: T. Bensley, 1802.

Simpson, Duncan. *C.F.A. Voysey, an Architect of Individuality.* New York: Watson-Guptill, 1981.

Spalding, Frances. *Roger Fry: Art and Life.* Berkeley and Los Angeles: University of California Press, 1980.

Spencer, Isobel. *Walter Crane.* New York: Macmillan, 1975.

Spencer, Robin. *The Aesthetic Movement: Theory and Practice.* London: Studio Vista; New York: E.P. Dutton, 1972.

Strauss, Walter L. *The German Single-Leaf Woodcut, 1550–1600,* vol. 1. New York: Abaris Books, 1975.

Sugden, A.V., and J.L. Edmondson. *A History of English Wallpaper, 1509–1914.* New York: Charles Scribner's Sons, 1926.

Taylor, Hilary. *James McNeill Whistler.* London: Studio Vista, 1978.

Teynac, Françoise, Pierre Nolot, and Jean-Denis Vivien. *Wallpaper: A History.* New York: Rizzoli, 1982.

Thornton, Peter. *Seventeenth-Century Interior Decoration in England, France, and Holland.* New Haven and London: Yale University Press and the Paul Mellon Center for Studies in British Art, 1978.

———. *Authentic Decor: The Domestic Interior 1620–1920.* New York: Viking, 1984.

Trappes-Lomax, M. *Pugin, a Medieval Victorian.* London: Sheed and Ward, 1932.

Troy, Nancy J. *The De Stijl Environment.* Cambridge, Mass.: MIT Press, 1983.

Tuchsherer, Jean-Michel. *Sonia Delaunay: Etoffes imprimées des années folles.* Mulhouse, France: Musée de l'Impression sur Etoffes, 1971.

———. *Raoul Dufy, créateur d'étoffes.* Mulhouse, France: Musée de l'Impression sur Etoffes, 1973.

Vallance, Aymer. *The Art of William Morris.* London: G. Bell and Sons, 1897.

———. *The Decorative Art of Sir Edward Burne-Jones, Baronet.* London: The Art Journal, Easter Art Annual, 1900.

van de Velde, Henry. "Artistic Wallpapers." *L'Art moderne* 13 (June 1893): 193–95.

———. "Essex and Co.'s Westminster Wallpapers." *L'Art moderne* 14 (1894): 254–55.

Varnedoe, Kirk. *Vienna 1900: Art, Architecture and Design.* New York: Museum of Modern Art; Boston: New York Graphic Society and Little, Brown, 1986.

Vellay, Marc, and Kenneth Frampton. *Pierre Chareau, Architect and Craftsman.* New York: Rizzoli, 1985.

Veronesi, Giulia. *Style and Design, 1909–1929.* New York: George Braziller, 1968.

Viollet-le-Duc, Eugène-Emmanuel. *How to Build a House.* Translated by Benjamin Bucknall. London: Sampson, Low, Marston, Low and Searle, 1874.

———. *Discourses on Architecture,* vol. 2. Boston: James R. Osgood and Co., 1875.

Völker, Angela. *Die Stoffe der Wiener Werkstätte 1910–1932.* Vienna: Österreichisches Museum für Angewandte Kunst and Verlag Christian Brandstätter, 1990.

Völker, Angela, and Ruperta Pichler. *Wallpaper Designs of the Wiener Werkstätte in the Österreichisches Museum für Angewandte Kunst, Vienna,* 2 vols. Tokyo: Gakken, 1989.

von Heusinger, Christian. "Ein Neuentidecktes Exemplar der Dürertapete auf schwarzen Grund." *Jahrbuch der Berliner Museen* 25 (1983): 143–59.

Voysey, C.F.A. "An Interview with Mr. Charles F. Annesley Voysey, Architect and Designer." *The Studio* 1 (September 1893): 231–37.

———. "Aims and Conditions of the Modern Decorator." *Journal of Decorative Art* 15 (April 1895): 82–90.

Walpole, Horace. *Strawberry Hill Accounts.* Edited by Paget Toynbee. Oxford: Clarendon Press, 1927.

Waters, William, and Martin Harrison. *Burne-Jones.* New York: Putnam, 1973.

Watkinson, Ray. *Pre-Raphaelite Art and Design.* London: Studio Vista; Greenwich, Conn.: New York Graphic Society, 1970.

———. *William Morris as Designer.* New York: Reinhold, 1967; London: Trefoil Books, 1983.

Wedgwood, Alexandra. *A.W.N. Pugin and the Pugin Family.* London: Victoria and Albert Museum, 1985.

Weisberg, Gabriel P., ed. *Japonisme: Japanese Influence on French Art, 1854–1910.* Cleveland: Cleveland Museum of Art, 1975.

Wells-Cole, Anthony. *Historic Paper Hangings from Temple Newsam and other English Houses.* Leeds, England: City Art Galleries, 1983.

Whistler, James A. McNeill. *The Gentle Art of Making Enemies.* London: Heinemann, 1892. Reprint. New York: Dover Publications, 1967.

White, Colin. *World of the Nursery.* London: Herbert Press, 1984.

White, Palmer. *Poiret.* London: Studio Vista, 1973.

Whitford, Frank. *Bauhaus.* London: Thames and Hudson, 1984.

Whitworth Art Gallery. *British Sources of Art Nouveau.* Manchester, England: Whitworth Art Gallery, 1969.

———. *Historic Wallpapers in the Whitworth Art Gallery.* Manchester, England: Whitworth Art Gallery, 1972.

———. *Walter Crane: Artist, Designer and Socialist.* London: Lund Humphries, 1989.

William Morris Gallery. *Catalogue of A.H. Mackmurdo and the Century Guild Collection.* Walthamstow, England: William Morris Gallery, 1967.

Windsor, Alan. *Peter Behrens, Architect and Designer.* London: The Architectural Press, 1981; New York: Watson-Guptill, 1982.

Wingler, Hans M. *The Bauhaus: Weimar, Dessau, Berlin, Chicago.* Cambridge, Mass.: MIT Press, 1969.

Wölfflin, Heinrich. *The Art of Albrecht Dürer.* Translated by Alastair Grieve and Heide Grieve. London: Phaidon Press, 1971.

Wong, Roberta. *Will H. Bradley: American Artist and Craftsman 1868–1962.* New York: Metropolitan Museum of Art, 1972.

Woods, Christine. "Pedigree Papers or Popular Patterns; the Curator versus the Consumer." *Apollo* 130 (October 1989): 248–52.

Wright, Frank Lloyd. "The Art and Craft of the Machine." In Edgar Kauffmann and Ben Raeburn, eds., *Frank Lloyd Wright: Writings and Buildings,* 55–73. New York: Horizon Press, 1960.

INDEX

Page numbers in *italics* refer to illustrations.

"Abstract" (Sutherland), 202, *202*

"Acanthus" (Morris), 61, *61*, 66, 96

"Afrique, L'" (Dufy, c. 1920), 150, *151*

"Afrique, L'" (Dufy, c. 1925), 150, *150*

"Age d'or, L'" (Dalí), 192, *193*

Age d'or, L' (film), 193

Aldin, Cecil, 245

Alt, Otmar, 256; work by, *256*

Altdorfer, Albrecht, 19; work by, *19*

"Amenophis" (Fry), *166*, 167

"American Revolution, The" (Deltil), 34, *34*

animal wallpaper borders (Mucha), *104*, 105

Apollinaire, Guillaume, 146, 152, 155

"Apollinaire" (Laurencin), 155, *157*

"Arbre en Fleur" (Matisse), 214, *214*

Art Deco, 126, 145–73

"Artist as Decorator, The" (article; Fry), 168, 169

Art Nouveau, 66, 68, 73, 77, 81, 85, 89–113

Arts and Crafts movement, 66, 77, 81, 135, 139

"Arums, L'" (Dufy), 148, *148*

Ashbee, C.R., 139

Attributes of the Studio (painting; Ensor), 228, *228*

Attwell, Mabel Lucie, 244–45

Audubon, John James, 39; work by, *40*

Au Paradis (painting; Denis), 102, *102*, 249

"Aviary" (drawing; Steinberg), *196*, 196–97

"Babies' Garden, The" (Bradley), 108

Baby's Bouquet, The (book; Crane), 237, 239

"Baby's Opera" (Crane), *238*

Baby's Opera, The (book; Crane), 237, 239

"Bachelor's Button" (Morris), 59

Badovici, Jean, 156

Balmoral Castle wallpaper (Morris), 65, *66*

Balzac, Honoré de, 36

"Bamboo" (Godwin), 84, *85*

Banalité (gravure print; Parry), 223, *224*

"Bateaux Jaunes" (Denis), 98, *98*

"Bateaux Roses, Les" (Denis), 98, *98*, 101, 102

Battersby, Martin, 172

Bauhaus, 113, 117, 132, 135, 173; work by, *135*

Bawden, Edward, 171–72; works by, *170*, *172*

Beardsley, Aubrey, 108–9

"Beauty" (Berges), 204, *204*

bedroom in the Berl House (drawing; Olbrich), 112, *113*

bedroom in the Primavesi Villa (Hoffmann), *120*, 121

Bedroom Nude with Black Choker and Wallpaper (sculpture; Wesselmann), *216*, 217

Beerbohm, Max, 84, 218; work by, *218*

Beham, Hans Sebald, 16, 18; works by, *1*, *17*, *18–19*

Behrens, Peter, 132; work by, *133*

Bell, Vanessa, 167, 168, 252; works by, *168*, *253*

Bénédictus, Edouard, 163; work by, *162*

Berges, Werner, 204; work by, *204*

Bestiaire, Le (Apollinaire), 146, *146*, 152, 156

"Biches, Les" (Denis), *100*, 101

Bing, Samuel, 96, 106

"Birches, The" (Burchfield), 179, *179*

"Bird" (Morris), *59*

"Birds" (drawing; Steinberg), *196*, 196–97

"Birds and Blossoms" (Burchfield), 177, *178*

Birge, M.H., and Co., 177–78, 179, 183

Black Brunswicker, The (painting; Millais), 220, *221*

Blake, William, 71

"Blé et Oiseaux" (Dufy), 146, *146*, 152

Blondel, Méry-Joseph, 33; work by, *32*

Bluebird and Cottonwoods (watercolor; Burchfield), 179, *179*

Blue Monk (painting; Zakanitch), *230*, 231

Blue Silk Dress, The (painting; Rossetti), 56

"Bo Peep" (Owen), *244*, 245

Boucher, François, 211; work by, *212*

"Bouquet de Mariée" (Laboureur), *154*, 155

Bradley, Will, 106, 108–9, 112, 251; works by, *106*, *108*

Bradley: His Book, *106*, 108, 251

"Bradley House, A," 109

Broc, Jean, 33; work by, *37*

"Brother Rabbit" (Morris), *245*

Buñuel, Luis, 193

Burchfield, Charles, 177–83; works by, *174–76*, *178–83*

Burges, William, 45–46; works by, *46*, *47*

Burne-Jones, Edward, 53, 66, 82; work by, *68–69*

Cabinet-Maker and Upholsterer's Drawing-Book (Sheraton), 23

Caldecott, Randolph, 239, 240; work by, *242*

Calder, Alexander, 134, 194–95, 214, 217; works by, *184–85*, *194*, *195*

"Calder #1" (Calder), 194, *194*

"Captain Cook" wallpaper (Charvet), *30–31*, 33

cardboard "wallpaper" (Mondrian), 134, *134*

Carlson, Cynthia, 231

cartoons for a wallpaper frieze (von Zülow), *250*

Castel Béranger, Le (album; Guimard), 89

Castelli, Leo, 205, 207

Cat among Pigeons (watercolor; Bawden), 172, *172*

"Celui qui aime ecrit sur les murs" (Lurçat), *164*, 165, 252

"Cervantes" (Dalí), 192, *193*

Chareau, Pierre, 252; work by, *253*

Charvet, Jean-Gabriel, 33; work by, *30–31*

Château-sur-Mer (Newport, R.I.), 46, *47*

"Cherubs" (Beham), 16, *17*

"Chinese Garden" (artists unknown), 40, *40*

"Chinese Garden" (Burchfield), 178, *178*

chinoiserie wallpaper (Stéphany), 160, *160*

"Chrysanthemum" (Morris), 64

Clemens, Samuel and Olivia, 237

"Cobweb" (Tiffany), 106, *107*

"Cockatoo" (Gaudier-Brzeska), 170, *170*

"Colombes, Les" (Denis), 101, *101*

Colour (magazine), 168

Column with acanthus wallpaper (Altdorfer), 19, *19*

Compositions, couleurs, idées (pochoir album; Delaunay), 160

"Coq et Perroquet" (Réveillon and Fay), *5*, 23, *23*

"Country Life and the Hunt" (Burchfield), *176*, 177

Couture, Thomas, 212; work by, *213*

"Cow" (Warhol), 10, *205*, 205–6, 207

Crace firm, 37, 39, 41, 42

Crane, Walter, 73–74, 77, 93, 237, 239; works by, *71–76*, *236*, *238–40*

"Cupid and Psyche" (Lafitte and Blondel), *32*, 33

Czeschka, Carl Otto, 125; work by, *124*

dado (Omega Workshops), *169*

"Daffodil" (Morris), 59, 61

"Daisy" (Morris), *50–51*, 57, 66, 246

Dalí, Salvador, 138, 192–93; work by, *193*

"Dance of the Wodehouses, The" (illumination; Froissart), 55

Dantis Amor (painting; Rossetti), *70*, 73

Dearle, John Henry, 59

De Chirico, Giorgio, 191

"Deer and Rabbits" (Crane), *72*

Delaunay, Sonia, 160; work by, *161*

Deltil, Jean-Julien, 33, 34; works by, *34*, *35*

"Demon, The" (Voysey), *78*, 79

Denis, Maurice, 96–98, 101–2, 113, 249; works by, *97*–*103*, *249*

Derngate house, *118*, 119

"Desert and Camels" (Bawden), *170*, 171

"Design for a Bedroom" (Bradley), *108*, 109

design for a girl's bedroom (Lurçat), *164*, 165, 252

Deskey, Donald: work by, *173*

De Stijl, 117, 132, 134–35

Deutsche Kunst und Dekoration (periodical), 125, 126

Deutscher Werkbund, 117, 132, 135

"Diamonds and Hexagonals" (O. Jones), 49, *49*

Dinner at Smith Square (painting; Hodgkin), 226, *226*

Documents Décoratifs (design album; Mucha), *104*, 105, *105*

Domela, César, 134–35

Domino wallpaper (artist unknown), 21, 22

"Don Quixote" (Dalí), 192, 193

"Dove and Rose" (Morris), 61

"Dragon and Bamboo" (R. Jones), 39, 39

Dufour, 33, 36

Dufy, Raoul, 57, 145, 146–50, 152; works by, 146, 148–51

Dulac, Edmund, 244; work by, 243

du Maurier, George; work by, 54

Dürer, Albrecht, 15–16, 19, 21–22, 29, 65; works by, 12–13, 14, 16, 20

"Eau et le feu, L'" (Réveillon), 23, 24

Eckert, Horst, 256; work by, 234–35

Eckmann, Otto, 109, 112; works by, 110, 111

Ecole Martine. See Martine

"Elaine" (Voysey), 94, 94

Enchanted Domain, The (mural; Magritte), 190

Ensor, James, 228; work by, 228

Entrelac design (Knox), 90, 93

Entry of Christ into Brussels in 1889 (painting; Ensor), 228

Ernst, Max, 217; work by, 217

"Eucalyptus, Les" (Martine), 144, 146

Exposition des Arts Décoratifs (1925; Paris), 145, 156, 163

fabric design (Delaunay), 160, 161

"Fasan" (Eckmann), 109, 111

Fay, Jean-Baptiste, 23; work by, 5, 23

Femme au singe, La (painting; Laurencin), 155

Femmes à leur toilette (collage; Picasso), 208–9, 217

"Fillettes, Les" (Denis), 102, 103, 249

Flachenschmuck (album), 120, 122

Fleurs, Les (pochoir album; Seguy), 163

"Flight" (Voysey), 94, 95

flock wallpaper, 22, 22, 65, 66

Flögl, Mathilde, 129

floral wallpaper (Riemerschmid), 132, 132

Floréal (pochoir album; Seguy), 163

Folon, Jean-Michel, 191–92; work by, 192

"Foultitude" (Folon), 192, 192

"Four and Twenty Blackbirds" (Voysey), 248, 249

"Four Winds" (Crane), 74

Fragonard, Jean-Honoré, 211; work by, 212

Friedmann, Maria: work by, 116

Froissart, Jean, 57; work by, 55

Frommel-Fochler, Lotte: work by, 120

"Fruit" (Morris), 59, 62, 63, 63

"Fruits de Mer, Les" (Ruhlmann), 159, 159

Fry, Roger, 167, 168, 169, 170; works by, 166, 167

"Fusées, Les" (Lurçat), 165–66, 142–43

Gaudier-Brzeska, Henri, 170; work by, 170

Gauguin, Paul, 10, 96

Gautier, Théophile, 33

"Gazelles, Les" (Martine), 147, 147

"Gentleman's Wallpaper, A" (Gibson), 109

George IV (Prince Regent, later king of England), 37, 39, 42

Gibson, Charles Dana: work by, 109

"Gibson Girl" (Gibson), 109

Gilbert and Sullivan, 54

Gill, Eric, 172

Gilman, Charlotte Perkins, 8

Gilman, Harold, 223; work by, 223

Gober, Robert, 231

Goblin Market (book; C. Rossetti), 73

Godwin, Edward William, 84–85; works by, 84, 85

Gogh, Vincent van, 223; work by, 96, 210

Golconde, La (painting; Magritte), 188, 190

"Golden Age, The" (Crane), 73, 75

"Goldene Schmetterlinge" (Moser), 121, 122

Goodwin house, 84, 85

Grammar of Ornament (book; O. Jones), 46, 47, 136

"Grange, The" (Burne-Jones house), 67

Grant, Duncan, 167, 168; work by, 168

Grasset, Eugène, 11, 90, 105, 136, 163

"Grategus" (Voysey), 78, 78

Great Triumphal Car (woodcut; Dürer), 21

Greenaway, Kate, 239–40; work by, 241

Grego, Joseph, 27

Grooms, Red, 217; work by, 216

Gropius, Walter, 117, 135, 139

"Grosse Girlande" (Beham), 16, 18, 18–19

"Grosse Säule" (woodcut; Dürer), 16, 16

"Grotesque Borders for Screens, Billiard Rooms, Dressing Rooms, etc." (Rowlandson), 27, 28

Guimard, Hector, 89–90; work by, 88

"Happy Cow, The" (Alt), 256, 256

Harmonies of Ruhlmann (album), 158, 159, 254

"Harpistes" (Denis), 97, 97

Harunobu, Suzuki, 225

Hassall, John, 245–46

Haus Bloemenwerf (van de Velde), 93, 93–94, 96

Haus Pickler, 124, 125

Hazy July Noon (watercolor; Burchfield), 180, 181

"Henrik Ibsen, Receiving Mr. William Archer in Audience" (cartoon; Beerbohm), 218, 218

"Hey Diddle Diddle" (Crane), 239, 239

Histoire d'une maison (book; Viollet-le-Duc), 90, 91

"History of a Woman" (Denis), 96–97

Hobby Horse (magazine), 81

"Hochwald" (Jungnickel), 251–52, 252

Hodgkin, Howard, 226; works by, 226, 227

Hoffmann, Josef, 117, 118, 119, 121–22, 123, 125, 126; works by, 116, 120, 122, 124, 125

"Hommage de l'Amerique à la France, L'" (Huet), 150

"Honeysuckle" (Morris), 60, 61

Horne, Herbert, 81

"Horses" (Steinberg), 200, 201

Horta, Victor, 78, 81, 90, 94; works by, 94, 95

Huet, Jean-Baptiste, 23, 150; work by, 150

"Humpty Dumpty" (Crane), 239, 239

"Innocent badinage, L'" (Watteau), 25

Intérieur chez Maurice Denis (painting; Vuillard), 102

Interior with Pink Wallpaper I, II, III (lithographs; Vuillard), 224, 225

"Isis" (Voysey), 77, 86–87, 93

Jackson, Andrew, 36

Jackson, John Baptist, 23, 211; work by, 25

"Jagdfalke" (Hoffmann), 116, 121

"Japanese Rose" (Vigers), 92, 93

"Jasmine" (Morris), 64, 66, 67

Jeffrey and Co., 65, 77, 81

Johnson, Philip, 230

Jones, Allen, 204; work by, 204

Jones, Owen, 46–47, 49, 90, 137; works by, 48, 49

Jones, Robert, 37, 39; works by, 38, 39

Jugendstil, 89, 132. See also Art Nouveau

Jungnickel, Ludwig Heinrich, 125, 251; work by, 252

Kelmscott House, 59, 62

Kelmscott Manor, 55, 56–57, 61, 246

"Kennet" (Morris), 56–57

Kitchen, The (painting; Grant), 168, 169

Knox, Archibald, 93; work by, 90

Kushner, Robert, 231

Laboureur, Jean-Emile, 152–53, 155, 252; work by, 152–55

Lafitte, Louis, 33; work by, 32

"Larkspur" (Morris), 58, 59, 61, 94

"Laube" (cabinet; Peche), 126, 129, 129

Laurencin, Marie, 155–56;

works by, 156, 157

Le Corbusier, 117, 135, 137–39, 141, 156, 172; works by, 136–39

Léger, Fernand, 134, 194

Leistikow, Walter, 109, 112; work by, 110

"Lesser Arts of Life, The" (essay; Morris), 53

Leyland, Frederick, 82

Light Switches (watercolor; Oldenburg), 228, 229

Likarz, Maria, 129; work by, 130–31

"Lion" (Pugin), 42, 42, 43

Lion and Vagrant (painting; Magritte), 190, 191

Little Tear Gland That Says Tic Tac (gouache; Ernst), 217, 217

"Long Ears" (Hoffmann), 122, 122

Loos, Adolf, 112, 122–23

Lurçat, Jean, 164–66, 252; works by, 142–43, 164, 165

"Macaw" (Crane), 76, 77

Mackintosh, Charles Rennie, 117–19; works by, 118–20

Mackmurdo, Arthur Heygate, 77, 81, 93; works by, 79, 80

Magritte, René, 187–88, 190–91, 230; works by, 186, 188, 190, 191

Maine Room (watercolor; Grooms), 216, 217

"Mao" (Warhol), 206, 206, 207

"Mardele, Le" (Guimard), 88, 89

"Marin, Le" (Laboureur), 152, 153

Martine, 145–47, 167, 252; works by, 2–3, 144, 147

Matisse, Henri, 214, 232–33; works by, 214, 231–33

Matta, Roberto, 214; work by, 215

"Mauer" (Le Corbusier), 137, 138, 138–39, 139

"Mauerblumchen" (Frommel-Fochler), 120

Maximilian I (Holy Roman emperor), 15, 19, 21

"Mazeraies, Les" (Lurçat), 165, 165, 252

"Mermaid" (Burne-Jones and Morris), 66, 68–69

"Mermaids" (Moser), 114–15, 122

Mies van der Rohe, Ludwig,

118, 132

Millais, John Everett, 71, 220; work by, *221*

Miró, Joan, 194, 214, 217; work by, *215*

"Miss Mouse at Home" (Crane), *236*, 237

"Modernistic" (Burchfield), 177, 182–83, *183*

Mondrian, Piet, 132, 134–35; work by, *134*

Monkton House, 171, *171*

Monroe, James, 36

"Months, The" (Greenaway), 240, *241*

"Monuments of Paris" (Broc), 37

Morris, Jane, 56, 61

Morris, May, 246

Morris, William, 8, 9, 10–11, 49, 53–54, 56–57, 59, 61–66, 73, 77, 78, 79, 81, 90, 93, 96, 121, 135, 139, 177, 178, 183, 232, 246; works by, *50–51, 52, 55–69, 245–47*

Morris, William, Gallery (London), 65

Morris, William, Society, 62

Morris and Co., 53, 59, 61, 66, 68

Moser, Koloman, 112, 118, 119, 121–22, 126; works by, *114–15, 121–23*

"Mouse, The" (Dufy), 146, *146*

Mucha, Alphonse Maria, 11, 105–6; works by, *104, 105*

Muthesius, Hermann, 118, 132

Nabis, 9–10, 96, 106, 225

"Nana" (Saint Phalle), 256, *256*

Nash, Paul, 170

Natanson, Misia, 225, *225*

Nicholson, Ben, 134

"Nicotine" (Deskey), *173*

Nouvelle Variations (pochoir album; Bénédictus), 163

#105 (Wright), *140*, 141

#103 (Wright), 141, *141*

#706 (Wright), 141, *141*

nursery (drawing; Olbrich), 251, *251*

nursery design (Chareau), 252, *253*

nursery design (Ruhlmann), 254, *254*

nursery for Omega Workshops (Bell), 252, *253*

"Nursery Rhymes" (Crane), 239, *239*

nursery wallpaper (drawing; Dulac), *243*, 244

nursery wallpaper (Ruhlmann), 254, *255*

"Oak, the Ash, and the Bonnie Ivy Tree, The" (Sumner), 81, *81*

Olbrich, Joseph Maria, 112, 121, 251; works by, *112, 113, 251*

Oldenburg, Claes, 228; work by, *229*

Omega Workshops, 167–70, 172, 252; work by, *169, 170*

On the Threshold of Liberty (painting; Magritte), 188, 190

"Ornament and Crime" (essay; Loos), 123

Owen, Will, 245; work by, *244*

OXO advertisement, 202, *202*

panoramic wallpapers, 30–31, *32*, 33–34, *34, 35, 36, 36–37, 37*

"Papiers Peints" (Stepanova and Popova), 160, *161*

Papillon, Jean, 22

Parakeet and the Mermaid, The (gouache; Matisse), *231–33, 232, 233*

"Paris Opera" (Steinberg), 201, *201*

Parry, Roger, 223; work by, *224*

Pasquier, Nathalie du, 230–31

Patience (operetta; Gilbert and Sullivan), 54

"Peacock" (Behrens), 132, *133*

Peacock Room (Whistler), 82, *82–83*

"Peacocks and Amorini" (Crane), *71*, 73

Peche, Dagobert, 126, 129, 177; works by, *126–29*

Peeters-Lacroix factory, 187

Personal Values (painting; Magritte), 190–91

Picasso, Pablo, 217; work by, *208–9*

Picture Books (Caldecott), 240

"Piece of My Workshop, A" (Calder), 214

Piper, John, 254

plain wallpapers (drawings; Le Corbusier), *136*

"Plentiful Catch" (Moser), 122, *123*

Poiret, Paul, 145, 146, 147, 149, 252

"Pomegranate" (Beham), *1*, 18, *18*

"Pomegranate" (Morris), 59, 63, *63*

Pompadour, Madame de, 22, 211

Popova, Lyubov, 160; work by, *161*

"Poppies with Roots" (Mucha), 105, *105*

Potter, Beatrix, 243–44

"Poussins, Les" (Denis), 249, *249*

Primavesi Villa, *120*, 121

print rooms, 23, 25, *26–27*

Prismes (pochoir album; Seguy), 163

"Prodigues, Les" (Couture), 212, *213*

"Psyche Intending to Stab the Sleeping Cupid" (Lafitte and Blondel), *32*, 33

Pugin, A.W.N., 37, 41–43, 45, 90; works by, *41, 42, 43, 44, 45*

"Pygmalion and His Statue" (Fragonard[?]), *212*

"Queen Jones" (O. Jones), *48*, 49

"Queen of Hearts" (Crane), 237, *238*

Queen's Drawing Room flock wallpaper (artist unknown), 22

Queen's Robing Room wallpaper (Pugin), 42, 44, 45, 90

"Rabbits" (Moser), 122, *122*

"Red Birds and Beech Trees" (Burchfield), *174–75*, 180

Red House (Morris), 53, 54, 56, 57

"Rediscovery of the Sandwich Islands" (Charvet), *30–31*, 33

"Red Library-Boudoir, The" (Ruhlmann), *158*, 159

Régates à Perros, Les (painting; Denis), *99*, 101

Relais (pochoir album; Bénédictus), 163

Réveillon, Jean-Baptiste, 23, 25, 152; works by, *5, 23, 24*

Riemerschmid, Richard, 132; work by, *132*

"Right-Hand Lady" (A. Jones), 204, *204*

"Robins and Crocuses" (Burchfield), 182, *182*

Rokeby Manor print room, *26–27*

Room and Book (Nash), 170

Roosevelt, Theodore, 109

"Rose and Butterfly" (Mackmurdo), *80*, 81

"Roses" (Ruhlmann), 159, *159*

"Roses roses, Les" (Martine), *2–3*

Rossetti, Dante Gabriel, 53, 56, 61, 66, 68, 71, 73; work by, *70*

Rowlandson, Thomas, 26–27, 29; works by, *28, 29*

Royal Gallery wallpaper (Pugin), 42, *45*

Royal Pavilion (Brighton), 37, 38, 39

Ruhlmann, Emile–Jacques, 156, 159, 252, 254; works by, *158, 159, 254, 255*

Ruskin, John, 81–82, 85, 121, 135

"Sahara" (Bawden), *170*, 171

"St. James" (Morris), 64, *64*, 65, *65*

St. James's Palace, 53, 63–64, *64*, 73

Saint Phalle, Niki de, 256; work by, *256*

Salomé (play; Wilde), 109

Samarkande (pochoir album; Seguy), 163, *163*

Sambourne house, *62*, 62–63

Samuel Sargent Family, The (anonymous), 219–20, *219*

Sandys, Frederick: work by, *60*

Satyr Family, The (engraving; Dürer), *14*, 15

"Satyr Family, The" (Dürer), *12–13*, 15–16, 29

Saudé, Jean, 163

"Savaric" (Voysey), 94, *95*

"Sauvages de la mer Pacifique" (Charvet), *30–31*, 33

"Scenic America" (Deltil), 34, 35

scenic wallpapers, 30–31, *32*, 33–34, *34, 35, 36, 36–37, 37*

"Schilf" (Peche), 126, *128*

Sea Nymph, The (painting; Burne-Jones), 66

Schumacher, *140*, 141

"Segelschiffe" ("Sailboat"), (Leistikow), 112

Seguy, E.A., 163; work by, *163*

self-portrait wallpaper (Warhol), 206, *207*

"Semiramis" (Peche), 129, *129*

Servranckx, Victor, 187; work by, *189*

Severini, Gino, 171; work by, *171*

Shaw, George Bernard, 167

Sheraton, Thomas, 23

"Ships" (Servranckx), 187, *189*

Shopping List, The (Gilman), 223, *223*

"Siam" (Likarz), 129, *130–31*

"Silverbrook" (Bradley), *106*, 108

"Simple Simon" (Owen), *244*

"Singes, Les" (Laurencin), 155, *156*

"Six-Mark Teapot, The" (cartoon; du Maurier), 54, *54*

sketch after Dürer's "Satyr Family" (Rowlandson), 29, *29*

"Sleeping Beauty" (Crane), 239, *240*

Small Triumphal Car (woodcut; Dürer), 21

"Sol, El" (Miró), 214, *215*

Solvay House (Horta), 94, *95*

Song of Love, The (painting; De Chirico), 191

Song of the Redbird (watercolor; Burchfield), 180, *180*

"Sparrow and Bamboo" (Godwin), 84, *84*

"Spitze" (Peche), 126, *126*

"Splotchy" (Calder), *184–85*, 194, *195*

"Squirrels" (Burges), 46, *46*

"Stagecoach and the Natural Bridge" (Deltil), 34, *35*

Standon house, 57, *57*, 59, 246

Stanway house, 246, *247*

Steig, William, 218; work by, *218*

Steinberg, Saul, 196–98, 201–2; works by, *196–201*

stencil design (Mackintosh), 119, *119*

stenciled wallpaper (Mackintosh), *118*, 119

Stepanova, Varvara, 160; work by, *161*

Stéphany, Henri, 156, 160; work by, *160*

Still Life, Jug and Eggs (painting; Fry), 167, *167*

Stoclet, Adolf, 123, 125

"Strohblumen" (Friedmann), *116*

"Summer" (Peche), 126, *127*

Sumner, George Heywood, 81; work by, *81*

"Sun-Dice" (Matta), 214, *215*

"Sunflower" (Morris), 56, *56, 57, 59,* 64

"Sunflowers" (Burchfield), 180, 182, *182*

Supper after the Masked Ball (painting; Couture), 212

Surrealism, 187–93

Sutherland, Graham, 202, 244; work by, *202*

"Swan" (Eckmann), 109, *110*

"Swirling Leaf" (Mackmurdo), *79,* 81

Tapis et tissus (pochoir album; Delaunay), 160

Tassel House (Horta), 81, 94, *94*

"Telemachus on Calypso's Isle" (artist unknown), 36, *36*

Tiffany, Louis Comfort, 106, 237; work by, *107*

Tinguely, Jean, 202; work by, *203*

Tissot, James, 220; work by, *220*

toile de Jouy, 150

"Tokyo" (Voysey), 96, *96*

Toorop, Jan, 94

Toulouse-Lautrec, Henri de, 152

"Trains" (Denis), 101, *101*

"Trains" (Steinberg), 198, *199*

Treasure Houses of Britain (exhibition), 22

"Trellis" (Morris), 56, *246*

30 ans ou la vie en rose (painting; Dufy), 149, *149*

"Tritons" (Beham), 16, *17*

Triumphal Arch for Maximilian I (woodcut; Dürer), *20, 21*

Triumphal Procession (frieze), 21

Trois Marins, Les (etching; Laboureur), 153, *153*

"Tudor" (Pugin), *41, 42*

"Tulip and Bird" (Voysey), *77, 77–78*

"Tulips" (Olbrich), 112, *112*

van de Velde, Henri, 78, 93–94, 96, 113, 132, 135; work by, *93*

van Doesburg, Theo, 134, 135, 139

Variations (pochoir album; Bénédictus), 163

Venturi, Robert, 230; work by, *227*

"Venus Rising from the Waters" (anonymous), *213*

Verkade, Jan, 96, 102

Ver Sacrum (periodical), 119

"Views in Paris" (Steinberg), 198, *198,* 201

Vigers, Allan Francis, 93; work by, *92*

Viollet-le-Duc, Eugène-Emmanuel, 90, 93; work by, *91*

"Vive la Liberté" (Tinguely), 202, *203*

von Zülow, Franz, 125, 251; work by, *250*

Voysey, C.F.A., 77–79, 81, 93, 94, 96, 121, 249; works by, *77, 78, 86–87, 94–96, 248*

"Vues d'Amérique du Nord" (Deltil), 34, *35*

Vuillard, Edouard, 102, 225; works by, *224, 225*

wall decorations (Omega Workshops), *169,* 170

wall hanging design (Viollet-le-Duc), *91,* 93

"Wallpaper" (cartoon; Steig), 218, *218*

wallpaper after Tintoretto's *Crucifixion* (Jackson), 23, *25*

wallpaper and Chinese painting (R. Jones), *38, 39*

wallpaper design (Seguy), 163, *163*

wallpaper designs (Magritte), 187, *188*

wallpaper for Haus Bloemenwerf (van de Velde), *93, 93–94*

wallpaper from *Nursery Books* (Caldecott), *240, 242*

wallpaper in Behrens house (Mackintosh), 119, *120*

wallpaper in Charleston Farmhouse (Grant and Bell), *168,* 169

wallpaper in Pickler house (Czeschka), *124,* 125

wallpaper panels (Réveillon and Fay), 23, *23*

wall textile (Severini), 171, *171*

Walpole, Horace, 23, 211

Warhol, Andy, 205–7; works by, *205–7*

Warner, Metford, 77

"Water" (Hodgkin), 226, *227*

"Water Snakes" (Voysey), 93

Watteau, Antoine, 25–26

Webb, Philip, 54, 57, 246

"Wedding" (Steinberg), 197, *197*

Wesselmann, Tom, 217; work by, *216*

Wheeler, Candace, 106

Whistler, James McNeill, 81–82, 84–85; work by, *82–83*

Wiener Werkstätte, 117, 119, 121–23, 125–26, 129, 132, 145, 167, 251; exhibition installation (Hoffmann), 125, *125*

Wightwick Manor, *60, 61, 61*

Wilde, Oscar, 8, 109

"Wild Swans" (Leistikow), 109, *110,* 112

"Wild Vine" (Eckmann), 109, *111*

"Willow" (Morris), *52, 55, 56,* 246

"Willow Boughs" (Morris), 56, 246, *247*

"Woodnotes" (Crane), 73, *73*

Woolf, Virginia, 168, 170

Wright, Frank Lloyd, 109, 117, 139, 141, 195; works by, *140, 141*

Wunderlich, Paul, 204

"Ye Frog He Would A-Wooing Go" (Crane), *236,* 237

Yellow Book (magazine), 108

Yellow Wallpaper, The (novel; Gilman), 8

Zakanitch, Robert S., 231; work by, *230*

"Zirkus" (Eckert), 234–35, 256

Zuber, 34, 36, 192

Photography Credits

Every effort has been made to contact the current owners of the works reproduced in this volume. We would appreciate hearing about any changes in ownership or credit lines so that we may update future editions. Please send this information to: Wallpaper and the Artist, c/o Abbeville Publishing Group, 488 Madison Avenue, New York, N.Y. 10022. The photographers and the sources of photographic material other than those indicated in the captions are as follows:

Arcaid: plates 42, 45, 46, 240; Copyright © 1991 ARS N.Y./Spadem: plate 136; Art Resource, New York: plate 55; Terry Beasley: plate 61; Copyright © Bianchini Férier, Lyons, France: plates 135, 139; Copyright © Bildarchiv Preussischer Kulturbesitz, Berlin, Germany: plates 100, 244; Jean Boucher, Brussels: plate 76; Courtesy of Bridgeman Art Library, London: plates 47, 62, 90; Courtesy of the Burchfield Art Center Archives, Buffalo: plates 167, 168 (Biff Henrich), 171, 172, 174, 175; Walter Carone: plate 227; Catalogue raisonné Maurice Denis: plates 80, 84, 85, 86, 242; Jean-Loup Charmet: plates 89, 153, 155, 203; John W. Corbett, Middletown, R.I.: plate 33; Prudence Cuming Associates Ltd.: plate 225; P. Delbo: plate 121; Giraudon/Art Resource, New York: plate 83; Biff Henrich: plates 169, 170, 173, 176; Idaka: plate 186; IMPF, Belgium: plate 182; Michael Jorge: plate 204; B.P. Keiser: page 1, plates 3, 4, 6, 7, 8; A.F. Kersting: plate 39; Copyright © The Metropolitan Museum of Art, New York, all rights reserved: plates 1, 2, 5, 93 (Copyright © 1991); Copyright © Musée départemental du Prieuré, Symbolistes et Nabis, Maurice Denis et son temps, Saint-Germain-en-Laye, France: plates 81, 82, 88; Copyright © Musée Horta, Brussels: plate 77; The Board of Trustees of the National Museums: plate 216; Ken Pelka: plates 25, 140, 187, 188, 192, 206, 207, 208, 232; Pieterse-Davison International, Ltd.: plate 213; Copyright © Photo R.M.N. (Réunion des Musées Nationaux), Paris: plates 87, 201, 215; Ottica Romeo: plate 10; Copyright © British Architectural Library, Royal Institute of British Architects, London/Geremy Butler: plates 64, 241; Robert D. Rubic: plate 239; Eddie Ryle-Hodges: plate 15; Elisabeth Schaumberger: plate 243; Marc Schuman: plate 209; Stephen Shore: plate 198; L. Sully-Jaulmes, all rights reserved: plates 130, 144, 154, 156, 183, 249; John Bigelow Taylor, New York: plate 125; P. Turcksin, Antwerp, Belgium: plate 180; Copyright © 1992 Tom Wesselmann/VAGA, New York: plate 210.

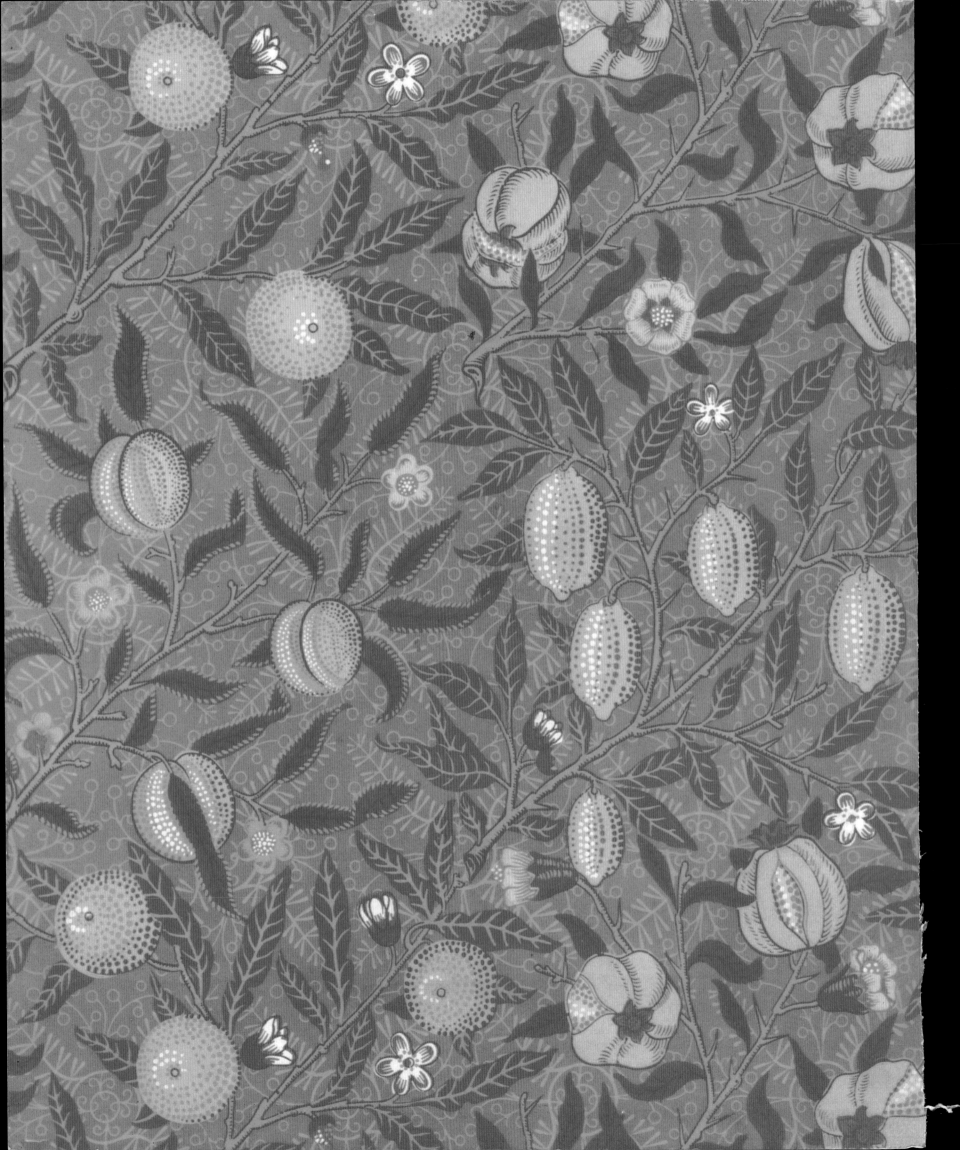